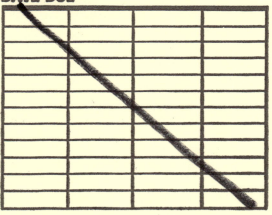

# LENIN
## AND THE
## END OF
## POLITICS

# LENIN
## AND THE
## END OF
## POLITICS

# A. J. POLAN

UNIVERSITY OF
CALIFORNIA PRESS
BERKELEY   LOS ANGELES

First published in the
United States by
The University of
California Press, 1984

© 1984 A. J. Polan

Typeset by
Scarborough Typesetting Services
and printed in Great Britain at the
University Press, Cambridge

Library of Congress Cataloging in
Publication Data

Polan, A. J.
    Lenin and the end of politics.
    Based on the author's thesis
(Ph. D.)—University of Durham.
    Bibliography: p.
    Includes index.
    1. Lenin, Vladimir Il'ich,
1870–1924. Gosudarstvo i
revoliūtsiia.    2. Marx, Karl,
1818–1883.    3. Socialism.
4. State, The.    5. Revolutions.
6. Soviet Union—Politics and
government—1917–        I. Title.
HX314.L3529P65    1984        320.1
84–2489
ISBN 0–520–05314–1
ISBN 0–520–053168 (pbk.)

# CONTENTS

**TO
MY MOTHER AND FATHER**

# ACKNOWLEDGEMENTS

This book originated as a piece of work which eventually became a PhD thesis for the University of Durham. Huw Beynon, as my supervisor, provided help, encouragement, advice, guidance and friendship just when these were most needed, as well as the opportunity to pursue the project in the first place. Thanks are also due to David Rosenberg, without whose constant pressure and comforting confidence in my capacities this work would certainly never have been started and probably not finished.

My greatest debt is to my friend of many years, Ted Jones. As a constant source of intellectual stimulation and fruitful argument, he contributed immeasurably to the ideas that are presented in the following pages, although, of course, he cannot be held responsible for those parts with which he might nevertheless disagree. Bob Miller, John Crook and Bob Greenwood were indispensable companions and critics throughout the project, and my gratitude also goes to Marilyn Polan, Terry Austrin, David Lister, Barbara Jones, Lisa Hilson, John Paterson, Liz Cantell, Andy Kellaher, Tony Morrison, Janet Hall and Claude Jean-Alexis, who helped in their different ways, perhaps when they least realized it. Professor Zygmunt Bauman of Leeds University, Irving Velody of Durham University, and Professor Bernard Crick suggested amendments which improved the style and the argument, and Gavin Kitching was remarkably effective in arranging for publication. My appreciation goes also to Nancy Marten of Methuen for her enthusiasm and encouragement.

Throughout the writing of the book I was a member of the staff of Heston Comprehensive School, Hounslow. This civilized and civilizing community contributed in no small measure to my ability to complete the project at the same time as doing a job which, throughout, remained enjoyable and compatible with the activity of research and writing. My acknowledgements therefore go to the headmaster, Mr M. C. Moulton, the deputies, Jill Isles and, again, John Crook, the rest of the staff past and present, and, in a special way, those Sixth Form groups who so often provided a stimulating and critical sounding-board for ideas. Financial assistance was generously provided by Hounslow Education Committee.

TONY POLAN
September 1983

# INTRODUCTION

To suffer woes which hope thinks infinite;
To forgive wrongs darker than death or night;
To defy power, which seems omnipotent;
To love and bear; to hope till hope creates
From its own wreck the thing it contemplates;
Neither to change nor falter nor repent;
This, like thy glory, Titan, is to be
Good, great and joyous, beautiful and free;
This is alone life, joy empire, and victory.

Shelley, *Prometheus Unbound*

Few would deny that the events in Poland in 1980 and 1981 were
among the most remarkable in recent history. From the shattered wreck

of the aspirations of those months, little perhaps is for the moment left, apart, indisputably, from that creative hope that Shelley celebrates. But it is necessary to think as well as to hope. One thing clearly worth thinking about is the strategy pursued by the Solidarity leadership, which on the face of it was, to say the least, puzzling and confusing. The apparent puzzle is that Solidarity displayed a remarkable and perhaps unprecedented confidence and aggressiveness in pursuance of its demands, while refusing nevertheless to translate this into a 'political' programme or movement. The stance adopted was in fact quite the reverse, the movement being apparently determined to resist any definition of its activities or aims as 'political'.

Such a stance might be open to at least two lines of criticism, both suggesting a problem of 'immaturity' or 'irresponsibility'. From one standpoint it may be argued that Solidarity's strategy, or lack of it, exacerbated Poland's social and economic crisis at a time when the union's right to exist had been established, and when a policy of militant activity was no longer relevant or useful. This stance can be seen as a causal factor in the military intervention, and indeed might even give some degree of legitimacy to that action. Once the fundamental right to exist had been won, it would seem that historical experience and practical logic should have dictated a new attitude. That is, having established an organization that could claim de facto loyalty and support from a huge part of the population, it was time to move from being an organization of dissent and protest advancing the interests of a specific social group. It was necessary for Solidarity to see itself as a partner in the power structure and make its own contribution to solving the social crisis that gripped the country. At the very least, some kind of 'social contract' was implied whereby an equilibrium could be established between the union and the party. Only in this way could the party be provided with the necessary assurances that would allow the process of reform to continue and consolidate. But the quality of magnanimity was unfortunately missing from Solidarity's strategy. Despite Walesa's assertions to the effect that 'Solidarity has declared its readiness to co-operate in implementing any rational programme aimed at overcoming the crisis and reforming the existing structures of the social and economic life of our country',[1] the way in which workers' representatives had been absorbed by the apparatus after previous crises showed the danger of a wholehearted adoption of such a course.

But if the magnanimity to effect the necessary compromise was lacking, so also was its opposite. For the second possible criticism is that

Solidarity failed to translate its awesome social power into a coherent and determined struggle for political power. It had deprived the party of the power to make decisions over vast areas of social and economic life, but it naively refused to openly challenge the power structure, and thus complete their victory.

From the standpoint of both criticisms, what is deemed to be lacking is politics: in the first case, politics sophisticated enough to establish a compromise; in the second case, politics tough enough to make a bid for the control of the state. As such, whatever the risks involved in either option (absorption in the first case, defeat in the second), the risk involved in opting for *neither* loomed even larger. Some force would have to step in and fulfil the responsibilities that Solidarity so studiously refused, and thus arrived the rule of the army.

It is possible, therefore, to see the career of Solidarity in terms of the consequences of tactical decisions that went wrong, this itself being attributable to the lack of maturity from which such a new movement will inevitably suffer. But, as Bauman has suggested, such a view would quite fail to grasp the originality of Solidarity's strategy, and the clarity of mind with which the union pursued it. Bauman points out that the refusal to become engaged in politics was deliberate,[2] and involved very careful and conscious definition of aims on the part of the leadership. Against the claims of both defenders and opponents of the regime that the union's activities were by their very nature political, the union offered a different definition of politics. It was advancing a concept of politics that was not about power, but about representation. It rejected the assumption that the articulation of specific interests by a particular social group automatically implied a claim for control of the state. This of course is distinctly at odds with the official culture of politics within the East European party regimes, which are built upon the assumption that there is no distinction between state and society. Such a distinction is the salient feature of liberal democracies, wherein politics is seen as the discourse of the necessary interplay between the interests and ideologies articulated in civil society and their representation in the decision-making processes that are allocated to the state. A concept of politics as identical with the issue of the possession of state power must of course abolish politics as activity and replace it with politics as apparatus.

A culture of 'politics as apparatus' might seem to dictate an inevitable strategy for any who criticize the existing regime: a direct challenge to the totality of existing power. But Solidarity rejected this imperative. Instead it attempted to uncouple certain areas of civil society from the machinery of state power. These were to constitute distinct and separate domains claiming rights to representation, arbitration and negotiation that did not necessarily impinge upon, or contradict, the legitimate prerogatives of a central administrative apparatus. Thus the withdrawal from politics was in another sense a reclamation of politics. It was a reclamation of a concept of politics redolent of the mainstream of European political theory, that based upon the separation between state and civil society. The writer, Jacek Kuron, indeed argued that the government and party should withdraw from certain areas of social life, while retaining control over the army, police and central administration. The resulting vacuum would not necessarily and automatically be filled by Solidarity members, but by the members of the particular social group involved – the professions, the media, the arts and, in the case of the trade unions, the members of the working class. Similarly, the withdrawal was reinforced from Solidarity's side by the ruling which forbade union officials to hold office in the state or municipal machinery.[3] This, as Bauman points out, was to re-establish the traditional distinction between state and civil society, and reclaim the autonomy of the latter.[4]

The trade unionists, then, in emphasizing autonomy for union activities, were not demanding an alternative form of state power: their 'autonomy' did not necessarily possess implications of the council-type state form, the reconstruction of the state along lines more in keeping with radical and putatively 'socialist' forms. What was involved instead was the rejection of a single-celled political structure and the evolution of a far more highly diversified organism. In other words, an organism that would be able to cope with the complex social problems and the multiform human aspirations that are the concomitant of a modernized society. Arato and Vajda make this the crucial distinction between possible paths to reform: 'While the goal of traditional Marxists . . . remains the negative Utopia of the politicization of the whole of society, the immense bulk of Eastern European dissidents seeks the creation or recreation of civil society.'[5] They expand on the implications of this in their indictment of

the traditional indifference or hostility of classical Marxist theory (based on the identification of capitalism and civil society) to the institutions that civil society in its capitalist form already possesses: market, parliamentarism, negative rights attached to possession and privacy, general and formal law, freedom of speech and press,

political pluralism, and, above all, those institutions of small-scale
public participation which are to mediate between the individual
and the representatives of political power.[6]

Thus the 'depoliticization' strategy may represent a withdrawal from
politics, but only from politics as it is officially defined by the state
culture. In the long run, such a withdrawal was bound to have political
effects of major dimensions. The greatest effect would be the overthrow
of the discourse that legitimated the party regime. Conversely, had
Solidarity itself adopted a strategy of power, it would not have been
immune to problems of legitimacy. The competing claims that the
party and the union could advance to such legitimate possession of
power might well *both* lack convincing authority.

But the existence of groups within society that manage to establish
for themselves some legitimate independence and distance from the
state apparatus must result in the generation of a field of politics
wherein such groups and interests operate. This is why the threat of
Solidarity was ultimately so profound. It challenged not merely an
institutional structure – and structures may after all be reformed or
reconstructed – but also a discourse. Bauman defines Solidarity's
refusal to engage in politics as a refusal to enter a discourse within
which it would be powerless and illegitimate: 'the rules of the political
game, the grammar of political language, are so constructed that they
automatically reproduce and perpetrate the party's domination.'[7]
Oppositional forces cannot win a debate upon the terrain prepared and
mastered by the party, because it is a discourse that legitimates only one
concept of politics. It is a concept of politics that must embarrass and
confuse the new participants, because within it their own very existence
is illegitimate. But to establish domains outside the reign of the party is
to subvert the official discourse by rendering its assumptions vacuous
and redundant. The creation of the elements of civil society in its own
way redefines the proper role and powers of the state, in the sense of
reducing these to the representative and administrative functions that
it possesses in democratic theory and practice.

The argument that I will seek to develop concerns the origins and
nature of the discourse of politics that obtains in countries like Poland.
This discourse originates in Marxism, but in some ways politics is an
unfortunate domain to investigate from the standpoint of Marx's work.
A study of his writings will find much analytical discussion of the
nature of politics at specific moments of modern history. But when

Althusser points out, on Marx's *Capital*, 'The reader will know how Volume Three ends. A title: Classes. Forty lines, then silence',[8] he is underlining a problem that faces any such investigation as this. Marx's discussions of the political domain are directed to specific historical events. Not, of course, that these are devoid of theoretical constructs; but we are left without any rigorous exposition of a theory of this domain, and, most notably of all, we are left without a substantive discussion of Marx's conceptualizations of the institutions of an emancipated society.

Marx, in common with contemporary radicals, was not disposed to separate the problem of political institutions from the 'social question' which was perhaps necessarily construed as the exclusive focus of the struggle for emancipation. It was, therefore, inevitable that this should be a neglected area of discussion, that questions of 'state and government' should be overwhelmed by this prior 'obsession'.[9] Nevertheless, the one state form to which Marx did declare allegiance was the Paris Commune of 1871 and it is the image of this institution that has entered into the theory, the vocabulary and the imagination of the Marxist tradition. Even here, Arendt and Anweiler have entered a reservation regarding Marx's commitment to this form, arguing that Marx envisaged for the Commune a role only as 'temporary organs in the political struggle to advance the revolution',[10] that is, *not* as the permanent organizational form for the politics of the future society. Nevertheless, Engels – reporting to Bebel the conclusions to which he and Marx had come in the light of the Commune – seems categorical:

> The whole talk about the state should be dropped, especially since the commune, which was no longer a state in the proper sense of the word . . . the state is only a transitional institution which is used in the struggle, in the revolution, to hold down one's adversaries by force . . . as soon as it becomes possible to speak of freedom the state as such ceases to exist. We would therefore propose to replace *state* everywhere by *Gemeinwesen*, a good old German word which can very well convey the meaning of the French word *commune*.[11]

These comments on the Gotha Programme of the German Social-Democratic Party are significant not only for their insistence on the idea of the commune. Even more interesting is the contradiction established between freedom and the state, and here the importance of the Commune to concepts of the socialist order is clearly more central than Arendt has allowed. What is involved, of course, is the assumption that the state is no more than the organization of 'bodies of armed men'. This refusal to allow the state any more complex articulation and any broader role is clearly a restrictive theoretical step, particularly in the light of the rich tradition of political philosophy, at very least since Hobbes, that has investigated the more realistic problem of the ambiguity and delicacy of the relationship between the state and freedom.

In the following chapters I shall seek to define the nature of the contemporary political forms and discourses of the 'Marxist' states through an investigation of that concept of the commune that evoked Marx's approval. In an echo of Engels' argument, the usual definition of the relation between these two entities – 'really-existing socialism' and the 'commune-state' – is one of contradiction. The two appear to represent the antipodean forms that state institutions might take. In contrast to this argument, however, I shall be trying to suggest an inescapable, and probably causal, link between the two. But the subject of my argument will be Lenin, not Marx. Such a substitution might ordinarily evoke a protest from those who consider that Leninism is but one of many possible versions of Marxism, and in itself not the most legitimate. But in the area I shall be discussing such a protest is perhaps weaker than it might otherwise be. For Marx endowed posterity with no other theory of the politics and government of socialist society than the commune-state; and Lenin incorporated into his politics the theory of the commune-state as elaborated by Marx, without additions and without omissions.[12] Here, at least, there seems to be a process, not of revision or development, but of straightforward inheritance.

## NOTES

1 Speech at ILO Conference in Geneva, 5 June 1981, printed in D. MacShane, *Solidarity: Poland's Independent Trade Union*, Nottingham, 1981, 161.
2 Z. Bauman, 'On the maturation of socialism', *Telos*, 47 (Spring 1981), 51.
3 MacShane, op. cit., 126, 128, 129.
4 Bauman, op. cit., 52.
5 A. Arato and M. Vajda, 'The limits of the Leninist opposition', *New German Critique*, 19 (Winter 1980), 167.
6 ibid., 168.
7 Bauman, op. cit., 51.
8 L. Althusser, *Reading Capital*, London, 1970, 193.
9 H. Arendt, *On Revolution*, London, 1963, 258.
10 ibid., 257. O. Anweiler, *The Soviets*, New York, 1974, 15, concurs with Arendt.

11  F. Engels, 'Letter to A. Bebel, March 1875', in Marx and Engels, *Selected Works*, Moscow, 1968, 339.

12  The extensive literature on the Commune of 1871 includes F. Jellinek, *The Paris Commune of 1871*, London, 1937; J. Hicks and R. Tucker, *Revolution and Reaction*, Amherst, Mass., 1973; E. Schulkind, *The Paris Commune of 1871 — The View from the Left*, London, 1972. Much of Marx's writings on the issue will be found in the Pelican Marx Library, vol. 3, *The First International and After*, London, 1974.

# ONE **LENIN'S THE STATE AND REVOLUTION**

## PROBLEMS OF A TEXT
## AND ITS DISCOURSE

The *Collected Works* of Lenin fill some forty-five volumes.[1] Yet, for the purpose of understanding Lenin and his impact upon the world we inhabit, the bulk of his work is redundant. It has relevance only for specialist academics, traditionalist revolutionaries and fastidious ideologues. For the rest of mankind, the importance of Lenin is contained in a handful of tracts. These are the writings that have functioned as definitive elements of contemporary political culture, the active elements that have shaped institutions, parties, states and peoples. *What Is To Be Done?* (1902) argues the need for a revolutionary party to combat the consciousness of the people and supply them with scientific and revolutionary politics. *One Step Forwards, Two Steps Back* (1904) propounds, if only by example, the necessary form of this party – tight, professional, disciplined, structured by 'democratic centralism'. *Imperialism* (1916) proposes a specific characterization and perspective on contemporary world society and economy, and proposes a theoretical conclusion to the capitalist epoch. *The State and Revolution* (1917) gives a prescription for what a real socialist revolution would have to achieve, and a model of the institutions it would construct. Finally, *Left-Wing Communism* (1920) articulates the approach necessary for the capture of power through the rest of the capitalist world, in a political handbook that established revolution as the highest principle, and flexibility as the only strategy.[2]

Within this group of texts, *The State and Revolution* stands apart. The unity of the other texts lies in that they are *practical* and *timely*: each originated as a response compelled by a specific political problem. The 1902 text was a reply to the threat posed by the so-called 'economist' trend. In 1903 the proposals of Axelrod and Martov for a party of an open type produced the dispute over the party rules that gave to history the dubiously accurate terms 'Bolshevik' and 'Menshevik'. *Imperialism* was dictated by the need to provide a characterization of the First World War that would condemn the pro-war positions of the European social democratic parties. In 1920 it was the immaturity and naivety of the new European communist parties that dictated the new handbook of revolutionary tactics. All the texts are resolutely practical. They display an overriding concern for the mechanics of power, of political survival and success, whereby illusions are demolished with an instinctive realism. They assault any thought that harbours a whiff of liberalism, utopianism, impracticality, abstract morality or ethical motivations.

There is no difficulty in placing the origin or import of these texts. This is not so with *The State and Revolution*. As we shall see, it has proven difficult to explain precisely why Lenin chose the moment of temporary lull in the storms of 1917 to write the book in his enforced Finland exile. And it is even more difficult to discover why he chose to propound the argument it contained. What possible connection these thoughts bore with what subsequently occurred under his leadership is the most obscure question of all.

But these problems do not confer upon the text the status of an aberration, standing at odds with the rest of the corpus. In fact the effect of the text is the reverse. *The State and Revolution* provides Lenin's legacy with a dimension that would otherwise be missing, and it is arguable that such an absence would debilitate the effectiveness of the artefact that is Lenin and Leninism. Without it, the whole canon of his writings would take on an entirely different aspect. The existence of *The State and Revolution* suggests that the rest of the corpus, on the face of it practical writings with an instrumental intent, are built upon a fundamentally emancipatory intent; and that the subsequent history of the Russian state under Stalin and his heirs can reasonably be interpreted as a violation of both the letter and spirit of Lenin's politics. Openly or implicitly, *The State and Revolution* has had a long career as Lenin's credentials as a revolutionary humanist, allying him with those who reject the pragmatism and brutality of subsequent Soviet history. The virtues of libertarianism, spontaneity, praxis, anti-authoritarianism, proletarian creativity, self-emancipation, all resound through the writing. And so at the very least *The State and Revolution* can lead to a consequent acceptance of all the less attractive elements of practical Leninism, and similarly prevent or delay the rejection of the whole Leninist ideology by those repelled by that ideology in action. At most, it lies at the very core of the effectiveness of Leninism as a mobilizing ideology of political movements. A political ideology based only upon a theory of vulgar *Realpolitik* (the rest of Lenin's writings) and a reality of disappointed hopes and bloody confusions (the history of the Soviet state) would be a weak one indeed. *The State and Revolution* inserts into this unconvincing ensemble all the humanist elements that are missing: the deeply felt aspirations for a truly free society based upon tolerance, equality and fraternity. An effective and practical politics which can guarantee the birth of Utopia is surely difficult to resist.

At the time he undertook his first researches into the theoretical problem of the state, Lenin was living in exile in Zurich. These preparations were modest, and amounted, in their published form, to about one hundred pages of extracts from Marx and Engels accompanied by Lenin's marginal notes.[3] The material was written in January and February of 1917 and was left for safe keeping in Stockholm when Lenin returned to Russia in April. Later in the year, in July, he instructed Kamenev to arrange their publication if he did not survive contemporary events.

The opportunity to complete the work on the state arose in the wake of the July Days. What amounted to a popular rising began on 3 July 1917, at the moment when the provisional government had ordered a large military offensive. The demonstrations lasted four days and developed into a serious threat to the government. Although the Bolsheviks considered that the moment was far too premature to attempt to supplant the provisional government, that government could not but see it as an attempt on their part to further destabilize the situation. Loyal troops were drafted into the capital, *Pravda* was suppressed and orders were issued for the arrest of the three chief Bolshevik leaders. Kamenev was taken, and Lenin and Zinoviev went into hiding and escaped to Finland. Lenin asked for his notebook to be brought to him, where he used parts but not all of it in the writing of *The State and Revolution*.

Although he maintained intimate contact with developments in Petrograd, Lenin's return to the city was delayed until 9 October. It was on the following day that the Bolshevik central committee was persuaded by Lenin's urgent insistence to decide to prepare for armed insurrection. A political bureau was appointed to carry out this decision, although the actual task of organizing the action fell to the military-revolutionary committee of the Petrograd soviet. This body, being a Menshevik initiative with solely defensive responsibilities, predated the decision of 10 October. After the decision, the Bolsheviks converted it to their own purposes, composed as it was exclusively of Bolsheviks with one Left Social Revolutionary. This was the instrument that organized the seizure of power later in the month. Lenin subsequently noted (30 November 1917) that the completion of *The State and Revolution* by the addition of a seventh chapter on 'The experience of the Russian revolutions 1905 and 1917' was interrupted by these events and commented that 'it is more pleasant and useful to go through the experience of revolution than to write about it'.[4]

In the *Collected Works*, the text is noted as being written in August–September 1917, although not published until 1918. This does not, however, mean that the ideas contained in it were not made public until after the October revolution. It appears that the actual writing of *The State and Revolution* was in itself little more than a formality; the central themes had already been articulated in various public writings throughout the year. In the interval between the February revolution and his return to Russia Lenin wrote his *Letters from Afar*, one of which contained the central idea of the need for a post-revolutionary state, but a 'State of a different type'. The Commune is advanced as exemplar. He returned to the theme in his article on 'The dual power', published in *Pravda* on 9 April, six days after his return from exile, and the Commune is further referred to in the *Letters on Tactics*, written between 8 and 13 April, and discussed in some detail in the pamphlet *The Tasks of the Proletariat in Our Revolution*, completed on 10 April, although not published until September.

Lenin's report to the Petrograd City Conference of the RSDLP (Bolsheviks) on 14 April presented the concept in some clarity to his comrades.[5] The theme became a consistent note in his public and private writings and his proposed revision of the party programme, which was published in June 1917, makes the innovations official. The most significant change Lenin proposed involved the removal of the clause that the 'RSDLP make its primary and immediate task to overthrow the Tsarist autocracy and set up in its place a democratic republic', in favour of one that stated, 'The party of the proletariat cannot remain content with a bourgeois parliamentary democratic republic. . . . The party fights for a more democratic workers' and peasants' republic.' The proposals then proceed to introduce the concepts of recallable delegates and elective officials, and envisages the emergence of the soviet form as the structure of the state: 'parliamentary representative institutions will be gradually replaced by Soviets of people's representatives (from various classes and professions, or from various localities) functioning as both legislative and executive bodies.'[6]

It is clear, therefore, that the ideas in *The State and Revolution* had already been propounded by Lenin some time before he had the opportunity to codify them in a 'theoretical' work. It should also not be forgotten that to attribute to him sole authorship of the ideas would be mistaken. It seems to have been Bukharin's earlier work that first brought the classical Marxian concept of the state to Lenin's attention, although he had until February 1917 displayed a sharp hostility towards the 'semi-anarchism' of Bukharin's call for the 'revolutionary destruction' of the bourgeois state.[7] At a different level, it is likely that such libertarian ideas had already been given currency by the political activity of anarchist and populist trends within the revolutionary movement, and it is quite probable that experiences since February had given rise to ideas, albeit imprecise, with similar libertarian and utopian yearnings among parts of the population itself. What Lenin did was to take the ideas out of the realm of romantic politics and emotive speculation and fuse them with a practical and seemingly successful politics. They were transformed, as a result, from the ephemera of social dislocation into the lineages of the state that was born later in the year.

## THE ARGUMENT AND ITS SIGNIFICANCE

The theses of the text can, without doing violence to the argument, be stated in summary form.

(a) All states are instruments for the oppression of one class, or set of classes, by another. They are, in the last resort, and in their most fundamental aspect, bodies of armed men.

(b) The state form constructed under the capitalist mode of production is appropriate for only that social system. For a new class power, it is therefore necessary that the old state machine be destroyed and a new one constructed.

(c) This new state regime is termed the 'dictatorship of the proletariat'.

(d) The dictatorship of the proletariat will, however, involve less need for a state machine than any previous regime. This is because (i) the ruling class will for the first time be the majority class in the population, and (ii) the administrative tasks of the state have been immensely simplified by the development of the forms and forces of production under capitalism.

(e) Nevertheless, a state of some form will be needed (i) to suppress the remnants of the old ruling classes, and (ii) to regulate the distribution of economic resources and rewards during the transitional period leading to a socialist economy.

(f) This new state will not recognize the division of tasks established by capitalist regimes. Distinctions between representative, legislative, executive, administrative and judicial functions will be removed.

(g) The state will therefore not be of a parliamentary type, but of a soviet or council type. The structure of parliaments establishes false barriers between the rulers and the ruled: the political system must become delegatory rather than representative. Parliaments also elevate the principle of separation of powers, thereby reducing or eliminating the possibility of democratic control over the functions of the state. All such functions will be conferred on a single institution.

(h) The tasks of running the state can be fulfilled by all and any member of society. To ensure maximum participation in these tasks, and remove the possibility of the development of a bureaucratic élite, the holding of office will be governed by the principles of rotation of office, instant recall for violation of mandate and payment of average salaries.

(i) This state will, from its very inception, be set on a course of withering away, as the conflicts it exists to resolve are eliminated in the course of development of the socialist economy.

On initial consideration, it is difficult to claim much significance for the work. Historians of Lenin's life and thought, of the Russian

Revolution and the Bolshevik regime, of political philosophies and practices, tend to devote little space to *The State and Revolution*. The piece appears to offer little opportunity for comment or discussion. It is usually merely necessary to summarize it, and the value of any further examination is not easy to establish. It is a brief, inelegant and confessedly derivative argument. It presents no problems of interpretation: there are no ambiguities in the text, no opportunities for conflicting readings. In that sense, it is not a *Capital*, not even a *What Is To Be Done?*. And, in contrast to those two examples, it does not require 'translation' for a modern audience: despite the frequent polemical references to unfamiliar contemporary figures, its concepts are not strange to a modern readership, its arguments are anything but subtle and its message is transparent. As political philosophy, it does no more than retail the themes of a much older and richer political tradition. E. H. Carr has pointed out its roots in More, Rousseau, Godwin, the early socialists, as well as Marx and Engels.[8]

But if a discussion of the work as political philosophy seems unrewarding, there is perhaps even less satisfaction to be derived from studying it as a historical object. Its status in the history of the time is unambiguous: it is marginal. It is not an official document, a government decree, a manifesto or a party programme. It was a subterranean, not a public document. By the time it was published real events in the life of the new regime had rendered it little more than a historical curiosity. Such is the discrepancy between the argument of the text and the manner in which the Bolshevik regime actually developed that it appears to offer no access to an understanding of what happened. Here were a set of utopian ideals rapidly erased by the brute necessities of political life. Carr presents the most popular explanation: he details the 'sullen obstruction' of the peasantry, which even 'carried a part of the urban workers with them into passive opposition', the failure of the European working class to make the revolutions which would rescue the new state, the siege laid by a 'capitalist world united in its hostility to Bolshevism'. And so 'Lenin never openly admitted these disappointments, or perhaps even admitted them to himself. But they were responsible for the apparent contradictions between the theory of *The State and Revolution* and the practice of the first year of the regime.'[9]

Despite the central role which the ability to quote appropriate texts from Lenin played in the inner-party disputes of the 1920s, even here *The State and Revolution* appears to be absent. None of the major oppositions seems to have deemed the work significant enough – or perhaps acceptable enough – to include it in its verbal armoury for combating Stalin's approach.[10] As history, then, the work seems to be of purely archaeological interest.

Yet these considerations perhaps mistake the nature of the object. The fact is that the significance of the text is derived from its contemporary political and social role, not from historical or philosophical considerations. The significance of Marxism–Leninism is as one of the most effective mobilizing ideologies and legitimating belief-systems in the history of parties, states and societies. It is an ideology widely subscribed to some sixty years after the death of its junior author, in strikingly diverse locales around the globe, albeit often to support ideas and actions that would somewhat surprise that author.[11] But the apparently huge distance between the original ideas and contemporary versions of them does not undermine the relevance of discussion of those originals. Such a connection would only be illegitimate if we presumed a rationality of discourse in historical action that cannot seriously be postulated so late in the twentieth century. Ideas have careers of their own, and if they are 'criminal' careers by the lights of their progenitors they nevertheless testify to what elements of the initial problematic have been found relevant by history. And, of course, the particular ideas under discussion lay more claim than most to an appeal to the judgement of the court of history.

Even if it is difficult to establish a precise connection via the genealogy of discourses between Lenin's interpretation of Marx and Engels and the political practices and institutions that characterize contemporary party regimes, it is possible to suggest that more profound processes are at work that establish a link. Historical events can easily be explained by reference to the most obvious influences: the consequences of a precisely articulated political programme, or a rigorously tabulated set of 'objective' and 'material' conditions. But they may not necessarily be most *adequately* explained by such means. Historical events must have elusive causes, or history would be far easier to direct than has proven to be the case, and historical explanation must often proceed by intuition rather than documentation. The most elusive of historical causations is 'culture', because culture is both the context and the co-conspirator of all human action, and what is problematic about it is that the most important elements of it are by definition unspoken and inexplicit. The 'ideas' that constitute it are obviously the most successful – that is, the most influential – of all ideas, because they have become 'second nature' to the members of a particular society. But because they are 'natural', they do not present themselves obviously for interrogation.

Cultural critique is problematic: culture is not only object, it is also subject. Culture cannot be thought of except through culture, through internalized norms, attitudes and values. How is it possible, then, to attempt a valid criticism of cultural objects? How is one to avoid the situation scathingly described by Adorno:

> The cultural critic is not happy with civilization, to which alone he owes his discontent. He speaks as if he represented either unadulterated nature or a higher historical stage. Yet he is necessarily of the same essence as that to which he fancies himself superior.[12]

Adorno offers a categorization of possible modes of critique, and analyses the dangers associated with each of them. An 'immanent critique', he explains, is achieved by 'confronting [the culture] with the norms which it itself has crystallized'[13] and revealing the discrepancy between the object and the claims of the object, and those claims and the social reality they criticize. What is involved is a minute and detailed investigation and dissection of every aspect of a particular cultural object; and criticism can claim such a dispassionate relationship to its object of study because the subject, the critic, claims an autonomy from the world that surrounds him; he claims to be more than a mere product of economic, social and cultural determinations. But there is no guarantee that such immanent criticism will not at least suffer from what may be called an unconscious failure of nerve. For 'the spontaneous movement of the object can be followed only by someone who is not entirely engulfed by it'.[14] This surely was the trap that awaited a conventional form of cultural criticism. It concealed the assumptions of the object of criticism and thus rendered itself complicit in its claims.

Marxism offered an example of an alternative mode of critique. This *transcendent* critique was able to insulate itself from the unwanted dictates of the indigenous culture. 'The transcendent critic assumes an as it were Archimedean position above culture.'[15] This was the basis of effective ideology critique, as it had been used to confront the social ideologies of the nineteenth-century bourgeois reality. And Adorno was aware of the achievements of such critiques. Indeed, it was an essential part of his initial formation as a Marxist. Classical liberalism, and its pretensions to effective social integration, had been confronted by the ability of Marxism to reveal the structure of power and partial social interests that propagated it. But, Adorno realized, this approach faced the uncomfortable question, from what standpoint does this critique take place? Even Archimedes needed a fulcrum. Transcendent critiques tend therefore to be based on teleologies which assume a certain end to the process of history, and of cultural change. Adorno, throughout his career, was profoundly suspicious of such systems of thought, which assumed an ontology and some form of identity between subject and object. Such approaches functioned often by reducing complex realities to a single organizing principle. Thus Marxism demonstrated an 'affinity with barbarism', that is, a willingness to confidently sweep away the claims of all and any cultural phenomena to some degree of independence, to have some legitimate statement to make that was not simply a product and reflection of existing power structures. Any Marxist definition of culture as superstructural reflection of the 'real' economic base compounded the cultural destruction inherent in any systemic thought. It resulted in a vulgar reductionism which denied culture any possibility of distance from the power of a ruling class and tended to 'wipe away the whole as with a sponge'.[16]

Adorno pointed to the paradox that it was precisely the project of contemporary social development to turn this philosophical assumption into a growing reality. It was the urgent desire of present and future administration to achieve this integration, as culture became an industry, and power became administration. Further, if 'the choice of a standpoint outside the sway of existing society is as fictitious as only the construction of abstract utopias can be',[17] the existence of a *really existing* society outside bourgeois society offered the practitioners of transcendent criticism the irresistible temptation to ground it in the only concrete alternative available: that of the 'socialist' regimes. And, paradoxically, it was precisely in the Soviet Union that culture had become, emphatically, administration. In sum, not only were the components of this alternative culture ethically so suspect as to disqualify it as a basis for the critique of anything, the critique made such an immoderately sweeping and immediate totalization of its object that no insights into its nature and complexities could be forthcoming.

Hegel, whose system provided the model for this approach, suffered the exposure of his pretensions at the hands of subsequent history. His sophisticated system proved less than adequate to its claim of revealing the true past, present and, above all, future of human reason. Adorno insisted that

> The matters of true philosophical interest at this point in history are those in which Hegel, agreeing with tradition, expressed his disinterest. These are non-conceptuality, individuality, and particularity – things which ever since Plato used to be dismissed as transitory and insignificant.[18]

The solution to this problem is unclear. It has been suggested that Adorno established a satisfactory path between the Scylla of immanent submergence and the Charybdis of transcendent barbarism in, at least, his sociology of music.

Beethoven's work provided the paradigm, the moment of certainty, against which all other moments of musical history, before or since, could be judged. This was not, it should be understood, because Beethoven's work represented some abstract ideal of form or beauty which other composers failed to attain due to an inadequate aesthetic talent. The uniqueness of Beethoven was his ability to express the antinomies and tensions of a point in history when the future was profoundly ruptured from the past. It fully explored the 'peculiar freedom in the social structure of his time'.[19] It is thus an expression of human freedom, but one which derives the expressiveness of its freedom from its intimate involvement with its situation in historical time. This freedom expresses Beethoven's emancipation from immanence; but its connection to lived history of the moment guarantees it from dissolution into the meaningless 'extreme autonomy and overripeness [of] the hypersubjective composers of the later 19th century – let Tchaikovsky stand as their archetype'.[20] Thus Beethoven is not conceived as some 'still point in a turning world', to whose *formal* qualities all other attempts at musical composition must aspire. It is rather this complex and ephemeral relationship between consciousness of, and independence from, the social reality in which the work is created that gives it the character of the supreme corpus of critical culture.

But does this offer a solution to the problem under discussion, that is, how to open a meaningful discussion of a document of political argument? Adorno's concept of Beethoven is certainly a striking and thought-provoking image, and it would be advantageous to the argument that follows were the reader to bear that image in mind. But inasmuch as we have no such artefact in the field of political discourse which will authoritatively inform and illumine the concerns of our

present historical age, we are still left without a clear path to follow. At this stage, therefore, all that I will take from Adorno's typology is an analogical classification of the treatments that have been given to Lenin's text.

Commentators on Lenin's text fall into two categories. There are what may be called the historians, who offer critiques and explanations of a 'transcendent' type. In other words, such authors are profoundly distanced from the assumptions of the text. This distance has, perhaps, surprisingly little to do with the 'ideological' commitment of the particular author: it is interesting that the more ideologically distant from Leninism an author is, the more generous his comments on the text tend to be. It is the Marxists or Marxisants such as Hill, Bahro and Carr who discern a certain insincerity and dissimulation where non-Marxists like Ulam and Conquest see innocent and sincere commitment. But what unites these authors for our present purposes is quite simply the historical approach, which produces similar readings as a consequence of a common manner of constituting the object of study. For all these writers the discrepancies between author, text and history are so profound and obvious as to deprive the text of any meaning and any genuine substance. The distance they establish, deliberately or otherwise, from the culture of Leninism makes it impossible for them to feel any pulse of life in the text they are examining. Thus they produce transcendent critiques that ultimately fail to plumb the complexity of the object.

The other approach is the 'political'; but here we stumble into the pitfalls of immanence. For the political writers the ideology of *The State and Revolution* is the very warp and weft of their own culture, and the unconscious and uninterrogated assumptions which they share with the text serve to transform it into something entirely unproblematic. Before the confrontation between text and critic ever occurs, the text has already suborned and conquered the critic.

This would seem to present an insoluble problem: a cultural object can only be grasped as *an* object from outside, but *the* object itself can only be grasped from inside, that culture. I shall later try to suggest a solution to this impasse, but before that is possible we must fully investigate the crisis of interpretation *The State and Revolution* presents.

## THE HISTORIANS' ASSESSMENT

I shall first consider assessments of the text offered by historians, that is, by those seeking to account for origins and features of the Soviet state and its development, and the relation of Lenin and his ideas to that process.[21] The authors are both Marxist and non-Marxist, but what they have in common is that they partake of a discourse on what happened, and why, and are thus distinguished from those we shall consider later as contributors to the 'political' discourse. The latter will be identified by an approach that, in contrast, takes the events the historians discuss as a 'given', and seeks to determine the relevance of that complex historical 'given' to contemporary political problems.

Conceptions of *The State and Revolution* put forward among historical writers vary: they range from suggestions that it is sincere but unconnected to anything that later transpired to the discovery in it of rather less sincere motives and find that the democratic instincts it espouses are a mask for something less attractive. Conquest finds both the content and the intention of the text hard to fault:

> The thesis presented in *The State and Revolution* is far from an ignoble one . . . the booklet was not published before the Revolution, so there can be no question of it being a piece of intellectual demagoguery. . . . It is not the product of anything so crude as hypocrisy . . . but rather of the paradoxes, the ambivalence of Lenin's whole political nature.[22]

– this, despite the fact that Conquest may be considered one of the commentators most out of sympathy with Lenin's thought and achievements.

Wilson's classic work on the origins and development of Bolshevism dismisses the piece with rather less sympathy:

> He had given so little thought to the ultimate goals of socialism . . . that when . . . he tries to formulate some notions of the subject, he can only look it up in Marx and Engels and repeat the meagre indications of the 'Critique of the Gotha Programme' in respect to inequality of wages and the withering away of the state. There is nothing in *The State and Revolution* except the qualified utopianism of his masters.[23]

Ulam construes the work as more serious in its selection of texts and ideas than Wilson has allowed. He stresses the fact that this was not something carelessly 'thrown off' in the heat of the moment, under the pressure of events: 'the length of its preparation and Lenin's extreme solicitude that the work be completed even if he were to be "bumped off" ' indicates that this is not a mere propaganda pamphlet addressed to the needs of the hour.'[24] Yet he clearly cannot locate the work comfortably in the Lenin he knows: 'no work could be more unrepresentative of the author's political philosophy and his general frame of mind than this one. . . . The unfortunate pamphlet is almost a straightforward profession of anarchism.'[25]

Ulam does not suggest that the work is 'insincere'. But he does argue that Lenin's approach to 'theory' is essentially conditional and pragmatic. Rather than his politics flowing from a consistent and coherent social and economic analysis, the demands of politics, of the imminent revolution, impose upon Lenin the need for a particular mode of theorizing:

> in the revolution, in the struggle for power, marxism subsists and conquers by an appeal to the anarchistic instincts. . . . Such was Lenin's absorption in the doctrine and its psychology that upon coming to power he could pass, as if unconsciously, from a denigration of the state to its staunch defence.[26]

Liebman disagrees with Ulam's estimate of the importance Lenin attached to the work, a necessary move perhaps in a book which attempts a sustained defence of Lenin's politics:

> It must be emphasised that *The State and Revolution* is an unfinished work, the writing of which was interrupted at the end of the summer of 1917 so that the author might engage in less theoretical work and prepare for the imminent coming of the state that would be born from the revolution.[27]

On the doctrine of the 'smashing of the state' Lenin advances, according to Liebman, 'nothing that was not in conformity with Marxist doctrine'. Liebman does, however, consider that on other issues Lenin makes an original contribution. On the building of socialist society, Lenin 'advancing beyond the realm of classical marxism ventured . . . into the unknown and dangerous territory in which criticism of society gives way to constructive work'.[28] And, on this count, Liebman judges the work a failure, and a dangerous one at that. He is a markedly sympathetic commentator, but feels compelled to underline the consequences of the 'unfinished' nature of the work. It shows

> glaring weaknesses where one of the most important and difficult problems is concerned, namely that of the dictatorship of the proletariat . . . it is surprising to see how lightly Lenin dealt with it . . . here

was a book that needed to be completed and developed, since, as it stood, it was silent about, or else overlooked, or even dodged, the gigantic problems that the building of socialist society must necessarily encounter.[29]

Liebman then briefly indicates what appear to him as problems in the application of such ideas to a complex society. But he comes to concur with Ulam's emphasis on the effect of the political moment: 'A democratic inspiration lies at the heart of Lenin's vision at the time, and gives it its "immoderate" character. This is the mark of the period.'[30]

The critics so far discussed have maintained an essentially generous interpretation of the work. The practical implications – for a mass democracy, for real power to the soviets – were genuinely conceived by Lenin as the aim of the revolutionary process. Albeit the work was inconsistent with all of Lenin's thought so far, and was to be effectively negated by his subsequent actions, it was a simple response to the spirit of the times, an infatuation with the vibrant creativity displayed by the Russian people. Others have detected more considered and less ingenuous motives behind the work. Schapiro boldly asserts that: 'It is unlikely that the more utopian parts of this represented Lenin's convictions.'[31] He does not attempt to define more specific motivations. Daniels is similarly dismissive:

> The book reads like a manifesto of left-wing Bolshevism, and indeed, that is its real significance. To consider *The State and Revolution* as the basic statement of Lenin's political philosophy – which non-communists as well as communists usually do – is a serious error. Its argument for utopian anarchism never actually became official policy after the revolution, as the Soviet leadership has always pretended.[32]

It can, however, be suggested that the 'over-emphasis' on the libertarian mode in the text was deliberate. First, it can be considered as part of a long-standing 'debate': the debate within the international socialist movement initiated by the 'betrayal' of the social democratic parties of Europe in August 1914. Thus E. H. Carr also appreciates the significance of the 'moment'; but for him the moment is defined not only by the imminence of revolution, but also by the need to settle the issues raised by the split in the international movement. For Lenin, these issues bore directly on the likely outcome of the 1917 events, and lack of clarity in perceiving them could constitute a danger to the success of the revolution. The classical Marxian concept of the state had contended with two deviations since being propounded by Marx and Engels: the 'reformist', which did not consider that the class nature of the state posed a problem under bourgeois democracy; and the anarchist, which denied any role for a state in the revolutionary transformation of society. The latter had been a minor trend; the former was a dominant tendency, responsible for the volte-face of 1914, whose dangerous nature must have been multiplied in Lenin's eyes by the conciliatory attitude of the Bolshevik party to the provisional government before his return in April. Thus Carr suggests that

> it was the loyalty of the so-called social democrats to the national state, their abandonment of the fundamental socialist tenet of hostility to the state, which had broken the international solidarity of the workers of Europe and driven them to engage in fratricidal strife at the behest of the ruling classes of their respective nations. Hence the emphasis in *The State and Revolution* . . . was somewhat one-sided.[33]

This in itself does not undermine the moral or theoretical integrity of the text. It does not put in question, rather it confirms, Lenin's adherence to the soviet form. Others, however, suggest that certain absences in the text, and the incongruity of the text itself, express a degree of 'dishonesty', and perhaps reproduce the consistently manipulative and opportunist character of Lenin's politics. The soviets are a means, and a transitory one, not an end. Hill places the emphasis on Lenin's clear perception of the political and social barriers that could obstruct the transformation of Russia under a Bolshevik leadership:

> Lenin wished above all to ensure that no respect for formal legality, or even for a constitutionally expressed majority, should prevent the Bolshevik Party from seizing a favourable opportunity for carrying out changes which he regarded as essential. He was convinced (rightly, as was made clear in October and November) that the policy of his party represented the will of the majority of the population: and even if this had not been so he would have argued that the pressure of existing institutions, the ruling class monopoly of education and propaganda before 1917, the age-long habits of submission and obedience, weighted the scales unduly in illiterate Russia. The dictatorship was needed as a weapon against inertia, force of habit.[34]

The authoritative historian of the Russian soviets, Anweiler, echoes the suggestion that Lenin's infatuation with the soviets was a short-term, tactical position derived from the necessity to gain state power. Previously, in 1905, he had been hostile to the soviets. He had been consistently suspicious of all attempts at proletarian, spontaneous self-organization, inasmuch as these were bound to conflict with his own party's right to lead.[35] The change of attitude in 1917 was of a specific nature. Lenin's acceptance of the soviets only extended as far as their role in the revolutionary moment, and did not legitimize them as structures for revolutionary self-government:

> Lenin's attitude to the soviets, like Marx's approach to the Paris Commune, was dominated by the politics of revolution; his blueprint of the socialist soviet state in *The State and Revolution* was the theoretic justification of the imminent seizure of power . . . the slogan of the soviets was primarily tactical in nature.[36]

Keep, who has translated the available records of the proceedings of the Central Executive Committee of the Soviet in the first months of Bolshevik power, points to what he considers to be a lack of seriousness in Lenin's writing. He stresses how little thought Lenin gave to the actual workings of soviet institutions, precisely how their administrative functions were to be fulfilled and their democratic procedures ensured. This he attributes largely to the demands of a strategy for obtaining power:

> The silence was in large part tactical: Lenin realised that by entering into too much detail he would spoil the bright image of the future that he was delineating . . . this appealing doctrine . . . enabled the Bolsheviks to seize the initiative in the Soviet movement.[37]

Bahro, the East German dissident, carries the argument one step further. For him, the actual totalitarian development of the future Soviet state was contained in the text. The 'democratic' arguments lack significance, and convince only the naive.

> Lenin's *The State and Revolution*, representing his immediate preparation for the capture of power, was fondly quoted against later developments by those illusionists who held in their polemic to the traditional elements of the position it developed. But on the decisive question it conceives Soviet power in just the way it was then being created.[38]

For Bahro this decisive question is Lenin's emphasis on the need to replace the smashed state machine with a new one, which will inherit the role of 'commanding' and 'governing'. In the final pages of the text, Lenin is enthusiastically concerned to stress that what will follow the revolution is the period of 'transition', and:

> Until the 'higher' phase of communism arrives, the socialists demand the strictest control by society and by the state over the measure of labour and the measure of consumption. . . . It follows that under communism there remains for a time not only bourgeois right, but even the bourgeois state, without the bourgeoisie.[39]

Bahro comments: 'Here is the unmistakeable voice of compulsion, a compulsion directed not against the former ruling classes, but one that can only be addressed to the "backward elements" of the working class and the people itself.'[40]

It may be objected that Bahro can hardly be classified among the 'historians'. He is a political writer, a dissident Marxist writing in a 'socialist' society, whose imposing book is concerned to approach the pressing political problems of that society. Nevertheless I include him in this survey because he similarly is concerned to view the object – the experience of Lenin and the Revolution – from outside, by means of an academic and highly theoretical mode of writing. In a sense he is transitional between the historical and the political mode of interrogating Lenin's text. This perhaps demonstrates the way in which the two modes are forced to meet to give life to an appreciation of the text; and, also, how rare are the attempts to combine, reconcile or transcend the two modes.

Perhaps the writer best qualified to span the space between the historical and political was Trotsky. Indeed, he seems uniquely qualified for this task. His mammoth *History of the Russian Revolution* represents an attempt by a central political actor to explain the experience in which he participated. But it is for our purposes a disappointment. To Lenin's major theoretical work of the period, to the work that was later to gain wider credence than perhaps any other, Trotsky devotes hardly one page out of a thousand. He will see nothing original in the work, nothing problematical in its origins and intentions, nor in its consequences. Its production was a rational act, and the work is a rational contribution to a rational process:

> With the same painstaking care which he dedicated to thinking about practical problems of the day, he here examines the theoretic

problems of the state. He cannot do otherwise: for him theory is in actual fact a guide to action. In this work Lenin has not for a minute proposed to introduce any new word into political theory. On the contrary, he gives the work an extraordinarily modest aspect, emphasising his position as a disciple.[41]

From Trotsky, the most ardent of Leninists, the most passionate propagator of the centrality of Lenin's theories to the task of revolution to which he, Trotsky, devoted his life, we have what amounts to silence; a silence which becomes all the more strange when it is remembered that one of Trotsky's central planks against the Stalin tendency was the struggle for democracy. Trotsky's silence bespeaks an embarrassment. What strange emotions must he have had if forced to contemplate this text from the historical shallows of 1932? His rigorous discourse, a discourse founded agonizingly upon the need to ensure the survival of the Soviet Union, will not allow such feelings to surface.

## THE POLITICAL ASSESSMENT

There is no evidence that those who came to rule the Soviet Union after Lenin felt any differently about the text than did Trotsky. But, of course, the society very rapidly atrophied into the most hermetic of authority systems. The public writings and statements of Stalin, his colleagues and successors can offer little of interest to those concerned with the problems of a genuine politics. In a peculiar irony on Engels' dictum, the 'government of people' had truly become the 'administration of things'. The absolute erasure of any public sphere consigned all ideology to redundancy or vacuity. The public discourse of the ruling group no longer had a function. In any society but one reduced to a hermetic administrative structure, such public discourse is essentially a mode of negotiation; of negotiating and rearranging the relations between élites, interests, groups, classes, fractions and parties. Where no such plurality of groups exists, public discourse is an absurd non-sense, a ghost without substance, without connection or role within the world of material corporeality.

Nevertheless the public discourse of Leninism overflowed into the world of Europe and Asia, and had its own effects on political culture. And thus the text under discussion became public, claimed a much higher profile and a more elevated stature. It affected the destinies of nations, manipulating and restructuring political cultures both sympathetic and hostile.

Colletti, in his 1967 defence of the text, testifies to the public career of *The State and Revolution*.[42] In particular, he stresses its success in Russia and in communist parties throughout the world during the Stalin era. The text achieved a cult status, which, given the actual practice of politics in the Soviet Union and the Comintern, was bizarre, to say the least. Colletti suggests that this success was simply based upon a misreading of the text, a reading which suggested only that 'The Revolution is violence', and its essential act is the smashing of the existing state machine. He implies that this reading was deliberately encouraged so as to produce a social amnesia about the radical-democratic implications of the soviet form. It can also be argued that the inculcation of such an attitude towards their native state machines among party members in the west was useful to the Russian government. Practically excluded as they were throughout the period from negotiating their role and defending their interests through the channels of diplomacy, the existence of a proletarian 'Trojan horse' to press the interests of the Soviet Union within these countries was invaluable. The most resonant element of the argument throughout this period was therefore probably the term 'the dictatorship of the proletariat': as a slogan it matched the temper of the times, when thinking people could easily and reasonably be convinced of the need for 'tough' solutions to the acute problems of struggle and survival which were posed throughout Europe.

The tradition which consistently stressed the 'democratic' as opposed to the 'violent' interpretation of the text was very much a dissident one. Within the Bolshevik party, Bukharin continued to express a respect for the ideas. Cohen reports his opposition to Lenin's attempts to curtail factory committees and establish hierarchical authority in the very language of Lenin's text: 'It is good that the cook will be taught to govern the state; but what will there be if a commissar is placed over the cook? Then he will never learn to govern the state',[43] and Bukharin may be found advocating steps towards the commune-state as late as 1928. Lukacs, the self-appointed, if officially disparaged, philosopher of the revolution, found the Soviet system an apt vehicle for the political project of the 'subject – object identical'. That is, if the Marxist project was epistemologically the final abolition of the separation between the knower and the known, sociologically this amounted to the construction of the 'transparent' society. This necessitated the dissolution of all institutions that effected separations and differences between people, that allowed corners to remain dark and private, and that assumed the continued existence of different and distinct practices. The Soviet system fulfilled these tasks by establishing the unity of economics and politics, by negating the division of labour, and by transforming all particularities into mere moments of a coherent and comprehensible totality.[44] In contrast to the problems that some writers have experienced in relating the concepts of direct democracy in the soviet form to other of Lenin's writings, for Lukacs they fit convincingly into his highly developed political framework. Indeed it was perhaps this consistency of Lukacs at the level of philosophical logic that led Lenin to castigate his writings as 'very left wing and very poor'.

Rosmer, the French syndicalist who was converted to the Bolshevik position, and later opposed the Stalin regime, has testified to the influence of the text in reconciling libertarian tendencies to Bolshevism and the 'dictatorship of the proletariat'.[45] Subsequently *The State and Revolution* found for itself a place in the radical tradition that has been sustained. Max Schachtman, in 1950 quite distanced from the Russian experience, declared that '*The State and Revolution* remain[s] an unassailable contribution to the socialist struggle for freedom.'[46] Two decades later, Colletti expressed the same sentiments:

> Marxist literature since Marx knows nothing that could even remotely compete with the seriousness of the critique of parliament contained in *The State and Revolution*; nor, at the same time, anything pervaded with such a profound democratic inspiration as that which animates Lenin's text from beginning to end.[47]

Not long after Colletti wrote his assessment, there occurred developments which at once revived the arguments over *The State and Revolution*. As Colletti has indicated, the text set the culture of the radical camp for several decades through to the 1950s. But by that time a process of evolution had occurred which had shifted the official communist movement towards a much less negative estimation of the institutions of the bourgeois polity. Various 'roads to socialism' had been legitimized which sought to take account of 'national characteristics'. Posed in this way, the change was subtle, and perhaps not total: the reassessment of democracy was a product of tactical necessities, and tied very much to the historical specificities of particular cultures. However, in the mid-1970s, in the light of the constant inability of communist parties to attain power in the west, and the constant inability of state regimes in the east to reform themselves in a democratic direction, a debate broke out which perforce involved an assessment of Lenin and

Lenin's texts. This was the 'Eurocommunism' debate, and the argument for a time centred on whether to abandon the slogan and concept of 'the dictatorship of the proletariat'.

In such a climate it is, paradoxically, not easy to escape the sway of Lenin's ideas. When his concept of 'dictatorship' is abandoned, his concepts of 'democracy' can gain in influence. Colletti has provided the interpretation which can justify this.

For Colletti, little time need be spent at the most primitive level of analysis and criticism in Lenin's work. The insistence that the state is in the last resort 'bodies of armed men' is worth noting only as a statement of fact, not an analytical point. To see this, and the prescription to 'smash the old state machine', as the nub of the argument is to miss the point. Colletti himself refers to the *image* conjured up by Lenin's mode and emphasis in writing: 'revolution . . . in its most elementary and external features: the capture of the Winter Palace, the Ministry of Interior in flames, the arrest and execution of the political personnel of the old government.'[48] He goes on to suggest 'all this may take place, but it is not the essential point'.

What is the essential point? Colletti's argument is about control. And it centres on the problem of control of governmental institutions not simply as an ethical choice, but as an essential element that makes possible the conceptions of a socialist social organization. For a political or technical élite to exercise control of the 'bodies of armed men' would fulfil the requirements for the termination of the old class rule, but would answer no questions about what was to replace it. Colletti advances a coherent and logically satisfying argument which bases itself on a distinct couplet of problems concerning the relationship between parliament and other entities. The first relationship is between parliament and the social relations of production that constitute a capitalist society. The second relationship is that between parliament and the subaltern classes. The most obvious, yet most superficial, critique of parliament, argues Colletti, is that which concentrates on the relationship between parliament and electorate. This is a simple problem of structure: one vote every five or so years, lack of accountability of representatives, and so on; and, by the same token, a problem of the *corruptibility* of parliament – electoral frauds, the absorption of radicals by the establishment, the power of patronage, and so forth.[49]

All that may, and clearly does, take place but it is not the point. It would, says Colletti, be theoretically possible for a parliamentary government to exist which had recallable MPs, the most representative of electoral systems, a complete absence of frauds, cheating, bribing and propaganda, and for this not to be genuine democracy but the most perfect expression of the dictatorship of the bourgeoisie.

For Colletti the relationship between the working class and parliament is subordinate to the problem of the relationship of parliament to the social relations of production. The heart of the matter is not the independence of the state apparatus – whether in its repressive, ideological or purely administrative forms – from parliament, but the independence of capital from parliament. This, he would suggest, is not a purely contingent independence, resulting from the manner in which the institutions may have historically developed. It is rather an immanent independence. If it were purely contingent, parliament could by the passing of laws extend its domain to include capital; as it is an immanent independence, i.e. as the inability of bourgeois democracy to dominate capital is inherent in the nature of the two entities, bourgeois democracy does not contain the possibility of subordinating and disciplining capital, and thus of running it in the interests of the subaltern classes. It could not do so even if it wanted to, i.e. even were there the equivalent of a Bolshevik government with a parliamentary majority.

For it is in the process of production that the key to capitalist society, the production of surplus value, lies. Yet it is precisely within the production process, by the very nature of that process itself, that the existence of exploitation is obscured. In Marx's words, the relationship between exploiter and exploited becomes a 'mysterious thing'. Bourgeois democracy can only exist because capital rules social life unperceived and uncontrolled. Because of the fetishized nature of the production process, a society whose central dynamic is exploitation can convince itself that it proceeds by the rule of reason, of freedom and of equality. In Colletti's language, the essence of the 'revisionist and reformist' prostration before bourgeois democracy is that

> For Marx, modern social inequality or capitalist exploitation occurs simultaneously with the fullest development of juridical-political equality; here, on the contrary, juridical-political equality – and hence the modern representative state – becomes the instrument for the progressive elimination and dissolution of real inequalities, which seem arbitrarily produced rather than an organic consequence of the system as such.[50]

Because of the peculiar, unique and critical nature of the disjuncture between capital and democracy, the relationship between democracy and the proletariat can for capital be quite flexible. Thus the parliamentary form can only reinforce capitalist power. Colletti does not deny the possibility and necessity of struggle in the parliamentary arena to reveal the contradictions that exist within it, and between it and the task of socialist transformation. But so long as a working class formulates its political perspective in terms of a parliamentary project, so long will that working class, equally, be distant from the appreciation of its fundamental social slavery and impotence. The project of confronting and overcoming the relationship of exploitation has to, at one and the same time, be the project for the rejection of parliament as an adequate, or even useful, vehicle for this project.

Colletti insists that *The State and Revolution* is essentially directed to a recognition of the substantial nature of this problem. The 'technical' problem of structure referred to above is subordinate, even though the answer to the problem will be found in what appear as technical measures:

> What is essential to the revolution is the destruction of the diaphragm that separates the working classes from power, the emancipation and self-determination of the former, the transmission of power directly into the hands of the people. . . . For Lenin, the revolution is not only the transfer of power from one class to another, it is also the passage from one type of power to another: for him the two things go together because the working class that seizes power is the working class that governs itself.[51]

And the corollary: the working class that cannot govern itself is a working class that is not capable of seizing power. Parliament, because its basic constituent element is the 'individual' citizen, divorced from his or her position in the process of production, is the succinct expression of the subordination to, and ignorance of, the rule of capital. The soviet form, because it reconstitutes the atomized individual as a member of a class standing in a specific relation to the process of production, and in so doing implicitly and limpidly states the exploitation relationship, is the only form that can express the political struggle that will overthrow capital. A socialist government whose lineaments are those of a struggle directed essentially towards and within a parliamentary institution will be the product of a struggle that has been deformed, directed into the parliamentary mentality. Thus will the old circle of exploitation and dependence reassert itself.

It is unlikely that an assessment could be penned today that found the implications of Lenin's argument so unambiguous. But many of the contributions to the Eurocommunism debate take the argument little further than that in which Lenin was engaged sixty years ago. Three texts will illustrate this. The difficulty in escaping the hegemony of Lenin is shown in the caution with which criticism is often addressed. To begin with an advocate of the Eurocommunist position, the general secretary of the Spanish Communist Party, Santiago Carrillo: in *Eurocommunism and the State* he is at pains to suggest that Lenin's writing tends to exaggeration and hyperbole due to the demands of political conjunctures, and this is above all true of the writings during the 1917 Revolution.[52] Carrillo's argument on the substance of the problem is obscure and somewhat tendentious. He chooses to take issue with a minor and subsidiary argument in Lenin's text, and not to confront the actual critique of bourgeois institutions, the purposes of this critique and the alternative which is suggested. Consequently, despite his defence of specific institutions (e.g. universal suffrage, on pp. 91 – 5) in the light of the tragic experience of Europe in the twentieth century, his argument fails to take the measure of the real power of the text: the way in which it articulates a critique of the limitations on human freedom and fulfilment which can, arguably, be attributed to the restricted nature of bourgeois democracy.

The response to the Eurocommunist argument cannot, however, be said to express appreciably more creativity and sensitivity. One of the most authoritative defences of a traditional position was developed by Balibar in a book published in 1976. This was intended as a contribution to the debate in the French Communist Party which led to the dropping of the term 'dictatorship of the proletariat'. Balibar's *On the Dictatorship of the Proletariat* is a disappointing piece of intellectual work (doing little more for Lenin than Lenin did for Marx and Engels, i.e. a rather lengthy exegesis and restatement of the original text in uncompromising terms). It is concerned to stress the continuing relevance of the concept of 'dictatorship' rather than any inherently democratic themes. The book is unlikely to have gained much credibility were it not implicitly based upon the work of Althusser. Althusser had already constructed a reputedly much more sophisticated analysis of the contemporary capitalist state than had been available to Marxists hitherto, and this analysis provided the intellectual justification for restoring the threatened concept of 'dictatorship of the proletariat' to its former authority. In the essay 'Ideology and ideological state apparatuses'[53] Althusser noted that the classical Marxian characterization of the state as an instrument of class repression, although correct, needed supplementing. The necessary supplement was the concept of 'ideological state apparatuses'. That is, if the function of the state was the reproduction of the conditions of production, it achieved its aims by ideological means as well as by coercion. Alongside the repressive arms stands a panoply of 'ideological' institutions.

This in itself hardly represents an original contribution to political sociology. Any acquaintance with the twentieth-century state reveals that it has developed major functions, which, whatever their specific roles, serve to strengthen the commitment of the populace to that state, and thereby to stabilize the existing political and socio-economic structures. Leaving aside the complex of problems associated with representative democracy, which might be legitimately excluded as conceptually different, the state apparatus as such clearly now has a crucial investment in the areas of economic management and welfare provision. In terms of costs these outweigh the repressive apparatus, and in terms of effectiveness in securing social stability their indispensability is obvious. Althusser is not, however, concerned to note these developments. The institutions that he identifies as the 'ideological state apparatuses' are quite different: the churches, the educational system, the family, the legal system, the political system, the trade union movement, the communications media, and the cultural domain.

Critical thought stands somewhat benumbed by this *coup de théâtre*. Refusing any intellectual discrimination or empirical verification, Althusser has simply included in his list practically every extant social institution. (His omissions are baffling. The only elements not included are those very structures that have undeniably become part of the state apparatus in the twentieth century: the welfare system and the economic management structures.) The economy, of course, remains an independent domain for it is the capitalist economy which this array of 'state institutions' is intended to service. It would indeed be hard to conceive of a more ludicrous way of resolving the problems of political sociology. But what can be the purpose of such a ploy? Notwithstanding the ignorance Althusser displays of social reality, the barbarism with which he approaches sociological theory, and the disdain he bestows upon sociological research, the argument achieves its purpose. By an act of theory, he has accomplished the absorption of civil society into the state; he has in fact abolished civil society by the simple expedient of redefining the state as including everything except the capitalist economy. This solves a lot of problems. Specifically it solves the problem of the Soviet Union. It subverts criticism that in the Soviet Union the state is identical with society, i.e. no institution exists which is not part of the state, no activity occurs which is not directed by the state and made to serve its purpose. Althusser demonstrates that exactly this state of affairs also obtains in the capitalist societies. Consequently, the Soviet Union can be seen to be a superior social formation, because at least the economy is socialized. Thus the argument for the dictatorship of the proletariat is restored. The populations of the capitalist states must realize that they already live under a dictatorship; that what they thought was private is in fact public; that what they believed to be public is in fact a tool of the state. All concepts of democracy, private life, civil rights, voluntary associations are consequently simply false consciousness. What we think are *ours*, and therefore worth protecting, are in fact already *theirs*. There can be no purpose in seeking to maintain them. Thus is the totalitarian state intellectually (although hardly convincingly) legitimated.

But other alternatives to Eurocommunism are similarly muted in their innovative attempts. Henri Weber, who in 'Eurocommunism, socialism and democracy' articulates a radical and anti-Stalinist tradition, accepts that the Leninist theses on democracy and socialism are in some ways flawed, and in some ways exaggerated.[54] He argues that Lenin's denunciation of 'bourgeois democracy' was a case of 'bending the stick'. Nevertheless his judgement on the question of institutions is ultimately uncomplicated – and unchanged:

> the historical conditions that produced the good old days of parliamentarism have now ceased to exist. It is really another institutional system which has to be built – one that will allow the distribution of power at the base of society and the active participation of the workers in managing their own affairs. . . . In the articulation of parliamentary and council-type institutions, the reality of power must pass to the latter.[55]

How can Weber, from the standpoint of his tradition, so confidently reaffirm the heritage of Lenin? It is because he refuses any problems inherent in the structure of Soviet institutions. The problems that have in the past led to the collapse of such institutions into the authoritarian state are weaknesses in the *populace*, not weaknesses in the *structures*. The implications of this proposition are clear, as are its intimate connections with authoritarian practices; institutions shall not be constructed to meet the needs of the people, but the people shall be reconstructed to make possible the functioning of the selected institutions. This is of course simply a muted version of the account which attributes the disappearance of democracy in the Soviet Union to objective conditions, that the culture of the population could not sustain it:

> We say [that power must pass the councils] . . . in full awareness of the difficulties involved in the establishment and functioning of socialist democracy. Such democracy must entail the reduction of working time by at least a half – otherwise the workers will have neither the energy nor the leisure to manage the economic units, and the state. It also entails satisfaction of the citizens' basic needs; relative consolidations of the new social order . . .; a high level of working class culture, skills, and consciousness; democratic traditions profoundly rooted in every sphere of social life, and so on.[56]

This whole argument begs the question as to how democracy is to be obtained and maintained in the period before these ideal conditions are available. The argument replicates the whole problematic of democracy in the Soviet Union under Lenin, and fails to advance beyond it. Thus the potent appeal of *The State and Revolution* is once more displayed.

What is the significance of these three contemporary texts, by Carrillo, Balibar and Weber? Clearly they do not represent all the contributions to the contemporary discussion, all the comments that have been made, the criticisms advanced, the developments and insights achieved. The purpose of citing the texts here is not to suggest that contemporary debate is limited to these parameters, and no more. Rather, they are symptomatic: of how this text can still dominate and bound three intellectually respectable and seemingly distinct discourses on problems of democracy; and, further, how each interpretation, or appreciation, of that text, can reinforce the failure of its own discourse to communicate with the other two and thus validate what are essentially partial appropriations of the substantive problem.

The three contributions are singled out as exemplary because each represents the way in which specifically political traditions of analysis (i.e. those which in some way acknowledge and seek to adapt Lenin's heritage for the resolution of contemporary political problems) appear to engage in a repetition without development. Each in its own way is trapped in terms of discussion and thinking initiated by Lenin himself; each consequently does not grasp what it is in Lenin that confronts their particular problematic.

Carrillo articulates a classical social democratic tradition: he desires socialism and believes that possession of state power is necessary to achieve it. He wants, however, the efficacy and innate value of West European institutions to be reconsidered and appreciated. His argument is directed against the term 'dictatorship of the proletariat' with its authoritarian implications of a monolithic and irremovable one-party regime. But he attacks Lenin's theory on its weaknesses and not on its strength. He leaves untouched its articulation of dissatisfaction with the formal limits of parliamentary democracy, its expression of libertarian aspirations, its insistence on the state forms in which those aspirations can be embodied. In this way Carrillo fails to grasp and engage the issues which opposing radical traditions consider to be essential: the inefficacy of parliaments as instruments of political participation and social transformation, and the possibility (central to the broadest radical tradition) of a truly egalitarian, emancipated and *self-governing* society.

Balibar is in no less of a trap. He articulates a traditional concept of the problem: not democracy, but power, is the issue. The concern for *institutions* which can guarantee democracy, central to both the traditions represented by Carrillo and Weber, is one he does not share. He represents a tradition on which the 'degeneration' of the Bolshevik regime has had little impact, and has consequently suggested no problems. Thus he simply refuses the problem that occupies the others:

> the necessary political foundations and the principal aspect of all these forms is what we can call *mass proletarian democracy*. Now this kind of democracy cannot be decreed, it cannot be 'guaranteed', in short, it does not depend mainly on institutions, however much freedom may characterise them; but it can be won, at the cost of a hard struggle, if the masses intervene in person on the political scene.[57]

Balibar expresses a consistent refusal to consider the impact of Bolshevik autocracy on European political thinking. He criticizes the Eurocommunist position on its weak point: it does not offer a clear means of achieving state power, nor guarantee that a party will be able to retain power in order to effect social transformation and contain its enemies while so doing. But he fails to appreciate its strong point: the experience of fascism *and* communism brought a new respect for democracy as something not lightly to be dismissed or dismantled. Carrillo is aware of what can be the devastating effects of a disregard for democratic institutions. To Balibar, democracy is still suspect, still a term with flavours of prostration before bourgeois ideology – or utopian leftism.

Weber's position completes this triangle of mutual incomprehension. On the issue of power, he is blind to the problem that the institutions he advocates have established a record of success far less impressive than those defended by Carrillo; and certainly have failed where Balibar's tradition registers marked success. Weber further cannot grasp the telling point of Carrillo's argument: whereas bourgeois democracy has shown an ability to sustain and replicate itself in the post-1945 period, there is no example of soviet- or council-based regimes avoiding the collapse into the authoritarian state; indeed, neither is there real evidence of such a strategy approaching seriously the problem of obtaining power. Thus Carrillo's argument guarantees democracy, if not power; Balibar's guarantees power if not democracy; Weber's promises both – but guarantees neither.

These, then, are the seemingly insoluble problems of the political discourse. We can see the contemporary status of *The State and Revolution* – one that exercises a peculiarly hegemonic power over the radical debate on democracy and the state, a status it has held since it was written. All participants feel they must acknowledge, contain, affirm or adjust Lenin's ideas: none can escape them. No real rupture is possible.

## ON READING TEXTS: A HERMENEUTIC SOLUTION?

It is perhaps simply a human failing to believe that where there is a problem, there must be *a* solution. Perhaps it is a product of the scientific culture, and the way the methods of science have been somewhat vulgarly appropriated by non-practitioners. But whatever the cause, there is a constant temptation to assume the existence of solutions not too far from one's immediate grasp. This gives the whole of radical political discourse an air of confidence that some would suggest appears increasingly misplaced. Nicos Poulantzas, in a unique and moving conclusion to his last book, expressed in full measure the anguish that confronts those who believe in a more real form of democracy and socialism, yet at the same time refuse to accept the traditional easy explanations and rationalizations of the twentieth-century experience. Poulantzas lays bare the problem, and its seemingly insoluble conflicts. He underlines the painful starting point for the whole discussion of Lenin and democracy: he grants, as one surely must, the likelihood of

Lenin being sincere in his desire for a democratic society. Lenin started from a desire to replace dead and formal democracy with something much more real and complete. But it is this very fact that

> leads me to the real question. Was it not this very line . . . which principally accounted for what happened in Lenin's lifetime in the Soviet Union, and which gave rise to the centralist and statist Lenin whose posterity is well enough known?[58]

There is no easy path out of such a realization. Poulantzas concludes his book thus:

> It can naturally always be argued, in the name of realism (either by proponents of the dictatorship of the proletariat or by the others, the orthodox neo-liberals), that if democratic socialism has never yet existed, this is because it is impossible. Maybe. We no longer share that belief in the millennium founded on a few iron laws concerning the inevitability of a democratic-socialist revolution; nor do we enjoy the support of a fatherland of democratic socialism. But one thing is certain: socialism will be democratic or it will not be at all. What is more, optimism about the democratic road to socialism should not lead us to consider it as a royal road, smooth and free of risk. Risks there are, although they are no longer quite what they used to be: at worst, we could be heading for camps and massacres as appointed victims. But to that I reply: if we weigh up the risks, that is in any case preferable to massacring other people only to end up ourselves beneath the blade of a Committee of Public Safety or some Dictator of the proletariat.[59]

In his preceding pages, Poulantzas discusses the responsibility of Lenin's ideas for the Russian state system. He suggests that the original intent of the concept 'dictatorship of the proletariat' was strategic, and that subsequent interpretations were of a similar nature. Thus the concept was bound to end up as an instrumental one, and no more. The Soviets were to become 'not so much an anti-state as a parallel state'.[60] I will argue, in the next chapter, that however non-instrumental the purpose of soviet forms may be, those forms themselves contain certain inadequacies which will subvert any particular intent. These inadequacies are at once more profound, and yet far simpler, than those suggested by Poulantzas. But, apart from anything else, the *tone* of Poulantzas' comments here is crucial. Its anguish is the anguish of an awareness of the *living consequences* of Lenin that confronts those with an interest in emancipation. It is from this that we might approach a suitable interpretation of Lenin's text, and escape the limitations of critique expressed in Adorno's concept of the immanent and the transcendent.

Adorno's attempts to define an escape from the unacceptable consequencies of both these forms of critique – dialectical criticism – appears unconvincing. The form of this dialectical criticism is vague: it must guard against 'perversion into delusion' and, on the other hand, 'enthrallment in the cultural object'. It must succumb neither to 'the cult of the mind' nor to 'hatred of the mind'. The cultural critic must 'both participate in culture and not participate'.[61] These are precautionary admonitions that amount to little in the way of an alternative. Perhaps the weakness of Adorno's alternative may be traced to the initial definition of the immanent and transcendent. His rejection of the available transcendent critique is, clearly, whole-hearted and sincere; but it is not absolute. He asserts that 'the *traditional* transcendent critique of ideology is obsolete'[62]; perhaps some different form of transcendent critique is still relevant and possible. And there are examples of its reappearance in his later work, sometimes to ludicrous and 'barbaric' effect. Thus in his 1963 critique of existentialism he is loftily dismissive of problems considered by Heidegger, Jaspers and others. His response to the problem of the sheer contingency of the life of the individual, in the context of a reality that is disturbing, and ultimately fatal, is to resort to the most simple and supercilious of Marxian solutions. Heidegger proposes the 'needs for residences' as one of the great difficulties of contemporary man: the anguished rootlessness of the children of the enlightenment. Adorno responds:

> that which announces itself, in the game about the need for residences, is more serious than the pose of existential seriousness. It is the fear of unemployment, lurking in all citizens of countries of high capitalism. This is a fear which is administratively fought off, and therefore nailed to the platonic firmament of the stars, a fear that remains even in the glorious times of full employment.[63]

What is this but an example of a 'diamat' reductionism that would have earned another writer Adorno's sternest rebuke?

It may be that the inability to find a more secure and serious stance for cultural criticism derives from the continued presence in Adorno's thought of the transcendent critique as the final arbiter of social phenomena. The inheritance of the Hegelian search for absolute knowledge is arguably present at a profound and unstated level throughout his career. Even for a social critic of Adorno's sophistication, such a commitment may readmit through the back door a crude Marxism which has been assertively dismissed via the front. His profound distaste for the age in which he lived – summed up by the 'dialectic of enlightenment' thesis and the alleged transformation of the whole world around him into a dull and manipulative positivity – left him with a yearning for a transcendent critique, a yearning that, as he himself would have been the first to recognize, could not possibly be fulfilled.

The very thesis of the dialectic of enlightenment itself displays the continuing temptation to write a totalizing history – even if the implications of that history are that one should resist the urge to totalize! The dialectic of enlightenment will be further considered later in this book. But how, in pursuing the task in hand, of coming to terms with this mysterious text, are we to avoid the traps into which even a thinker with the cunning of Adorno was wont to fall?

Some kind of solution to this problem may be available by moving beyond Adorno's somewhat simple dichotomy. The immanent and transcendent critiques may be accepted as 'ideal types', but may be supplemented by a realization that the possibility of genuine critique lies within the terrain that separates the two. It is necessary to abandon the idea of the transcendent critique as a methodological possibility, and occupy the gap it leaves with a realization of the historicity of all knowledge.

This may be approached by the path of hermeneutics. The task of hermeneutics is the same as Adorno's cultural criticism: to interrogate texts and historical or cultural artefacts, and find some standards by which to assess them. The original hermeneutic project was itself critical; it originated in the Protestant Reformation, which was confronted by the problem of the interpretation of biblical texts. The Catholic Church claimed that the original fragmentary Scriptures were obscure in their meanings. Correct interpretation, therefore, could only be ensured by reliance upon the established tradition of interpretation, which was embodied and institutionalized in the Catholic Church. To ground their oppositional and critical practice, the Lutherans had to present a mode of reinterpreting the Scriptures which could derive a universally valid interpretation from the fragmentary texts themselves.

The biblical hermeneutists attempted to provide such a valid interpretation of fragmentary texts by treating a text as a unity. A problematic single section of a work could be interpreted from the intention and composition of the whole. The established linguistic usage of any time and place provided the key to obscure passages. Grammar, philology and style could further be buttressed as the keys to a text by the appreciation of the text's own local characteristics, and an understanding of historical circumstances became part of the hermeneutic method. Such methods, of course, are not immune to problems of the historicity and distance of the interpreter, but aid was available in the form of 'thriving Christian practice' which provided the interpreter with a common and continuous context in which was situated both the text and the historian himself.

The subsequent school of historical hermeneutics dealt with these problems, but they were necessarily transformed. In broad terms, the hermeneutic technique was an attempted empathy with cultures distant in time. Outside biblical and classical interpretation, the task was no longer one of the technical reconstruction of partial texts, but an attempt to decipher the meaning and significance and origin of texts that often were available in their entirety. This produced a concentration on the context of a text rather than its content, and in particular on the position of the author in historical time. This suggested psychological reconstructions, and such reconstructions were necessary for another reason. The 'thriving Christian practice' that aided the original biblical scholars could not be available to the interpreter of more secular texts. Where, then, could be found the continuity that would guarantee some communication between historian and text? This could in fact be reduced to a non-question. Logically, no understanding at all is possible between totally strange and unconnected worlds. Bauman illustrates this with a sentence from Wittgenstein: 'If lions could speak, we would not understand them.'[64] Some ontological continuity between the historian and his object may therefore be legitimately assumed, by the very act of constituting the text as a problematic object to be interpreted. Thus before the research process is initiated, some degree of comprehension is guaranteed by the initial understanding that that particular text exists as an object to be interpreted. Past and present are thus conjoined by some continuum which will make the meaning of the historical act available to the investigator.

This was defined by Schleiermacher as inherent in the nature of understanding itself. That which makes understanding between human beings possible at all is a 'common human nature'. Differences between people are not 'qualitative', but only 'differences in degree in their mental processes'. By projection, the interpreter can stress and reinforce those qualities he has in common with another person, time and place, and thus 'bring about a reconstruction of an alien life within himself'. Dilthey thus speaks of the 'possibility of an interpretation that will be universally valid'.[65] But it is a possibility suffering still from considerable limitations. Not all historical artefacts are accessible to interpretation. There are moments of the past whose meaning we cannot grasp: the failures with which history is littered. Has a text which has no significance, other than the motives and aspirations of its author, a meaning for us? Dilthey makes a crucial point when he asserts that 'a moment of the past is meaningful insofar as it binds the future'.[66]

Texts which have had no impact beyond their immediate situation, which have not entered into the *tradition* that is the channel of communication between us and the past, are dead texts. Perhaps such a fate is inescapable for many human endeavours. There is, yet, a possibility that dead texts may come to life, but such a successful resuscitation is the task of history, not of the historian. The history of Marxism itself provides illustration of this. It is recognized that the publication of Marx's early writings some fifty years after his death coincided with and legitimized an entirely new interpretation of his whole body of work. Arguably the philosophical currents loosely grouped under the title 'western Marxism' would not have struck root without these texts. Their relevance to the humanist project of writers since Lukacs and Korsch was confirmed in Marcuse's exclamation that they 'put the entire theory of "scientific socialism" on a new footing'.[67] Althusser's determination, as part of the restoration of scientific Marxism, to establish the 'epistemological break' that would consign these texts once again to obscurity, is a further, negative, confirmation of their significance in this development.

But the 'accident' of the absence of these texts, and the irony of their eventual publication by the Moscow State Publishing House in 1932, should not suggest that their lack of significance prior to the first blossomings of western Marxism was itself accidental. We need only ask *to whom* these texts would have addressed themselves before the 1920s and 1930s (perhaps to Labriola, but who else?) and to *what perceived and felt social, political and historical problems* they would have been construed as relevant. Thus it was necessary for 'history to do its work' on the available, consensus interpretation of Marx (and, conversely, for the established interpretation of Marx to do its work on history) before the early writings could speak. The scientific positivism of 'iron-law' Marxism of the Second International and its disinherited child, the voluntarist *Realpolitik* 'concrete analysis of the concrete situation' Marxism of the Third International, had first to run their course. Both these interpretations worked intimately with the culture of their times: the optimism bestowed upon the nineteenth-century politicians by the successes of the natural sciences; and the bitter desperation and millenarianism born of the catastrophe that struck the heart of European culture, the First World War. Only subsequently – and then only among a handful of European Marxian intellectuals who failed to partake of the enthusiasm for the costly march of Soviet socialism – was the retrieval of the themes of an earlier Marx a possibility.

The argument here is not one of cause and effect, but of historical affinities. Lukacs' and Korsch's return to Hegelian Marxism predated the publication of the manuscripts by ten years or more (although, given that their publication was made possible by the dispatch of the photocopied manuscripts to Moscow by the early Frankfurt Institute, it is possible that they were familiar to some writers before their official publication[68]). Conversely, it is obvious that the texts themselves carried little implications for those who felt no qualms about the current state of the socialist movement. Clearly, if the texts were *inherently* subversive of official orthodox Marxism, the Moscow publishers would have thought twice about making them available. Thus, had it not been for the crisis of Marxian thought that spanned the period, the early writings would have had no more than archival significance. As indeed was the case, and presumably still is, with those copies that sit in massed numbers on the bookshelves of party members in the party states. Thus, texts may be available in editions of millions and still be dead texts.

Of course, even in the period of the birth of western Marxism the early writings had meaning for very few. It was not until the grand public crisis of official Marxism after 1956 that the themes of those writings found a wider audience and became effective in history. They presented a substantial challenge, at least in the west, to the intellectual and ethical respectability of diamat Marxism, and indirectly, particularly via the work of Marcuse, fuelled the radical movements of the 1960s.

The story may be taken one step further. A disappointment with the apparent inefficacy of humanist Marxism as a politics for the appropriation of power may have contributed after 1968 to a significant counter to Hegelian themes and a return to the project of a 'scientific' Marxism in the work of the Althusserian school. Thus, whatever the personal impulses behind Althusser's writings (which, of course, all predated the peaks of 1960s radicalism), it is probably inappropriate to see the brief Althusserian hegemony after 1968 as simply a 'police action' designed to restore the authority of classical Stalinism, as E. P. Thompson suggests.[69] Its renaissance has perhaps more understandable roots in the perceived limitations of humanist Marxism following the radical wave of the 1960s, and a consequent return of the desire for a politics that could successfully address the problem of power.

This story of the changing interpretations of Marxism (piquantly confirmed by Althusser's insistence upon his particular *readings* of texts), intimately linked to the specific historical problems displayed by any given period, confirms the unlikeliness of readings of texts that will give them a final apodictic interpretation, a genuine and final historical objectivity. The historian, therefore, must judge and assess from his own position as a contemporary of a specific historical period, which has its own definition of the meaningful and the meaningless. This inescapable particularity of any historical age may only be overcome if one is willing to assume a future situation of a different order, that is, a situation where history itself has come to an end. From the standpoint of such an authoritative position, the historian would be able to draw up the final balance sheet of the significance of all that which is past. By implication the adoption of a teleological philosophy of history can provide the historian with the standpoint for such an operation before the final consummation has itself come to pass. It should, however, be clear from many parts of this argument, both the preceding pages and those that are to follow, that I believe such an assumption to be unacceptable, both methodologically and in its political and intellectual consequences. I shall not here attempt to justify the rejection of that assumption specifically, but rather to suggest the consequences of such a rejection for the project of a historical understanding of our present text. If we insist that history is characterized by changing cultures, values and, consequently, interpretations, and the only possibility of an objective understanding of history, true for all future time and place, is the advent of the end of history itself, we are faced with the problem: is there any escape from an undifferentiated historical relativism?

Gadamer has offered a means to the dissolution of this problem. He also dismisses any claims that historical knowledge might have of an absolute nature. The 'romantic' hermeneutists believed that it was possible for the historian to gain a knowledge of a text that was superior to the understanding possessed by its author. They, after all, had not only the text to study, but also the knowledge of the totality of the age in which the author lived. They could draw out the impulses and constraints which produced the text, factors of which an author at the time could be only dimly aware, if at all. Gadamer is, however, content to relinquish any claim to 'superior understanding': 'It is enough to say that we understand in a different way, if we understand at all.'[70] He dismisses also any temptation for a philosophy that will provide 'an end to history' and thus guarantee apodictic knowledge of history. But Gadamer does not *regret* the temporal distance that separates the historian and his text. It is not, for him, 'something that must be overcome'. For a historian to regret time and its effects is like a doctor regretting the fact that the human body has a specific set of organs, and wishing instead that it possessed the structural simplicity of an amoeba. It is the complications that produce the possibility of knowledge, that offer the historian something to work on, and, by extension, provide human beings with the possibility of intellect and imagination. If, at some point in the future, it were to become possible to reveal history as transparent, no more than the workings of a single-celled uncomplicated essence or mechanism, the consequences for the human intellect would be truly frightening. And if we are conversely tempted by the hermeneutic antipodes of such a scientific Holy Grail, we need only ask the following question: if it did become possible to shed all the products and prejudices of our situation in present time, and enter a dialogue with the historical text or event completely on its own terms, within its own culture, devoid of any anachronistic pollutions – what then would we gain? Surely nothing but the collapse into immanence; surely nothing that could inform our understanding of our present. For when the observer becomes identical with the observed, he is by definition dissolved into the object. It is our present that must be the driving concern of the historian: otherwise the historian is a poor substitute for the time-travellers of science fiction, and our best hope is to await the development of the appropriate piece of technology.

Thus the attempt to recapture completely the spirit of a past age and to erase the preconceptions of the contemporary age from our questioning is unnecessary: 'In fact, the important thing is to recognize the distance in time as a positive and productive possibility of understanding.'[71] That distance is not an empty gap, a 'yawning abyss', but is filled with historical continuity and custom, that is, that which has produced the object that now presents itself to us in a *specific* and *contemporary* way. By the passage of time, the investigation of the text is protected from some possible sources of 'error' – those revealed by straightforward historical research, as well as those produced by an excessively close subjective involvement with the text and its times. But, valuable as these gains are, they do not thereby finally convert a text into a pristine object safely located within a securely defined context, the 'past'. This would simply return us to the comfort of a traditional and unreflective objective history, facing an object safely dead in the past, devoid of any ability to influence and subvert our understanding through its effect on our tradition and inheritance. Thus Gadamer insistently reasserts Dilthey's theme: a text can have meaning only to the extent that it, itself, addresses us. Its ability to do so derives from its vitality as a living and creative element in our tradition; and inasmuch as it is, therefore, part of the subject (the historian) as well as the object (the text), it will refuse all claims of those who would reveal and possess its meaning as absolute knowledge.

Gadamer suggests that the passage of time may diminish the problems described in Adorno's version of immanent critique:

> It is only this temporal distance that can solve the really critical question of hermeneutics, namely of distinguishing the true prejudices, by which we understand, from the false ones by which we misunderstand.[72]

True historical knowledge is that which takes account of its own situation in history, its inevitable saturation with its own contemporaneity. Historical objectivism may indeed claim some superiority to versions of a hermeneutic method which results only in arbitrary 'cosy recreations of the past'.[73] But to fail to recognize the existence of historically produced presuppositions in our own thought is to 'fall short of reaching that truth which, despite the finite nature of our understanding, could be reached'.

This is not a call to purge our consciousness of everything that we have not ourselves invented. Quite the reverse. The role of reason here is simply more subtle and inconclusive. Gadamer insists there can be no final *escape* from prejudices, nor, and this is the point, is the desire for one legitimate. What instead is necessary is to distinguish those prejudices which will help us to an understanding from those that will obscure it. The failure to understand *historically*, and therefore often at all, derives from an error of the Enlightenment. This distinguished between two possible sources of error: that of acceptance of authority and that of over-hasty judgement in the use of reason. Prejudice deriving from authority was identified with blind obedience to authority, in the form of *authorities*, such as the Church. This source of error could be rapidly disposed of by the reconsideration of all problems from the standpoint of reason. Pure reason alone could produce truth, and, having dispensed with prejudices derived from authority, philosophy and science could now advance. It was necessary only to be aware of the temptation to over-hasty judgement, to drawing conclusions without having obtained and examined all the possible evidence.

This, claims Gadamer, was too simple a solution. We can see it as the foundation of 'scientism', the overweening and excessive confidence in the powers of pure reason, and the evidence of its inadequacy lies in the very 'crisis of European sciences' that Gadamer, following Husserl and Heidegger, is investigating. Gadamer insists that it is now necessary to attempt a rehabilitation of the legitimacy of authority, if we are to escape the increasingly attenuated and one-dimensional mode of interpretation that Enlightenment prejudices have produced. We must summon from their premature graves all those valid elements of truth embodied in tradition that can help us to genuine historical understanding. Authority, especially and increasingly in the times we live in, is suspect. Authority is seen as being opposed to 'reason and freedom: to be, in fact, blind obedience'. That has often been its modern reality, especially in political life. But this, says Gadamer, is not true authority. True authority – and here his philosophy of knowledge parallels elements of Weber's political sociology – is based on something other than a simple and unquestioned claim to domination.

> authority . . . is based, ultimately, not on the subjection and abdication of reason, but on recognition and knowledge – knowledge, namely, that the other is superior to oneself in judgement and insight. . . . Authority is acquired [and] rests on recognition, and hence [is] an act of reason itself, which, aware of its own limitations, accepts that others have better understanding. Authority, in this sense, properly understood, has nothing to do with blind obedience to a command . . . but rather with knowledge.[74]

Thus the ever-already-given understandings and meanings into which we are born, the cultural biases and assumptions to which Adorno fearfully pointed, are something we may be able to come to terms with and utilize in the search for truth. Not, of course, if they remain, as in the ordinary run of daily life, unperceived and unin-terrogated assumptions. They must be scrutinized by reason. But it is a reason less commanding, less arrogant, less legislative, than that deployed by those who wish only to examine the past in order to expose its redundancy, its illegitimacy, its immorality, its irrelevance. The organizing principle of understanding, therefore, is not *rupture*, as in Marx, as in Lenin, as in Althusser, but *continuity*; the reasoned in-terrogation of tradition *and* the traditional interrogation of reason. The failure of radical political theorizing – its capitulation in the face of *The State and Revolution* – lies in its peculiar inversion of the appro-priate modalities of understanding. First, traditional authority is rejected, both in the forms of European political philosophy (bourgeois ideology) and in the form of the instinctual norms of political actors (false consciousness). Second, reason is let loose to construct anew the concept of politics. But the reign of reason is short-lived: only Marx himself is allowed to indulge in it. The conclusions of Marx's reasoning then become authority, tradition, genuine uninterrogated prejudice. And if Marx's reason at least allowed more than one possible path for later reasoning to pursue, the effect of Lenin's text is to close down all those possible paths but one. Having effected the first and sufficient rupture with the western philosophical tradition (which only 'inter-preted' the world), the new science strides into the world, proclaiming its virgin birth as its supreme and irrefutable justification. And, for those who come after, the authority of Marx's axioms *does* become illegitimate authority, something close to blind obedience, even if it is unconscious – as blind obedience usually is.

For my argument, the attempt to rehabilitate tradition has a twofold import. First, it is necessary to insist that Lenin's apparently trivial or transparent work is itself part of tradition: not a tradition in the sense of accumulated intellect and understanding, but in the sense of an un-acknowledged permeation of the world in which we live. The forms of this may vary. The historians fail when they seek a dispassionate account, when they refuse to contemplate *The State and Revolution* as an active agent and current component in the creation of subsequent history, and thus in ourselves, and in themselves. The radicals fail when they assume the text to be a product of reason, and a possession of reason, and assume a radical difference between this 'prophetic' state-ment and the actual course of Soviet history; they also fail when they ignore the historically produced presuppositions in their own thought, and assume their thought operations to be purely the activity of reason, and not in fact profoundly polluted by unacknowledged assumptions, often the very assumptions embedded in and produced by the text they are examining.

The second reason for reinstating tradition in more straightforward. It is necessary to deny the legitimacy of the rupture that Marx and Lenin claimed to have made in the discourse of political philosophy, political behaviour and political institutions. It is therefore necessary and legitimate to bring to bear upon their arguments precisely the thoughts of those philosophers whose contribution had been rejected as amounting to no more than unconscious prejudice and irrelevant tradition. This is not a matter of simply comparing and contrasting Lenin's text with the work of, say, Mill, or Locke, or Hobbes. The approach I will adopt will seek to do no more than to let the relevant and valid insights of western political thought come to bear upon Lenin's text where their authority seems to me to be justified by reason. This will doubtless be somewhat eclectic. But there is really no other alternative to such a non-rigorous methodology if, on the one hand, we accept a version of the concept of totality – in other words that a thing cannot be understood in itself, in its own terms, but only within the context of the complex inputs and determinations that have produced it; but, on the other hand, we reject the possibility that this complexity can be resolved and disciplined by the adoption of a holistic and monological theory of causality – in other words, the process by which Marxism claims to produce a total understanding of an object. If such a simple resolution is rejected – and I do reject it, for reasons which by now should be becoming clear – the direction the investigation must take seems evident. In contrast to the Marxist process of sealing off possible paths, and erecting borders beyond which the process of critique may not pass – whether by 'active forgetting' or by 'social amnesia' – it is necessary to open the borders and allow entry to whatever comes knocking. No passport will be demanded, save relevance.

Gadamer argues for what he calls 'effective-history'. Effective history escapes the complacency of the immanent critique and the barbarism of the transcendent by being prepared to accept the costs that follow from refusing to adhere to either. The cost of rejecting the immanent critique is a loss of intimacy with the object; but it is not a total loss, because such a total loss only occurs if one instead adopts the transcendent critique. The cost of rejecting the transcendent critique is the abandonment of the possibility of absolute truth. But it does not amount to the absence of *all* truth, because such an absence will arise only if we capitulate in the face of the object, if we are ready to accept it in its own terms, if we relinquish the entire project of critique, if we submerge our reason in immanence. Effective history is capable of providing a limited truth. 'To exist historically means that knowledge of oneself can never be complete', but 'every age has to understand a transmitted text in its own way, for the text is part of the whole of the tradition in which the age takes an objective interest and in which it seeks to understand itself.'[75]

This does not perhaps solve Adorno's problem of the criticism of *contemporary* cultural products. Lacking any separation in time from his object, he cannot find satisfactory criteria by which to judge it. Time has not had time to elect the important and disenfranchize the meaningless and ephemeral. It is almost inevitable, therefore, that the cultural critic shall confuse the important with the trivial and arrive at judgements that later will seem eccentric. But the cultural critic has no choice but to take this risk. The historian's situation may provide more comfort. The effects of history will have done their work, and separated the meaningful from the meaningless.

But history does not write itself. Historians disagree about interpretations, and a large part of this argument is a disagreement with accepted interpretations. Can one interpretation – the one that follows – claim any privilege over the others? It is my contention that existing interpretations have failed to trace the effect of *The State and Revolution* in history, and therefore its complicity in contemporary culture. If we return to Dilthey's axiom that 'a moment of the past is meaningful insofar as it binds the future', we can identify the mystery of Lenin's text in the corollary: *we may only grasp the meaning of the past by identifying how it bound the future, i.e. our present.* Now, in both schools of interpretation that we have examined, such a binding is lacking. The text does not enter into history, either due to its absurdity – an impossible utopianism – or its innocence – a valid libertarianism betrayed by the brutal necessities of subsequent history, or the bad faith of historical actors. Consequently the text is either *meaningless* – dead, historical, objective, a moment in one man's biography – or *excessively* meaningful, saturated with meaning, in fact sacred.

The 'meaningless' interpretations fall into two categories. First, the *absurd*, whereby not only can no connection be established between text and consequences, but no connection can even be established between text and author. Thus Conquest ascribes the text to the

'ambivalence' of Lenin's whole being, Wilson attributes its form to
'little thought', Ulam regards it as 'unrepresentative' and 'unfortunate', Liebman identifies 'glaring weaknesses' that reveal a 'surprising'
lack of thought. Schapiro and Daniels reinforce this version. The text
consequently had no meaning for its times or even for its author. The
second version may be described as the *cynical*. This interpretation puts
the author back in control of the text. The text could not mean what it
said, but was a ploy directed to another end than that revealed in the
text itself. It was designed to win the debate with the 'revisionists'
(Carr), to legitimate the dictatorship necessary to overcome the inertia
of Russian society (Hill), to legitimate the seizure of power itself
(Anweiler), to garner the political support necessary for that seizure
(Keep), to justify the subsequent compulsion of the population
(Bahro). Thus, in the first interpretation, the text is opaque, allowing
no meaning to shine through; in the second, the meaning is distorted,
but may be deciphered by attributing deliberate and rational
motivations to its author.

By contrast, the 'meaningful' interpretation asserts the transparency
of the text: meaning shines through it. Put differently, there is no
meaning that is separate from the surface of the text itself, and the text
escapes interrogation because of its honesty. The text is unassailable,
and consequently *sacred*. Lenin is the channel by which the truth may
express itself. And because the truth *has not yet come to pass*, it is not
*in* history. And that which is not *in* history cannot be examined as a
historical object. It has the status of a myth, and a myth may only be
*told*. It may not be examined. We may remember Lévi-Strauss's definition of a myth as a machine for the suppression of time. The mythical
status of *The State and Revolution* within the radical tradition has been
effective in suppressing aspects of the nature of Soviet authoritarianism, and, indeed, the myth of *The State and Revolution* has ensured
that the *history* of *The State and Revolution* remains unwritten. The
'history' of *The State and Revolution* has very little to do with its
origins, its motivations or its intentions. It must be realized that its
*history* is temporally situated *after* the appearance of the text, not prior
to and simultaneous with its production. Only if we can read the
history of *The State and Revolution* in the subsequent history of the
Soviet Union and of mankind will it have a history that contains any
*meaning*.

Thus, sixty years later, we have the benefit of temporal distance from
the historical text. What is more, that distance will give us access to the

effective history of the text; if, that is, it can be suggested that the text has participated in creating our contemporary reality. If this proves possible, then it may be possible to resist the efforts of the historians to turn the text into a dead and alien object. The next chapter, therefore, will attempt to suggest the continuing effectiveness of *The State and Revolution* in the Russia of the Gulag.

## NOTES

1 V. I. Lenin, *Collected Works (CW)*, 45 vols, Moscow and London, 1960–70. All references are to this edition.

2 Lenin, *What Is To Be Done?* (1902), *CW*, 5; *One Step Forwards, Two Steps Back* (1904), *CW*, 7; *Imperialism, the Highest State of Capitalism* (1916), *CW*, 22; *The State and Revolution* (1917), *CW*, 25; *Left-Wing Communism – An Infantile Disorder* (1920), *CW*, 31. It is possible to suggest two other texts of such historical significance – *Two Tactics of Social Democracy in the Democratic Revolution* (1905), *CW*, 9, on the tactic of class alliances; and the *April Theses* (1917), *CW*, 24, on the strategy for undermining the democratic revolution – but I can think of no others, although readers will doubtless have their own candidates.

3 Published as Lenin, *Marxism and the State*, Moscow, 1972.

4 Lenin, 'Postscript to the first edition', *The State and Revolution*, 30 November 1917, *CW*, 25, 492.

5 Lenin, *Letters from Afar*, *CW*, 23, 3rd letter, 320–32; *The Dual Power*, *CW*, 24, 38–41; *Letters on Tactics*, *CW*, 24, 42; *The Tasks of the Proletariat in Our Revolution*, *CW*, 24, 67–71; *Report on the Present Situation and the Attitude Towards the Provisional Government*, *CW*, 24, 145–6.

6 Lenin, *Draft of the Revised Programme*, *CW*, 24, 471.

7 S. F. Cohen, *Bukharin and the Bolshevik Revolution*, New York, 1975, 39, 40.

8 E. H. Carr, *The Bolshevik Revolution*, London, 1950, 1, 238–9.

9 ibid., 252.

10 I have been unable to discover any specific reference to *The State and Revolution* in Trotsky's writings of the 1920s. Stalin himself cites from the book a handful of times in the debate with the opposition, using the arguments supporting the concept of proletarian dictatorship. By contrast, in his 900 pages of printed text, *Left-Wing Communism* is cited repeatedly and exhaustively (J. V. Stalin, *On the Opposition 1921–7*, Peking, 1974).

11 This situation is piquantly summed up by Lukes and Piccone when they remind us 'that the Russians are drinking Pepsi and driving Fiats [while] only historical backwaters like Afghanistan, Angola, and Ethiopia, which even capitalism

left undisturbed, are having
"proletarian revolutions" these
days'. T. Lukes and P. Piccone,
'Debrizzi's undimensionality',
*Telos*, 37 (Fall 1978), 151.

12 T. W. Adorno, 'Cultural
criticism and society', *Prisms*,
London, 1967, 19.

13 ibid., 31.

14 ibid., 29.

15 ibid., 31.

16 ibid., 32.

17 ibid., 31.

18 T. W. Adorno, *Negative Dialectics*, London, 1973, 8.

19 F. Jameson, *Marxism and Form*,
Princeton, 1974, 42.

20 ibid., 40.

21 Apart from the works on Lenin's
life and works cited in the body
of this chapter, the following are
of some relevance: A. Besançon,
*The Intellectual Origins of
Leninism*, Oxford, 1981;
F. Claudin, *The Communist
Movement*, London, 1975;
T. Cliff, *Lenin*, 4 vols, London,
1975, 76, 78, 79; N. Harding,
*Lenin's Political Thought*,
London, 1981; L. Kochan, *Russia
in Revolution*, London, 1967;
D. Lane, *Leninism – A
Sociological Interpretation*,
Cambridge, 1981; M. Lewin,
*Lenin's Last Struggle*, New York,
1969; R. Medvedyev, *Let History
Judge*, London, 1971, and
*Leninism and Western Socialism*,
London, 1981; R. Pethybridge,
*The Social Prelude to Stalinism*,
London, 1974; P. Reddaway and
L. Schapiro, *Lenin: The Man,
the Theorist, the Leader*,
London, 1970; V. Serge,
*Memoirs of a Revolutionary*,
Oxford, 1967 and *Year One of*

*the Russian Revolution*, London,
1972; D. Shub, *Lenin*, London,
1966; B. D. Wolfe, *Three who
Made a Revolution*, London,
1966.

22 R. Conquest, *Lenin*, London,
1972, 86, 87.

23 E. Wilson, *To the Finland
Station*, London, 1972, 455, 456.

24 A. Ulam, *Lenin and the Bolsheviks*, London, 1969, 462.

25 ibid.

26 ibid., 463.

27 M. Liebman, *Leninism under
Lenin*, London, 1975, 192, 193.

28 ibid.

29 ibid.

30 ibid., 195.

31 L. Schapiro, *The Communist
Party of the Soviet Union*,
London, 1970, 209.

32 R. V. Daniels, *The Conscience of
the Revolution*, New York, 1960,
51, 52.

33 Carr, *The Bolshevik Revolution*,
246.

34 C. Hill, *Lenin and the Russian
Revolution*, London, 1971, 87.

35 O. Anweiler, *The Soviets*, New
York, 1974, 151.

36 ibid., 160, 161.

37 J. H. L. Keep, *The Debate on
Soviet Power*, Oxford, 1979, 22.

38 R. Bahro, *The Alternative in
Eastern Europe*, London, 1978,
95.

39 ibid.

40 ibid., 96.

41 L. Trotsky, *The History of the
Russian Revolution*, vol. 3,
London, 1967, 121.

42 L. Colletti, 'Lenin's The State
and Revolution', *From Rousseau
to Lenin*, London, 1972, 219.

43 Cited in Cohen, *Bukharin and
the Bolshevik Revolution*, 75.

44 G. Lukacs, *Lenin*, London, 1972,
67, 68. The 'subject–object
identical' is, of course, just
another name for God. Western
thought should be grateful for
Lukacs' contributions to intellectual history, but perhaps not
least for his unambiguous and
incontrovertible demonstration
of the theological consequences
of a rigorous development of
Marx's philosophical system. The
consequences of proletarian
monotheism are discussed in
chapter 4. I am grateful to Bob
Miller for pointing out to me this
consequence of Lukacs' system.
The quote below of Lenin on
Lukacs is from *Kommunismus*,
*CW*, 31, 165.
45 A. Rosmer, *Lenin's Moscow*,
London, 1971, 46–9.
46 M. Schachtman, *The
Bureaucratic Revolution*, New
York, 1962, p. 197.
47 Colletti, op. cit., 255.
48 ibid., 219.
49 ibid., 223.
50 ibid., 93.
51 ibid., 221.
52 S. Carrillo, *Eurocommunism and
the State*, London, 1977, 87.
53 In L. Althusser, *Lenin and
Philosophy*, London, 1971,
135–41.
54 H. Weber, 'Eurocommunism,
socialism and democracy', *New
Left Review*, 110 (1979), 5.
55 ibid., 11.
56 ibid.
57 E. Balibar, *On the Dictatorship
of the Proletariat*, London, 1977,
111.
58 N. Poulantzas, *State, Power,
Socialism*, London, 1978, 252.
59 ibid., 265.

60 ibid., 255.
61 Adorno, 'Cultural criticism and
society', 33.
62 ibid. (my emphasis).
63 Adorno, *The Jargon of Authen-
ticity*, London, 1973, 34.
64 Z. Bauman, *Hermeneutics and
Social Science*, London, 1978,
27. This is an incisive and indispensable account of the relevance
of hermeneutic thought to social
theory.
65 W. Dilthey, 'The rise of hermeneutics', in P. Connerton (ed.),
*Critical Sociology*, London, 1976,
114, 115.
66 Quoted in Bauman, op. cit., 40.
67 Cited in P. Anderson, *Considerations on Western Marxism*,
London, 1976, 50. The journal
*Telos* has contributed
immeasurably to our understanding of the intellectual and
political crisis of Marxism that
erupted in the 1920s. Relevant
articles include: R. Jacoby,
'Towards a critique of automatic
Marxism: the politics of
philosophy from Lukacs to the
Frankfurt school', 10 (1971), and
'The politics of the crisis theory',
23 (1975); P. Piccone, 'Dialectic
and materialism in Lukacs', 11
(1972), and 'Phenomenological
Marxism', 9 (1970); A. Arato,
'Re-examining the Second International', 18 (1973), and
'Lukacs' theory of reification', 11
(1972); M. Jay, 'The concept of
totality in Lukacs and Adorno',
32 (1977); P. Breines, 'Praxis
and its theorists: the impact of
Lukacs and Korsch in the 1920s',
11 (1972), and 'Korsch's road to
Marx', 26 (1975–6); F. George,
'Forgetting Lenin', 18 (1973–4);

P. Mattick, 'Anti-Bolshevist communism in Germany', 26 (1975 – 6).

68  M. Jay, *The Dialectical Imagination*, London, 1973, 12, 13.

69  E. P. Thompson, *The Poverty of Theory*, London, 1979, *passim*.

70  H. G. Gadamer, *Truth and Method*, London, 1975, 264.

71  ibid.

72  ibid., 266.

73  ibid., 268.

74  ibid., 248.

75  ibid., 263.

# TWO THE TEXT AND ITS CONSEQUENCES

## A SUBTERRANEAN AUTHORITARIANISM

It is necessary at this point to consider the content of Lenin's text in detail. The purpose will be to reveal the effect of Lenin's arguments in reality; for I believe that those arguments had effects that are demonstrable and consequences that were profound. The Soviet state that emerged after 1917 bore the stamp of *The State and Revolution* in all its subsequent phases, before *and* after the Bolsheviks secured the monopoly of power, before *and* after the decline of the Soviets as significant institutions, before *and* after the rise of Stalin. In this my argument differs from the interpretations discussed in the previous chapter.

This will be a selective consideration; and in it I will hope to 'attack' Lenin's position on its strong points and not its weak ones. The 'weak' points are those whereby Lenin implicitly gives some credibility and authority to subsequent authoritarian developments: the phrase 'dictatorship of the proletariat', and its consequences – the insistence on the temporary need for the state as an instrument of repression; the acceptance that 'bourgeois' norms of distribution will temporarily continue and have to be enforced. These are largely specific to the Russian situation, or at least they are in the degree of their intensity. Lenin's theses retain their power at least to some extent because it is always possible to conceive of the attempt at socialist construction taking place in conditions much less chaotic and underdeveloped than post-Tsarist Russia.

The arguments I present will not deal with the openly authoritarian echoes that are occasionally present in the text. Similarly, the evidence I will seek to present from the history of the Soviet state is intended to have general implications. The evidence itself must of necessity refer to a situation where utopian ideas were implemented in an almost 'worst possible case' situation. But it is my contention that the arguments this evidence seeks to illustrate are in no way confined to the exigencies of such a difficult situation. What follows may be read as relevant to utopian politics under *any* conditions, even the 'best possible case', and the reader is invited to bear this consideration in mind at all points.

## THE PROBLEM OF BUREAUCRACY

*The State and Revolution* argues that it is possible to establish a state which will be more democratic than any previously conceived. Partly this will derive from the fact that the state will be for the first time the property of the majority, not a minority. But this assumption alone will not produce the *profoundly* radical concept of democracy that Lenin has in mind. It will, perhaps, make possible a state that is less repressive, less secretive, less manipulative, less repulsive, and the implications of that change might in themselves be profoundly emancipatory. But such a limited conception of the new regime was not Lenin's; in fact, the reformist social democratic parties already adhered to such a vision, as they anticipated the day when the mass working-class parties would attain control of the state by means of the franchise. Lenin, it is well known, rejected their perspective by insisting on the unreliability of the bourgeois state machine: it would resist, sabotage and destroy social democratic movements that appeared to be within reach of majority office. It was consequently, he argued, necessary to 'smash the state machine'. But Lenin does not recommend the most straightforward alternative: that would necessitate little more than replacing the staff of the state apparatus with those loyal to the new regime. It is unnecessary to limit the aim to this. The conditions are present that make it possible to reject the very idea of the modern state.

His fundamental assumption concerns the functions of the state: a socialist society will cause a radical reduction in those functions. This, then, is the conceptual starting-point for the model of the radical state that will be elaborated in the pages of the text:

> Capitalist culture has created large scale production, factories, railways, the postal services, telephones, etc., and on this basis the great majority of the functions of the old 'state power' have become so simplified and can be reduced to such exceedingly simple operations of registration, filing, and checking that they can be easily performed by every literate person. . . . A witty German Social-Democrat of the seventies of the last century called the postal service an example of the socialist economic system. This is very true. At present the postal service is a business organised along the lines of a state capitalist monopoly. Imperialism is gradually transforming all trusts into organisations of a similar type. . . . Once we have overthrown the capitalists . . . and smashed the bureaucratic machine of the modern state, we shall have a splendidly equipped mechanism . . . which can very well be set going by the united workers themselves, who will hire technicians, foremen, and accountants, and pay them all workmen's wages.[1]

Only a minimum of the functions that the capitalist state performs are therefore actually necessary. The greater part of that apparatus is devoted to a task that will clearly be redundant in the future society – the oppression of the working class:

> The imperialist war has immensely accelerated and intensified the process of transformation of monopoly capitalism into state monopoly capitalism. The monstrous oppression of the working people by the state, which is merging more and more with the all-powerful capitalist associations, is becoming increasingly monstrous. The advanced countries . . . are becoming military convict prisons for the workers.[2]

Thus, when Lenin *was* later confronted with the fact of bureaucratization in the state that *he* established after the revolution he attributed it to a specific cause that had nothing in common with the capitalist state regimes. The *Soviet* bureaucracy was the product of economic backwardness:

> In our country bureaucratic practices have different economic roots, namely the atomised and scattered state of the small producer with his poverty, illiteracy, lack of culture, the absence of roads and exchange between agriculture and industry, the absence of connection and interaction between them.[3]

Lenin's argument stands in contrast to other work on the problem of bureaucracy that was developing during the same period. Lenin is not noted as the most penetrating theorist of this problem; that title must be given to Max Weber. Weber's work took a contrary line to that of Lenin. He suggested that the phenomenon of the state had taken on a new complexity, not simplicity. Weber postulated a link between development and bureaucracy by suggesting the extension of administrative tasks in qualitative and quantitative forms. The 'qualitative' argument proposes:

> It is obvious that technically the large modern state is absolutely dependent upon a bureaucratic basis. The larger the state, and the more it is a great power, the more unconditionally is this the case. The United States still bears the character of a polity which, at least in the technical sense, is not fully bureaucratized. But the greater the zones of friction with the outside, and the more urgent the needs for administrative unity at home become, the more this character is inevitably and gradually giving way formally to the bureaucratic structure.[4]

Arguably, Lenin's thesis is undamaged by this proposition. It was no part of his vision to achieve 'great power' status for Russia, and his vision of a socialist and fraternal world system, while naive, cannot be accused of any lack of coherence with his theory of the declining tasks of the state. This, however, will not prove to be the case with the other core of his thesis: the effect of industrialization and modernization. Weber's argument on the 'qualitative' development of administrative tasks suggests that:

> increasing bureaucratization is a function of the increasing possession of consumption goods, and of an increasingly sophisticated technique of fashioning external life – a technique which corresponds to the opportunities provided by such wealth. This reacts

upon the standard of living and makes for an increasing subjective indispensability of public, inter-local, and thus bureaucratic provision for the most varied wants which previously were either unknown or were satisfied locally or by the private economy. . . . Among essentially technical factors the specifically modern means of communication enter the picture as pacemakers of bureaucratization. [They] can only be administered publicly.[5]

The disagreement between the assumptions of Lenin and Weber could therefore not be sharper. For Weber, the space for bureaucracy is provided by the *disappearance* of the 'small-scale and scattered producer', the *increase* in literacy and education, the *rise* in the general level of culture, the *extension* of methods of communication and the growing *interdependence* of the various sectors of the economy.

It is now perhaps easy to assert the superiority of Weber's diagnosis over Lenin's. But it is also clear that the evidence for this argument was already present at the time both men were writing. The governments of all relatively modernized societies were coming to a realization that the traditional and limited tasks of administration were being replaced by something rather more complex and intractable. These traditional tasks indeed amounted to little more than 'registration, filing and checking' in the performance of essentially limited tasks. But the nature of the new administrative problematic was characterized by a change in function: the administrative machine would have a much greater role in the guidance and resolution of conflicts of competing interests, and of performance of problematic tasks which had previously been the domain of the automatic and unconscious processes of culture and civil society. Family and community had performed the tasks now undertaken by the nascent welfare systems of Britain and Germany, had performed them according to norms and calculations unquantifiable in terms of rational administrative processes. Similarly, Lenin mistook his object when considering the 'economic system' itself. Functionally, an economic system, capitalist or socialist, is a mechanism for the allocation of economic resources and the distribution of rewards from those resources. Lenin seems to suggest that the economic problem that can be resolved by the adoption of the model of the 'postal service' is simply one of efficiency: where the multi-faceted confusions of the competitive mechanism have been removed, there is no 'economic' problem of organization. However, the problem remains that the capitalist mechanism, in the form of the market, accomplished the task of allocation and distribution of rewards and resources, while this task remains to be performed in the absence of the market. Confident assertions of the possibility of extending the 'postal' model to embrace the whole economy ignore the fact that the absence of a market forces the state to inherit a task of immense complexity. Again, it is the case that such problems were already being presented to the European capitalist states, not least in the problems of economic management arising from the experience of total war.

The fact that all these tasks had been autonomously fulfilled by family, community and market did not make their execution one whit less complicated once they became the province of the rationalized procedures of administrative processes. Lenin's framework was not equipped to cope with these considerations; and it is of course arguable that precisely these considerations made themselves very strongly felt in short order, playing no small part in the multiplication of tasks that was to fall to the Soviet government in its formative years. The process of industrialization upon which all Russian revolutionaries were determined to embark could not but emphatically contribute to the decisive destruction of non-administrative means of social provision, involving as it did large-scale rural depopulation, destruction of traditional forms of social organization and rapid occupational mobility. And the allocation of resources to competing interests within the fields of social provision and economic activity is a decision-making process: it is more than the simply mechanical processes of 'registration, filing and checking'.

Weber believed that the nature of even the simple and routine tasks provided a basis of power for the administrators that was potentially dangerous. If it can be further established that the complexity and technical content of these tasks increase to the point of transformation as development proceeds, such dangers are obviously magnified. It is necessary, therefore, at this point to take note of these dangers as Weber initially defined them.

## WEBER'S BUREAUCRACY

Weber defined a series of features which gave his concept of bureaucracy a specific character. The following account of these features is by no means exhaustive, but provides the elements that this argument will attempt to bring to bear on Lenin's model. According to Weber, a modern state exists where a political community possesses the characteristics of an administrative and legal order that is subject to change by legislation; an administrative apparatus that conducts official business in accordance with legislative regulation; binding authority over all persons and over most actions taking place within its jurisdiction; the legitimation to use force within this area if coercion is permitted or prescribed by legal authority.

The legal authority of the modern state thus implies that:

(a) Any norm may be enacted as law with the claim and expectation that it will be obeyed by all those who are subject to the authority of the political community.

(b) The law as a whole constitutes a system of abstract rules, and governmental administration is bounded by rules of law and conducted in accordance with generally formulated principles that are approved or at least accepted.

(c) The people who occupy positions of authority are not personal rulers, but superiors who temporarily hold an office by virtue of which they possess limited authority.

(d) The people who obey the legally constituted authority do so as citizens, not subjects, and obey the law rather than the official who enforces it.

Where the rule of law thus prevails, a bureaucratic organization is governed by the following principles:

(a) Official business is conducted on a continuous basis.

(b) It is conducted according to the rules that (i) the duty of each official to do certain types of work is delimited in terms of impersonal criteria, (ii) the official is given the authority necessary to carry out his assigned functions, (iii) the means of compulsion at his disposal are strictly limited, and the conditions of their legitimate employment are clearly defined.

(c) Every official's responsibilities and authority are part of a hierarchy of authority.[6]

Weber then analysed the dangers presented by this social institution: the institution *itself* has certain regrettable features. Bureaucracy is part and parcel of the process of 'dis-enchantment' that was central to his analysis. Bureaucratic decision-making tends by definition to be 'inflexible'. It is difficult to adapt the processes of rationalized thought to particular cases of particular individuals, when this might be precisely what is required if a humane and sensible decision is to be reached. We might consequently feel ambivalent about 'the old-type ruler who is moved by sympathy, favour, grace, and gratitude'[7] when faced with the modern bureaucrat who adheres rigidly to established rules and the principle of calculability, sometimes to the point of obvious absurdity. This 'depersonalization' of decision-making underlies the common complaints about 'faceless bureaucrats'.

A further regrettable, and at times apparently irresistible, feature of the bureaucracy is the tendency to 'the concentration of the means of administration'. The general tendency for pre-modern forms of social provision and decision to be replaced by bureaucratic forms may sweep up in its flood such forms that are still viable and should not be relinquished. Not all administrative functions must by their nature be performed by state officials; many may reasonably be claimed by those involved in the institutions of a local, voluntary or autonomous nature. But the bureaucracy has an impulse to absorb all these, an impulse which it may be difficult to refuse because that bureaucracy can so often do the task more efficiently and cheaply. Or at least, it can pretend so, even if its real colonizing power derives only from the momentum of the already established bureaucratic machine.

These two problems are inevitable when a bureaucracy does no more than strictly follow its prescribed and legitimate role. However, we are faced with a far greater set of problems in the possibility of the bureaucracy overstepping the boundaries that a democratic society would wish to set for it. Bureaucracies may move into a realm where they have no right to be: they may aggregate to themselves powers of political decision-making. If there is any normative content to Weber's work on bureaucracy it must be understood as a theory of appropriate limitations. Weber's work does not propose a rejection of the bureaucratic institution: such a rejection would be an impotent gesture, and he had anyway clearly spelled out that bureaucracy came as part of a historical 'package'. Modernity brings improved health, genuine popular access to education, a standard of living previously denied to all but a small majority, a rise in the level of culture and opportunities, and so on. It also brings bureaucracy. This is, at least in part, a cost.[8] But before the cost is judged, the value of the commodities it pays for must be appreciated. Of this basic value, Weber seems to have had little doubt.

Weber also pointed out that the rise of bureaucracy was associated with the rise of democracy. Bendix summarized the argument:

> Bureaucracy developed with the support of democratic movements that demanded equality before the law and legal guarantees against

arbitrariness in judicial and administrative decisions. . . . In meeting these demands bureaucratic organisations had a levelling effect: the people subject to the law and the officials who exercised authority under the law became formally equal.[9]

This did not tempt Weber to anodyne and vacuous conclusions about the innocuous nature of bureaucratic power. His theory establishes two symbiotic but distinct domains. As we shall see, problems ominous for democracy arise from the blurring of divisions between these domains, or the colonizing of one domain by the other. One domain is that of *bureaucratic administration*, which is ruled by the considerations of rationality and calculability: it is the domain of instrumental values, and its responsibility is to seek the most effective and economical implementation of policies and decisions that have been arrived at elsewhere. It coexists with the *public, or political, domain*. This domain cannot expect its policies to arrive from elsewhere. Those decisions are the prerogative of the political domain and of no other. It is here that the basic value orientations of the society must be determined, and this, ideally, is achieved by a process of 'discursive will-formation', as Habermas has termed it.

This distinction is an important one for Weber, who speaks to the widespread fear of bureaucracies that exists in the modern world. It is common in popular culture and in radical political theory to conceive of bureaucracy only as a standing abuse to the principles and practice of democracy. For Weber, it is the relationship *between* bureaucrat and politician that is crucial. For while the latter is legally master, the relationship is easily tilted. Experts de facto carve out for themselves spheres of discretion and control despite their formal subordination to a political will:

> The power position of a fully developed bureaucracy is always great, under normal conditions overtowering. The political 'master' always finds himself, *vis-à-vis* the trained official, in the position of a dilettante facing an expert.[10]

Given that day-to-day authority rests in the hands of the administrators, every public political struggle in which a politician engages – election, parliamentary vote – must, if successful, be followed by a private struggle to ensure implementation by the bureaucracy. If the politician is the loser in such a struggle – and it is, as we have pointed out, often an uneven one – then the bureaucracy has usurped the process of political decision-making. Bureaucracies have a 'fundamental tendency to turn all problems of politics into problems of administration'.[11]

Gouldner has attempted to elaborate more fully the source of the bureaucrat's power over the politician: this power may be seen as undergoing subtle but profound changes as the bureaucracy responds to changing tasks. The ability of the traditional bureaucratic official to escape from political control was a result of the complexity of the tasks assigned, however routine and mundane the skills involved in the performance of those tasks might have been. In most instances, the old bureaucrat conformed to Lenin's picture of the regulator, the filer, the checker. He was no more than an *agent*, whose golden rule was that of obedience to higher authority. His skills consequently, were little more than those of being able to read, write, count and file. But the role of the 'modern' bureaucracy makes it less and less a clerical phenomenon, and increasingly part of an intelligentsia. This 'new intelligentsia' possess 'extensive cultural capital', which 'increases their mobility', and thus their potential independence from and lack of subordination to the specific norms of a bureaucratic culture:

> The technical intelligentsia . . . is controlled by those incompetent to judge its performance and whose control, therefore, it experiences as irrational. . . . In contrast to the bureaucrats . . . the intelligentsia seek nothing for its own sake, gives reasons without invoking authority, and regards nothing as settled once and for all. To them, nothing is exempt from re-examination. Unlike the bureaucrats, the intelligentsia are not 'ritualists' pursuing something without regard for effectiveness.[12]

If the power of the old bureaucracy rested on its 'mystery', its detailed knowledge of the procedures and possibilities, the history and the complexity of the administrative apparatus, the power of the new bureaucracy derives from contrary themes. The new bureaucracy possesses an *interrogative* capacity. This perhaps makes it less susceptible to the routinism of formal rationality and secrecy that Weber identified as the inherent failing of bureaucracy; by the same token, however, it describes an administrative machine that can possess an ethic of independence and decision-making that is strongly counterposed to the idea of control by political masters. Indeed, Gouldner sees this new potential as intimately connected with the attempt of a new ruling class to establish itself. Prerogatives of political decision-making will be claimed with increasing openness, and not just assumed by stealth. The viability of this prognosis is a matter for debate, but it is clear that if Gouldner's typology of the new bureaucracy is close to the truth, the problems of democratic control can only be intensified.

## BUREAUCRACY IN 'THE STATE AND REVOLUTION'

For Lenin economic development demanded a reduction in the tasks and responsibilities of the state. It is, then, perhaps not surprising that to the developments in the European state form in the early twentieth century, which included the first major attempts at welfare provision, economic management and planning, and political participation, he can only ascribe a uniformly negative character. But if it is accepted that Lenin's conception of the tasks that any state must *at a minimum* perform is inadequate, the consequences must be examined. Such a weakness must put in question the integrity of the model of the radical state that he expounded. We must consider whether Lenin's prescriptions for democratic control, for policing the power, and the boundaries, of the bureaucracy are rendered unacceptably naive by this growth of the administrative function.

Despite his extremely modest assessment of the functions of the modern state apparatus, Lenin *was* aware of the tendency of the administrative organs to establish their own autonomy – whether in their separate territories or over society as a whole. However, when he turns to this it appears that it is the issue over which he feels least impelled to extend or improve on the writings of Marx and Engels. He gives a lengthy quotation from Engels:

'Against this transformation of the state and the organs of the state from servants of society into masters of society – an inevitable transformation in all previous states – the Commune used two infallible means. In the first place, it filled all posts – administrative, judicial, and educational, by election and on the basis of universal suffrage of all concerned subject to recall at any time by the electors. And, in the second place, it paid all officials, high or low, only the wages received by other workers. . . . In this way a dependable barrier to place-hunting and careerism was set up, even apart from the binding mandates to delegates to representative bodies, which were added besides.'[13]

The theme of 'careerism' and 'place-hunting' is a pregnant one: it replicates the mistaking of the object that Lenin's critique of bureaucracy has already shown. After Engels' comments Lenin underlines the centrality of this problem for him: a career in bureaucracy is no more than an avenue to *economic* gains of the most vulgar kinds:

> if careerism is to be abolished completely, it must be made *impossible* for 'honorable' though profitless posts in the Civil Service to be used as a springboard to highly lucrative posts in banks or joint-stock companies, as constantly happens in all the freest capitalist countries.[14]

It is in fact remarkable that the only prescription for the control of officials that receives detailed attention – some two full pages – is that of the reduction of 'the remuneration of all servants of the state to the level of "workman's wages" '. The unquestionably more complex issues of the election of all officials, the constant right of recall and the necessity for binding mandates for delegates receive no further elaboration. Lenin's thought in this whole area is constantly voided of relevance to the real problem by the re-emergence of a theory of motivation cast solely in terms of cash.

Lenin's theoretical failure was later to produce a practical failure. When the bureaucratic corruption of his state was finally borne in on him, his only solution was to intensify the concentration of power. It was impossible to distribute power, inasmuch as the source of corruption came from sources external to the state machine itself. Recall Lenin's definition of the roots of bureaucracy: economic underdevelopment. Translated into political sociology, this meant the penetration of the administrative strata by the 'low cultural level' of the populace. Whether this refers to 'bourgeois' technical specialists retained from the old regime, or to somewhat uneducated recruits from the working class or peasantry, or to 'careerists' of all and any social origin, the analysis is the same: these people are polluted by bourgeois norms. In such a situation, Lenin's answer to the problem of bureaucracy was 'to fall back on the more advanced workers, on the proletarian elite, or, rather, on the Party'.[15] In the light of a more sophisticated analysis of bureaucracy this was, of course, to make the cure worse than the disease.

It is of some interest that Trotsky's theory of the bureaucracy, markedly more sophisticated in content than Lenin's, reproduced this fallacious theory of motivation. In his concern to pronounce anathema on the Soviet bureaucracy, Trotsky insisted on its 'parasitic' nature. It had, he stressed, no necessary role in the process of production, no valid economic role at all. To have claimed otherwise would not only have undermined Trotsky's refusal to define the bureaucracy as a class, but would, in his eyes, have questioned the very validity of October as a revolution for proletarian emancipation in the first place. The bureaucracy is therefore no more than a group of people who have a natural interest in maintaining their privileged access to consumption in a situation of grave material scarcity. To secure this, they practically 'invent' a job for themselves. This insistence on the parasitic – and unnecessary – role of the bureaucracy, on the fact that their sole *real* function was the regulation of consumption, in their own interests, must of course be a misconception of the processes actually going on. The manner in which they enforced and surveilled the process of industrialization during Stalin's 'second revolution' leaves little doubt about the real and major role they performed in production, however crassly, incompetently and barbarously.[16]

The point is that Trotsky's inadequate understanding of the role of bureaucracy within a modern economy prevents him from discovering any measures that will effectively cope with the problem. His immense labours on the problem and, indeed, the sincerity with which he condemns the bureaucracy for its gigantic 'betrayals' and later 'crimes' end up in a minimization of the problem itself. Lenin's solution to the problem of bureaucracy is modest: maintain standards of behaviour until rescued by the development of the forces of production and the elevation of the nation's culture. Trotsky's solution appears altogether more serious and committed. He made a defence of the soviet a central part of his programme for combating bureaucracy, and as such the institution occupies an important place in the 1927 Platform of the Joint Opposition. Yet what is clear is that Trotsky can propose no constitutional or institutional *changes* to the existing state of affairs. The oppositionists are reduced to anodyne suggestions whose guarantee of implementation lies only in willpower and good faith. It is necessary to 'adopt a firm policy of struggle with officialdom', to wage this struggle on the basis 'of a consistent development of workers' democracy in the party, trade unions, and Soviets' ('as Lenin would'); it is necessary to 'adopt a slogan', to 'heighten class activity', to 'draw the broad mass of people in', to 'bring it about' that the working people are 'convinced by experience' that the state institutions are on their side. Even the constitutional demand for 'a complete stop to the removal of elected Soviet officials' is rendered vacuous by the proviso 'except in the case of real and absolute necessity'.[17] Trotsky's solution later became profoundly radical: a political revolution to overthrow the bureaucracy.

But a solution of such magnitude is, paradoxically, just as simple as Lenin's – and as misdirected. Such an act of brutal rupture could certainly have removed that specific bureaucracy at that specific time; but only if that bureaucracy is seen as the unique product of a unique conjuncture will such a solution satisfy. For if the re-establishment of a stable situation were once again to present complex tasks which demanded the operation of those necessary functions which the bureaucracy had indeed performed, the situation returns to square one. The inadequacy of both Lenin and Trotsky's solutions is perhaps adequately expressed by the complete failure of either to take root in the Soviet Union.

An unsophisticated anti-bureaucratism ends up conspiring with the bureaucracy in the maintenance of its power. Lenin sees bureaucracy in terms of careerism, which allows the bureaucrat to 'cash in' on his service to the state through directorships. Trotsky sees that the bureaucracy of an administered society has direct access to material privilege. Both construe the motivation of the bureaucrat as economic gain. Their inability to avoid this reduction of the bureaucratic interest to something *outside* the specific function of the bureaucrat robs them of the insight that has made an alternative body of work, from Weber to Habermas, so fruitful. That insight involves the recognition that the bureaucrat – expert, administrator or intellectual technician – derives a motivation from the function he performs, and a power from the necessity of that function and the skills that he possesses to fulfil it. Thus a reasoned understanding of the problem of bureaucracy depends upon an acceptance of the necessity of the function of that group, rather than an assertion of it as an unambiguous evil.

Lenin's 'right of recall' will not overcome the power and moral authority granted to the bureaucrat who can lay claim to some measure of expertise. If the power of the bureaucrat comes from knowledge, if knowledge is power, the situation will evade the control of procedures designed to monitor a situation where the only commodity involved is power itself. Power, construed as simple authority deriving from the holding of office, can easily be transferred from one holder to the other. Power deriving from the possession of knowledge and skills may exercise two defences against such simple control procedures: the bureaucrat has the power of 'sabotage' in its widest sense, i.e. he can extract concessions in return for the obedient fulfilment of his functions; and the citizen will be vulnerable to an awareness of the imbalance in the power relationship he inhabits with the bureaucrat, and thus grant to the bureaucrat licence to perform his tasks without constant supervision. Thus, to set up crude mechanisms of control as a result of seeing the bureaucrat's power as deriving only from position is to allow the genuine power of the bureaucrat to garner strength unchecked by realistic balances. Only as a result of conceding to the bureaucracy its genuine, legitimate and distinct functions can one begin to determine the boundaries of its powers and construct political control procedures that may successfully police those boundaries. It is this concern with 'bureaucratic forms' as necessary objects of analysis which is almost entirely absent from the work of Lenin and Engels.

The Engels/Lenin model has further problems. I have just suggested that the misunderstanding of the nature of bureaucratic power is likely to result in the mechanism of recall, of mandating, and so on, falling into disuse. This, as ever, is not an absolute case. We can consider the possible effects where such measures do in fact become the norms of political practice.

It is worth noting, to start with, that the consequent instability of office-holders will obviously hinder the smooth working of an apparatus whose functions are by definition continuous. It will further set limits upon the freedom of action of the official – indeed it is designed to achieve precisely that. Clearly the possibility of a conflict between the general interest and the particular interest, however these are construed, does arise. A state machine that is avowedly charged with the task of administering a *transition* from an old way of life to a new one will face this problem rather acutely. The industrialization process itself unfortunately has the character of a 'command' situation, just as does any attempt to affect radical social and cultural change in an already developed economy. To propose no judgements on the moral acceptability of such attempts, the attempt itself simply raises issues of *conflict* between the interests on each side of the attempt. It should be recognized that when the position of the bureaucrat is unstable and temporary, as it would inevitably be under the commune formula, the curse of 'careerism' *could* become a genuine one. I have suggested that such concepts are not very helpful in understanding the culture and motivation of an established administrative stratum. But a situation where position is *constantly* threatened could well have the consequence of making the official constantly concerned about how to maintain his position; his knowledge of the indispensability of his particular skills in the face of popular ignorance could only reinforce an opportunist and populist attitude to those who held power over him.

We are thus faced with the possibility of corruption becoming an institutionalized practice: by corruption I mean a tendency to give undue weight to the interests of the prominent and powerful in the decision-making process. The removal of the membrane between the world of rational administration and the world of value-laden practical interests which is involved in Engels' proposal harbours the risk that the latter will overwhelm the former – not by a considered process of political change, but by counterposing opinion to legality. Bureaucrats may by such means be prevented from actions which their electors find unpalatable. They may also be induced to initiate actions which their constituents find desirable, but are not in fact within the powers granted to them by whatever constitutional processes the society has seen fit to construct. De Tocqueville noted such possibilities in his study of the society which makes the widest use of the principle of election to administrative office:

> In general the American functionaries are far more independent than the French civil officers within the sphere which is prescribed to them. Sometimes even they are allowed *by popular authority* to exceed these bounds; and as they are protected by the opinion and backed by the cooperation, of the majority, they venture upon manifestations of their power as astonish a European. By this means are formed habits in the heart of a free country which may some day prove fatal to its liberties.[18]

Such weaknesses in Engels' scheme can only be dismissed in a model of society which presumes a degree of conflict far more limited than is reasonable. It must presuppose within the citizenry the existence of a single will, with conflict arising, if at all, only between citizenry and bureaucracy. Rousseau asserted the existence of such a 'general will'. However, this general will was an entity viable, if at all, only in the functioning of small-scale city-states like his adopted Geneva; and the larger a state or nation became, the more likely was the possibility of 'dysfunctional' dissidence. For this purpose it was necessary for Rousseau to make a distinction between the 'general will' and the 'will of all'. The latter is the sum of 'particular wills', which may be misled, while the 'general will' derives only from an original contract and from the subsequent accumulated wisdom of a developing society, which cannot fall into error. Much has been made of the ambiguity of Rousseau's legacy, but one can certainly detect in various parts of *The Social Contract* the seeds of the Soviet regime's legitimation process.[19]

The history of the Soviet Union is the history of the *construction* of a general will. It had to be constructed, it was not given. The general will was constructed first by defining certain classes of people as non-citizens, i.e. class enemies, and then by embodying in the Bolshevik party the quality of the 'accumulated wisdom' which constituted the general will as against the 'will of all' that might arise from the 'contradictions among the people'. The party's understanding of the general will derived from the possession of 'scientific' Marxism. Differences within the leadership of the Bolshevik regime in its early years were disagreements over the interpretation of the general will, not over the legitimacy of such a concept as the basis of the state.

It may, however, be argued that the usurpation of power by a bureaucracy was rooted in its substitution of an incorrect version of the general will for a correct one. Lenin's strictures on the growth of a bureaucratic culture and Trotsky's later attempts to attribute the consolidation of bureaucracy to a matter of self-interest of a materially privileged stratum are examples of such arguments. But such views simply continue the legitimation of the bureaucracy: it possesses the general will, it assumes omniscience in the determination of values as well as techniques. Lenin and Trotsky criticize the bureaucracy for misinterpreting the general will (i.e. Marxism), or reading their self-interests as identical to the general will. But the real error lies in their possession of the right to determine the general will at all, and that error is inescapable as long as the idea of a general will itself is not rejected as politically authoritarian and sociologically nonsensical.

A bureaucracy that has acquired illegitimate power is one that has short-circuited the normal processes of the articulation and resolution of conflicts that are properly the domain of a public sphere. We have seen that bureaucracies contain natural tendencies to do this as a result of wider developments in twentieth-century economy, society and culture. But for such tendencies to be consummated, other determinations must be present. One such tendency is simply the cultural legitimation of such a domination. Whatever the material and conjunctural conditions that constrained Soviet society in its early years – and much has been made of this by observers – the weight of this cultural legitimation must be appreciated. The bureaucracy did not have to provide this cultural legitimation; it was provided in full measure by the culture of Bolshevism.

The Bolsheviks had a particular and specific theory of political differences. Political differences among the citizenry were defined as the remnants of alien class forces, or as symptoms of inadequate political culture demanding educational correction, or as historical 'contradictions among the people' which in time would find a suitable *aufhebung* at the hands of economic development. At various times in the early history of the Soviet Union the response to political problems in the public sphere involved one, or a combination, of these three options. If particular initiatives were identifiable as directly or indirectly the product of bourgeois forces, repression provided a straightforward answer – as with non-Bolshevik parties and institutions from the dissolution of the constituent assembly onwards. Kronstadt is the most obvious example. With issues in which the enemy and source were not personally so immediately identifiable, as with the situation resulting from war communism and leading to the New Economic Policy (NEP), the problems were handled with a combination of direct repression, educational initiatives, and administrative and policy adjustments to ameliorate the conditions of the unhappy peasantry.

An exception to this 'administrative politics' may be found in some of the arguments of Bukharin. It may be significant that Bukharin was one of the few Bolsheviks who had any acquaintance with contemporary developments in European social theory. He was clearly familiar with the work of Michels and Weber, and was prepared to quote Weber in support of his arguments in *Historical Materialism*, albeit only in the more academic parts of his argument. The last pages of that work take the form of an attempted refutation of Michels' theories of bureaucracy.[20] Doubtless Bukharin would have had only a hostile response to suggestions that the problems these writers discussed were relevant to the problems of the Soviet Union. But it is perhaps not too much to assume that Bukharin might have from this encounter absorbed some of the important and relevant insights embodied in their work. For it is only in Bukharin that we faintly hear any echo of the real problems of bureaucracy, politics and industrialization.

Those who are commonly regarded as the natural and democratic opponents of Lenin's bureaucracy shared the same naive assumptions as Lenin, demonstrating a resurgent intolerance. The Workers' Opposition of 1921 stressed heavily the need for a purge to effect the wholesale removal of non-proletarian elements from the party; the Democratic Centralists proposed measures to guarantee high proletarian representation on party committees. Their analysis of the problem of bureaucracy here foreshadowed Lenin's: the guarantee of democracy lay in the preservation of the purity of an élite, albeit an élite as widely defined as consisting of a whole class. In the wake of the Kronstadt revolt, the Bolsheviks' solution to political crisis was both repression and compromise.[21] The repression was directed against the critics on the Left. The compromise involved was the NEP. For Lenin and the Bolsheviks, these compromises were of a specific kind. They involved the exchange of political rights for economic ones. The peasantry would be allowed a degree of freedom of action in selling his surplus to markets, and even determining the fate of that surplus, in return for accepting the Bolsheviks' monopoly of political power. These were concessions granted as purely tactical steps, a retreat in the face of necessity, and nothing is clearer in the thoughts of the leading Bolsheviks than the understanding that these were temporary compromises which would be dispensed with as soon as possible. But Bukharin's appreciation seems to have been different:

> Bukharin did not interpret the granting of rights to the peasants as 'concessions', as purely tactical steps. In Bukharin's implicit and explicit interpretations, both the NEP and the market ceased to be seen as tactical retreats; they were good strategy for the entire 'transition period', if not longer.[22]

Such a position, once thought through, would have had major implications for the political processes of the Soviet regime. The continued existence of the NEP would surely have meant the emergence of definite interest groups which would at some point have been able to articulate positions – of whatever sort – which would have contested the Bolsheviks' claim to define the 'middle-range' objectives and policies of the society. Thus the problem at the end of the 1920s was that not only were the Bolsheviks forced to rapid collectivization, but the previous policy of the NEP had generated a distinct interest group – if not a class – against whose bitter opposition collectivization would have to proceed.

The consequences of the decision to resolve this problem are well known. But it can be argued that the path that Bukharin suggested would have obviated the fantastic human – and economic – losses sustained during the collectivization drive. A policy of fostering agrarian capitalism was not incompatible with some degree of directed industrialization; nor was it even hostile to the long-term strategy of a socialist society. It was, however, utterly incompatible with the maintenance of the Bolshevik monopoly of political power. A group as powerfully based economically as the capitalist farmers would have become would have demanded some participation in the policy-formulating processes of the government. But it is unnecessary to assume – and Deutscher points this out in his discussion of the 1928 crisis[23] – that such political groups would necessarily have been committed to the ending of the socialist project.

It is difficult to know what might have become of the Soviet regime had Bukharin's conception of the NEP been accepted and the development of the Soviet economy allowed to proceed in a different direction to that imposed on it after 1929. Lewin argues that the NEP was bound up with certain 'nonstatist' consequences: cultural and relative political pluralism, curtailment of the terror apparatus, the absence of a rigid ideology. More definitively:

> Whereas NEP had erected an elaborate legal edifice and seriously strived to achieve 'socialist legality', during the Five Year Plan this framework was utterly destroyed and replaced by a system of extra-legal, crude coercion and mass terror.[24]

This may well be an overstatement of the benefits that the NEP brought; compared with the period of war communism that preceded it and the Second Revolution that followed, it is bound to appear as an oasis of legality and civilization in a desert of arbitrariness. Even with the NEP we are still talking about a political process almost hermetically confined to the Bolshevik élite. Nevertheless Bukharin's model of the NEP in the 'transition' underlines the 'elective affinities' between the existence of differing interest groups and the viability, even necessity, of relatively open and democratic political processes. It, conversely, underlines the consequences of the orthodox Bolshevik interpretation of the NEP: just as in the economic field any concessions were merely temporary 'retreats', so in the political field any consequent liberalization was counted as a clear cost, not a gain.

The contrast between Bukharin and mainstream Bolshevik thought is nowhere clearer than in the discussion of the problem of bureaucracy. By the end of the 1920s, Lenin's primitive analysis had become an article of faith. In 1929 the central committee submitted to the sixteenth party congress the first – and probably the last – resolution specifically devoted to the problem of combating bureaucratism. In presenting it to the congress, Yavkovlev, the deputy commissar of the Rabkrin (the Workers' and Peasants' Inspectorate, set up by Lenin to combat bureaucracy and corruption) reaffirmed the analysis of the problem: 'He who is against industrialization, he who is against collectivization, stands, whether he means or does not mean to, for the perpetuation of the roots of bureaucratism.'[25]

Lewin expounds Bukharin's analysis, which was counterposed to such 'nonsensical ascription of every unpalatable fact of life to "bourgeois survivals" or to "petit bourgeois pressures" '.[26] Bukharin wanted to defend the craftsmen, small merchants, small industrialists and small agricultural producers, as well as co-operative and governmental small-scale enterprises and services, against their 'crushing' and absorption by the state. For the state to take on these tasks unnecessarily, along with the tasks which of necessity it had assumed due to the government's long-term project, was to fuel the source of bureaucracy. Bukharin thus made in passing a silent acknowledgement of Weber's connection between bureaucracy and industrialization, and this was clearly connected with his far more subtle appreciation of the complexities of Soviet problems. His argument, however, was subject to furious rebuttals, and what might have been the consequences of the insights he displayed about the NEP and about bureaucracy can only be a matter for speculation. It must be remembered that it was Bukharin, of all the Bolsheviks, who held faith with the model of the commune-state. In 1928 he reiterated the theme: 'We are far too centralized; we must ask ourselves whether we cannot take a few steps towards Lenin's state of the Commune.'[27] Whether, given time and experience, he would have arrived at a more sophisticated and appropriate model for the correction of the mistakes and problems that he saw must similarly remain a matter of speculation. For us, the real educational value of Bukharin's protests is the light they throw on the arguments he was opposing.

None of these responses crossed the threshold that divides administration from politics. Administration concerns the carrying out of an already determined policy; politics involves the discussion and negotiation of such policies. The Bolshevik government delegitimized politics within the citizenry. Such differences were either criminal (bourgeois class remnants), due to ignorance (low political culture of the masses) or transitory (the peasants were a historically doomed class, therefore their grievances had to be catered for, but not legitimized). What the Bolsheviks could not do was accept a characterization of any political differences as genuine, i.e. an opinion which a person or group had a right to hold and negotiate over as an equal partner in the process of will-formation. There could be only one genuine politics among the masses, a politics which coincided with the politics of the government, and consequently with the administrative bureaucracy. Clearly, this is the path to the authoritarian state. Because the government and the bureaucracy were already the expression of that one genuine politics, and by definition a more coherent and profound expression than could be found among the people themselves, the politics of the people were rendered redundant. Politically, the people were abolished. Thus the analysis suggested here is not the classic model of a bureaucracy establishing itself as a ruling class or caste over subaltern classes. Such subtle concepts of hegemony are not necessary. The bureaucracy necessarily became, not the ruling class, but the *only* class.

It was, after all, the case that the bureaucracy / party / government was the only location where differences could in fact be debated and discussed as differences, i.e. debates on practical questions, rather than as deviations from an increasingly narrowly constituted and defined general will, at least until the logic of domination finally worked itself out in the dictatorship of Stalin. Surely the submission of all oppositions to the concept of the single party, and, even more fatally, to the illegitimacy of taking discussions beyond the central committee, let alone the party, indicates a tabu whose strength cannot derive only from some misguided sense of loyalty or group solidarity. To appeal to the masses is to implicitly revive them from the mortuary whence they have been consigned by the dictates of the general will: it is to call in question the viability of such a general will itself. And that is to bring down the whole edifice of legitimation which sustained the Bolshevik regime, not the Stalin faction alone.

Thus Lenin's possible response to Weber's problems, his simple mechanisms for control of the state, are profoundly flawed. Instant recall of administrators initially dissolves the administration into the people, and makes them subject to the same norms of political interest as obtained in the public sphere. The consequence of that is corrupt administration, where instrumental rationality is prevented from applying in the areas where its writ must, for the sake of even-handedness and stability, run. This threatens not only the performance of the necessary functions of administration, but, further, the safeguarding of the access of minority opinions to the decision-making process. If this problem is overcome by the denial of the existence of such minority opinions, i.e. by denying the legitimate existence of political differences, then the rights not only of minorities but also of the majority are threatened. Only the existence of minorities gives meaning to the concept of a majority. A citizenry which displays no special and particular interests separate from and even discordant with the general interest has no need of politics. And thus the rule of the bureaucracy is logically ensured and embedded in a nation's culture.

## LENIN'S DEMOCRACY

Lenin's model does not, however, lack putative institutions for the expression of the will of the citizenry. So far, the discussion has dealt with the administrative machinery and the relationship of the citizens to it. Lenin also discusses directly political forms of confronting the problem, a substitute for the parliamentary form which attempts to fulfil that task in bourgeois democracies. His theme is once again taken directly from Marx:

> 'The Commune', wrote Marx, 'was to be a working not a parliamentary body, executive and legislative at the same time.'

Lenin expands into a critique of parliamentarianism:

> The way out of parliamentarianism is not, of course, the abolition of representative institutions and the elective principle, but the conversion of the representative institutions from talking shops into 'working' bodies. . . .
> 'A working, not a parliamentary body' – this is a blow straight from the shoulder at the present day parliamentarians and parliamentary lap-dogs of Social Democracy! Take any parliamentary country, from America to Switzerland, from France to Britain, Norway, and so forth – in these countries the real business of state is performed behind the scenes and is carried on by the departments, chancelleries and General Staffs. Parliament is given up to talk for the special purpose of fooling the 'common people'.

But this criticism applies to radical democratic forms as well. Even the soviets have reproduced the problem:

> The heroes of rotten philistinism . . . have even succeeded in polluting the Soviets after the fashion of the most disgusting bourgeois parliamentarianism, in converting them into mere talking shops. In the Soviets, the 'socialist' Ministers are fooling the credulous rustics with phrase-mongering and resolutions. In the government itself a sort of permanent shuffle is going on in order that, on the one hand, as many Socialist-Revolutionaries and Mensheviks as possible may in

turn get near the 'pie', the lucrative and honourable posts, and that, on the other hand, the 'attention' of the people may be 'engaged'. Meanwhile, the chancelleries and army staffs 'do' the business of 'state'.

Lenin proposes an alternative that will negate the possibility of such deceptions:

> The commune substitutes for the venal and rotten parliamentarian-ism of bourgeois society institutions in which freedom of opinion and discussion does not degenerate into deception, for the parlia-mentarians themselves have to work, have to execute their own laws, have themselves to test the results achieved in reality, and to account directly to their constituents. Representative institutions themselves remain, but there is *no* parliamentarianism here as a special system, as the division of labour between the legislative and the executive, as a privileged position for the deputies.[28]

There is here an intimate connection with previous elements of the discussion. If the 'parliamentarians' of the soviet system have to 'execute their own laws' then we are here talking about the same *people* as in the discussion of administrators and bureaucrats. The section of Lenin's work cited above, titled 'The abolition of parliamen-tarianism', is in fact composed mainly of the discussions on the 'postal service' concept and the payment of 'workmen's wages', etc. There is clearly no conceptual distinction in Lenin's mind between the nature of the 'representative' institutions and any other branch of the state apparatus. Lenin is talking about deputies as much as about function-aries when he pauses to remind us, immediately after the paragraph containing the above quotation, that:

> It is extremely instructive to note that, in speaking of the functions of those officials who are necessary for the Commune and for proletarian democracy, Marx compares them to the workers of 'every other employer', that is of the ordinary capitalist enterprise, with its 'workers, foremen, and accountants'.
>
> There is no trace of utopianism in Marx, in the sense that he made up or invented a 'new' society. No, he studied the birth of the new society out of the old, and the forms of transition from the former to the latter, as a natural-historical process.[29]

This is certainly no utopianism, if Lenin is serious in recommending the relationship of wage labour as ideally suited to effective democratic institutions. Baudrillard has elaborated a persuasive argument here, insisting that Marx's thought ultimately fails to be radical because it is no more than the 'mirror of production'. That is, all the fundamental categories upon which Marx chose to construct his theory of emancipation were simply the categories of the capitalist mode: production, value, humans as tool-making and labouring animals, and so on.[30] His mature criticism of existing society was based not upon the rejection of such conceptions of humanity, but upon a demand that they be allowed to speak liberated from the fetters that bourgeois society hypocritically laid on them. Baudrillard would argue that it came as no surprise that a new society constructed upon such estimations of the human subject turned out to be the most obsessively 'productivist' and 'reductionist' imaginable. Whatever the virtues of Baudrillard's argument, it is certainly striking to note how Lenin's ideas are permeated with, first, a concept of people as helplessly programmed for the pursuance of cash and acquisition; and, second, an admiration of the most instrumental elements of industrial and factory production as the condign mode for the management of human affairs. This most emancipatory and optimistic of documents is based upon a vision of human beings perhaps more bleak and demeaning than can be found in any previous work of political theorizing.

To return to the substance of Lenin's new version of parliamentarianism, the suggestion that this is a formula for successful democratic control of governmental machinery is quite vacuous. The elected deputies are to be civil servants, ministers and representatives of their constituents at one and the same time. They have to make the laws, carry them out *and* criticize them. Here Lenin summarily overthrows any previous claim he might have had to treating bureaucratization as a serious problem. If he is accepting that there are dangerous potentialities in the roles of a representative, of a legislator, of a civil servant and of a minister, his answer to those dangers borders on the absurd: conflate all these roles into one, embody them in a single individual. No grounds are offered for presupposing that the norms of the representative would win out against the norms appropriate to the other functions allocated to the individual. (The only question seems to be of what such an individual would die: overwork or multiple schizophrenia.)

Further, of course, and the implications here are major, there is no conceptual space for a parliamentary *opposition*. Delegates are described as being representatives, legislators and executives. A delegate who is *only* a representative, who wishes to bear no responsibility for legislation with which he or his constituents disagree, but claims the right for his opposing and critical arguments to be heard, who refuses both a legislative and executive role, is not catered for within such a system. In fact he is specifically ruled out: he it would be who conceived parliament as a 'talking shop' and his job as going there to talk persistently against those who were 'doing'. So here again we have the insistent emergence of the theme of the impossibility of divisions among the people: the people must have a unitary set of interests and the possibility of political conflict – which can result only from representatives becoming careerists – is to be avoided by the tight bonds between representatives and electors. Here the very possibility of *party* – that is of organizations expressing diverse views and value orientations – is abolished long before any exigencies of the 'particularly hostile' conjuncture persuaded the Bolsheviks to get round to it in practice. Liebman has constructed an apparently painstaking account of the process by which the Bolsheviks reluctantly eradicated the Mensheviks, social revolutionaries and anarchists, tragically forced to repression by the pusillanimous and hostile activities of those groups. The existence in Bolshevik theory and culture of the norms we have just discussed indicates that such an account should be treated with considerable caution.[31]

Lenin's criticisms are of course constructed around a grain of truth. Parliaments *are* unsatisfactory, by their very nature: they cannot transform government into a purely transparent process. The business of government is too complex and the interests involved too diverse to make that possible. But, as I have argued, it is this very complexity and diversity that renders desires for transparency redundant in theory and authoritarian if translated into practice. Certainly, then, any 'separation of powers' must result in *opportunities* for 'undemocratic' activities and domains to develop. In the grey areas where domains overlap, in the no-man's-land where domains fail to connect, in all manner of corners and behind any closed door, power may be exercised without responsibility and corruption may flourish in subterranean fashions. Apart from constant vigilance and a readiness to reform existing procedures and institutions to correct those abuses that come to light, there is no answer to such problems – so long, that is, as one wishes to continue to enjoy the fruits of modernity. It is not difficult to argue that the benefits outweigh the costs.

Lenin's condemnation of 'talking-shops' may also be granted a degree of relevance for one writing when he did. But here the discussion rapidly collapses into hopeless confusion. It is true that parliamentarianism, even in Europe (although much more should be said about the British, and perhaps especially the American, experiences), was in many aspects underdeveloped, compromised and ineffective. Weber made the same criticism of 'a merely speech making parliament' in Germany and argued for a 'working' institution.[32] The phrases are identical to Lenin's, but the argument is of a trenchancy and sophistication of quite a different order. For the solution to underdevelopment was not abolition – and posed in these terms we can see the absurdity of Lenin's position – but development. Parliament had to be turned into a body which could do its job, but this had to be done without evacuating the concept of all meaning in Lenin's manner. To collapse parliament into administration was a solution of such irrelevance that it did not occur to Weber. He pointed instead to the need for the parliamentary selection of leaders, the parliamentary accountability of leaders and the parliamentary control of the administration, in the sense of permanent surveillance.[33] These perhaps do not exhaust the list of necessary prescriptions for genuine parliamentarianism, but they do demonstrate the appropriate subtlety of approach, they point to the opportunities for improvement that even the most circumscribed parliament may contain, and they highlight the thoughtlessness of Lenin's approach. A division of labour does, and *must*, remain between the legislature and executive, and in his rejection of this fundamental provision Lenin displays his ignorance of European political philosophy, his weak grasp of contemporary history, his unconcern for the nature of genuinely democratic possibilities, and his reluctance to engage in intellectual inquiry in any serious manner.

As Lenin's hermetic model slowly seals itself before our eyes, we should perhaps take into account one possible objection. It is wrong to consider the soviet as a single institution on the model of bourgeois parliaments. The commune is after all a *local* body, both in linguistic origin and arguably in Marx's original intent. Is there not therefore a possibility of oppositional politics proceeding through local oppositions to central authority? Lenin is concerned specifically to deny that possibility. The commune-state is emphatically not a federalist state. Bernstein had so characterized the commune, and criticized Marx's adherence to it on those grounds. Lenin will have none of it:

Federalism as a principle follows logically from the petty-bourgeois views of anarchism. Marx was a centralist. There is no departure whatever from centralism in his observations . . . if the proletariat and poor peasants take state power unto their own hands, organise themselves quite freely in communes, and *unite* the actions of all the communes in striking at capital, in crushing the resistance of the capitalists, and in transferring the privately owned railways, factories, and land and so on to the entire nation, to the whole of society, won't that be centralism? Won't that be the most consistent democratic centralism, and moreover, proletarian centralism?[34]

Bernstein's objection was that the decentralization of power and administration inevitable in a commune-state contradicted the necessity for centralized state action, which he construed to be essential for socialist development. Lenin does not disagree with Bernstein over this aspect of socialism. He is simply insistent that the commune-state itself *will*, nevertheless, be centralized and unitary. What Bernstein fails to see – with, one might add, good reason – is that the communes, with all their local powers, interests and differences, will voluntarily transform themselves into a single-willed pervasive state structure, abandoning any federalist pretensions that *might* be suggested by the commune form itself:

Bernstein simply cannot conceive of the possibility of voluntary centralism, of the voluntary amalgamation of the communes into a nation, of the voluntary fusion of the proletarian communes, for the purpose of destroying bourgeois rule and the bourgeois state machine.[35]

Perhaps caution is necessary here, as Lenin's points seem to deal exclusively with the need for centralized action to effect the revolutionary act itself, i.e. destroying bourgeois rule. This could be a transitory need, still leaving open the possibility of a 'voluntary' reclamation of local powers and interests by the local communes once a relatively stable situation is established. Lenin himself, however, nowhere makes such a point, and the discussion of the federalist commune-state is practically concluded with the above quotation. Other parts of the text, in fact, leave no room to assume that Lenin entertains any reversal of this 'centralism' and 'amalgamation' of the communes. Chapter 4, part 4, of *The State and Revolution* attempts a refutation of the virtues of federalism under any circumstances, apart perhaps from being a temporary stage in the 'transition from a monarchy to a centralised republic'.[36]

Otherwise, a federal republic, even under bourgeois rule, is definitely less preferable than any centralized form:

> It is extremely important to note that Engels . . . disproved . . . the prejudice that is very widespread . . . that a federal republic necessarily means a greater amount of freedom than a centralised republic. This is wrong. It is disproved by the facts cited by Engels regarding the centralised French Republic of 1792–98 and the federal Swiss Republic. The really democratic centralised republic gave *more* freedom than the federal republic. In other words, the greatest amount of local, regional, and other freedom known in history was accorded by a *centralised* and not by a federal republic.[37]

Whether Engels' facts really disproved this 'prejudice' is none of our concern. The quotation simply illustrates *Lenin*'s own 'prejudice' against federalism and reinforces the assumption that his commune-state, even in a situation of established proletarian power, would be devoid of federalist features. Thus does Lenin rescue his commune-state from the one remaining threat to its effectiveness as a monolithic authority structure.

The attentive reader might at this point protest at my treatment of the argument on federalism and the possibility of localized structures as organs of dissent and opposition. I have only explained *Lenin*'s hostility towards such concepts as the federal state; I have not, as I have attempted in other parts of this argument, offered the 'best possible case' analysis I promised at the start of this chapter. In other words, might it not yet be possible that a central government *without* Lenin's particular prejudices would make such a central authority/local opposition structure viable? I would argue that such is not the case, and that such oppositional structures must either be rendered vacuous in short order or produce divisive tendencies incompatible with the survival of the modern democratic state and society. I believe that the experience of the United States, and of various developing nations, shows that such institutions cannot bear this profoundly weighty burden with any degree of success. This argument, however, will be developed in greater depth towards the end of the next chapter.

### NOTES

1 Lenin, *The State and Revolution* (1917), *Collected Works*, Moscow and London, 1960–70, vol. 25, 420, 421, 426, 427.

2 ibid., 383.

3 Lenin, *The Tax in Kind* (1921), *CW*, 32, 351.

4 Max Weber, *Economy and Society*, 2 vols, Berkeley, 1978, 971.

5 ibid., 972.

6 This outline is derived from R. Bendix, *Max Weber: An Intellectual Portrait*, London, 1966, 417, 422, 424. The *locus classicus* of discussion on bureaucracy, politics and the state is Weber, *Economy and Society*, 956–1002, while probably the most stimulating and trenchant defence of the legitimate roles of administration and politics is found ibid., Appendix 2, 'Parliament and government in a reconstructed Germany', 1381–462. Useful accounts and interpretations of Weber's work in this area include D. Beetham, *Max Weber and the Theory of Modern Politics*, London, 1970; A. Giddens, *Politics and Sociology in the Thought of Max Weber*, London, 1982; J. Habermas, *Towards a Rational Society*, London, 1971, and *Legitimation Crisis*, London, 1976; W. Mommsen, *The Age of Bureaucracy*, Oxford, 1974; B. Turner, *For Weber*, London, 1981; G. Poggi, *The Development of the Modern State*, London, 1978, is also relevant.

7 Bendix, *op. cit.*, 427.

8 Peter Berger's *Pyramids of Sacrifice*, London, 1977, is an indispensable and moving reflection on the costs of modernity and the transition to it.

9 Bendix, *op. cit.*, 437.

10 Weber, *Economy and Society*, 991.

11 Bendix, *op. cit.*, 440. The phrase is a quote from Mannheim.

12 A. Gouldner, *The Future of the Intellectuals and the Rise of the New Class*, London, 1979, 51. G. Konrad and I. Szelenyi, *The Intellectuals on the Road to Class Power*, Brighton, 1979, provides a view of the same process from the east. In fact the 'bureaucrats' of the early twentieth-century state, as Weber understood them perhaps already had more in common with Gouldner's definition of their role and culture than with Lenin's:

> Independent decision-making and imaginative organisational capabilities in matters of detail are usually also demanded of the bureaucrat, and very often expected even in larger matters. The idea that the bureaucrat is absorbed in subaltern routine and that only the 'director' performs the interesting, intellectually demanding tasks is a preconceived notion of the literati and only possible in a country that has no insight into the manner in which its affairs and the work of its officialdom are conducted. (Weber, 'Politics and government in a reconstructed Germany', 1404)

Weber's criticism is directed at German writers: how much more lacking in 'insight' must have been those who wrote in and of Russia!

13 Lenin, *The State and Revolution*, 451.

14 ibid., 452.
15 M. Lewin, *Lenin's Last Struggle*, London, 1969, 29.
16 The literature by and about Trotsky on the question of the bureaucracy is vast. Trotsky's mature and most detailed argument is *The Revolution Betrayed*, New York, 1972. The development of Trotsky's analysis is exhaustively pursued in I. Deutscher, *The Prophet Unarmed*, Oxford, 1959, and *The Prophet Outcast*, Oxford, 1963. Tony Cliff, *Russia: A Marxist Analysis*, London, 1970, offers a passionate if inelegant refutation of Trotsky's thesis. N. Mouzelis gives a succinct account of Trotsky's position in *Organisation and Bureaucracy*, London, 1975, 12–15.
17 L. Trotsky *et al.*, *Platform of the Joint Opposition* (1927), London, 1973, 51, 52.
18 A. de Tocqueville, *Democracy in America*, Oxford, 1965, 191.
19 J. J. Rousseau, *The Social Contract*, London, 1968; for example, 'Whether the general will can err', book II, chapter 3, 72–4, and 'That the general will is indestructible', book IV, chapter 1, 149–51. Rousseau does in fact say that 'if the general will is to be clearly expressed, it is imperative that there should be no sectional associations in the state'. But he *is* subtle enough to add the qualification, 'But if there are sectional associations, it is wise to multiply their number and prevent inequality among them' (73, 74). In this way the accumulated differences of sectional interests will cancel out each other, and the will of all will resemble a fair approximation of the 'general will' itself. Given his fear of the divisive, and ultimately violent, consequences of 'democratic' politics, Rousseau in this way, albeit grudgingly, offers a basis for the justification of a pluralist politics. Nevertheless the authoritarian implications of the metaphysical concept of the general will were to be his most disturbing legacy.
20 N. Bukharin, *Historical Materialism*, Ann Arbor, 1969, 309–11.
21 See R. V. Daniels, *The Conscience of the Revolution*, New York, 1969, 137–43.
22 M. Lewin, *Political Undercurrents in Soviet Economic Debates*, London, 1975, 45, 46.
23 I. Deutscher, *Stalin*, London, 1966, 319. The most lucid concise account of the economic policies and problems of the NEP is probably to be found in A. Nove, *An Economic History of the USSR*, London, 1969, chapters 4–6.
24 Lewin, *Political Undercurrents*, 97, 98.
25 E. H. Carr, *Foundations of a Planned Economy*, 2, London, 1976, 327.
26 Lewin, *Political Undercurrents*, 63.
27 Carr, *Foundations of a Planned Economy*, 324.
28 Lenin, *The State and Revolution*, 423, 424.
29 ibid., 425.
30 J. Baudrillard, *The Mirror of Production*, St Louis, Missouri, 1975.

31 M. Lewin, *Leninism under Lenin*, London, 1975, 238–57.

32 Weber, 'Parliament and government in a reconstructed Germany', 1416.

33 ibid., 1408. Weber then develops a complex and stimulating discussion of these themes.

34 Lenin, *The State and Revolution*, 429, 430.

35 ibid., 430.

36 ibid., 466.

37 ibid., 448.

# THREE **THE TEXT AND ITS ASSUMPTIONS**

## THE MISUNDERSTANDING OF A CENTURY

My argument has deliberately treated the field of political practices and institutions as a distinct and relatively independent domain. This approach departs perhaps from standard interpretations of Soviet history; it is also open to accusations of an 'idealist' approach to a problem whose determinations must be found in more profound roots, notably the economic sphere. I have noted in passing the arguments that attribute the decay of Soviet democracy to economic *practicalities*: the low productivity of labour, the atomization of the working class, the desperate administrative needs of a disrupted economy. Despite the undoubted relevance of such factors, I have sought to argue that a distinct, specific and major responsibility lies in another domain, that of the theoretical assumptions and cultural norms of the Bolsheviks with regard to the question of the state form. It seems to me that unless the question of political, institutional and constitutional forms is regarded as a distinct and separate subject for examination, there is an overwhelming tendency and temptation for the very significance of the question of political forms to be forgotten. I want now to support this contention by considering how later writers, by succumbing to this temptation, have contributed to a continuing misunderstanding of the world Lenin made.

To start with, there are arguments that attribute the authoritarian outcome of Lenin's activities to an insufficiency of radicalism at the core of his thought, in his conception of the economic (arguments which do not, however, question the position of such a domain as the organizing principle of a radical politics). Colletti argues that the conservative nature of the politics of the parties of the Second International was due to their appropriation of a positivist version of Marxism which sought to reduce all phenomena, social and natural, to the abstract laws of a 'dialectical materialism'. Such a Marxism was resolutely determinist, and could contain no element of the dialectic of subject and object. It found its paradigm in the base–superstructure metaphor, and the economic activity of human societies was reduced from a problem of social relationships to one of mere technique. Human practice and action become irrelevant to an understanding of history, and 'the materialist conception of history tends to become a technological conception of history'.[1]

Subsequently, Santamaria and Manville,[2] and Corrigan, Ramsay and Sayer, among others, have rooted the degeneration of the Russian Revolution in Lenin's adoption of capitalist industrial technique and management methods. Within a 'positivist' Marxism, such capitalist innovations would be regarded as unproblematic. Corrigan, Ramsay and Sayer attempt a radical critique of Bolshevism by opposing this version of Marxism. Their thesis is suitably bold: all radical critiques of the contemporary Soviet state fail, because 'Bolshevism as such is rarely invoked, anywhere on the left, in the explanation of the alleged Soviet malaise. It figures solely and monotonously as that which was betrayed.'[3] Citing the 'vulgar and naive conception of the "economy"' that Colletti has identified, the authors find the source of Bolshevik failure in the fact that

the emancipation of labour within production was never contemplated by the Bolsheviks. Their programmes on the contrary without exception enforced various relations, and experiences, of production reminiscent of the regime of capital: experiences that replicated capital's division of labour, capital's hierarchies of technical and managerial 'expertise', capital's divisive 'incentives', capital's inequalities, and, by no means least, capital's coercion of surplus labour and appropriation of its product to fuel an incessant and insatiable accumulation.[4]

Much of this is valid. The whole of the Marxist movement to Lenin's time partook of the same naive approach which held science, technology, production, efficiency and rationalization as unambiguous in essence and open to criticism only in terms of their use or misuse by specific social agents; and the Bolshevik regime hardly displayed a concern for 'job satisfaction', let alone workers' control of production. But does this really identify the *differentia specifica* of Bolshevism as a state philosophy? That difference, whoever the authors and whatever their standpoint, must have something to do with the ability of Bolshevism to bring about the physical liquidation of problematic social classes and political oppositions in very large numbers, and to the present day deny to the average citizen the protection afforded by basic democratic freedoms and human rights, the rule of law, freedom of movement, and so forth. It is, therefore, a serious assertion when the authors attribute to the theoretical error outlined in the quotations above those aspects of the Soviet political system to which they object: 'In short, and unsurprisingly, to foster capitalist forms of productive activity eventuates in the reproduction of various defining relations of the bourgeois state form that is their condition and consequence.'[5]

This seems to show a fine lack of conceptual discrimination. It is of course possible to see the political norms that prevail in the Soviet Union as identical in essence to those of a 'bourgeois state form', but only if certain major assumptions are made. It is necessary to assume that the particular *form* of the state is immaterial, epiphenomenal and insignificant, and what counts is a supposed *essence*. This assumption constitutes all non-Soviet regimes within the twentieth-century world system as unified by their essence as bourgeois regimes, with the essence being the subordination of certain specific classes to one specific class. By this assumption it is possible to elide the differences between liberal democracies and other more authoritarian and repulsive regimes of a fascist or totalitarian nature. No doubt such a distinction is heuristically viable, focusing as it does on the putative alternative of the transparent and self-governing society of the radical vision. But such an approach is intellectually dubious, leaping to the most general level without seriously pausing to consider the particular. For what is this concept of 'bourgeois state form' that is introduced so diffidently into the discussion?

The distinguishing features of the bourgeois state form are precisely *those that are most absent from the Soviet regime.* To wit, the separation of state and civil society: the competitive electoral process inscribed in the norms of social life; the right to form political – and other – organizations without obtaining permission from the state apparatus; the right within very broadly defined restrictions on obscenity and libel to publish and distribute material without sanction of the state apparatus; the formal and actual separation of powers; the absence of a single and hegemonic ideology and restricted political process embodied in a unique ruling institution; the protection of an independent judiciary under legislation duly and constitutionally established. It is in fact the case – and the case is presented by Marx, among others – that it was the introduction of these forms that marked the specifically bourgeois form of the state – not the simple rule of one class over another. This latter, of course, is a fairly common characteristic of state forms throughout history – and nowhere is this point made more strongly than in the Marxian canon.

The authors thus fail to grasp the real object of their study, the very thing they are at such pains to explain. Before it is necessary to discuss why and how it has come about that existing regimes of a socialist type fail to achieve the radical vision of freedom, it is logically a prior necessity to explain how those regimes fail even to provide a system of juridical and political freedoms to any degree equivalent to those prevailing in the western capitalisms. It is, after all, the absence in the Soviet Union of the latter, and not the former, political forms that confirms among the populations of contemporary capitalist societies a hostility to radical political change.

Arguably, capitalism has been able to utilize all of the productive practices itemized by Corrigan, Ramsay and Sayer, and utilize them to a far greater and more effective degree than has the Soviet Union. While the brutal history of various capitalist regimes gives proof enough that there is no guaranteed connection between contemporary industrial technique and political liberties, there is enough evidence to suggest that they are not incompatible. There *is* a distinct lack of evidence to support the author's theory that the existence of such techniques can account for the degeneration of the Soviet regime.

This argument has implications which Corrigan, Ramsay and Sayer have since made explicit. This is despite the fact that these implications, once made clear, will illustrate how this critique of Bolshevism ultimately justifies the Bolshevik regime. The authors buttress their demonstrated indifference to the institutional specifics of the bourgeois state by defining Soviet political processes as, in a distorted form, superior.

> The empty and ritualistic character of much 'official' Soviet political life – single candidate elections, a rubber stamp 'parliament' (the Supreme Soviet) – is . . . double edged in its significance. Too often it is taken as simply another index of the Soviet workers' powerlessness. What this ignores, in the simple-mindedness of the search for equivalents of 'our' institutions, is that the formality of Soviet politics *also* testifies to a diffusion of politics *throughout* the society and a partial overcoming of capitalism's separation of the political sphere. Soviet politics is largely ritual because most areas of Soviet life are subject to direct, though not necessarily democratic, political discussion and control. There is less place for a separate polity.[6]

The lack of discrimination referred to above is here applied to the Soviet regime. The authors believe that a distinction between the democratic control of social life, and direct state control of the same, can be in good conscience passed over in a subordinate clause. Doubtless the argument does rest on a feature of Soviet society that any argument must take into account. Lane has argued that the actual degree of participation and involvement in organizations on the part of Soviet workers *is* far greater than any comparable phenomenon in the west. He cites sources to the effect that the average amount of time spent on 'socio-political' activity has increased seven times over the period of Soviet rule, and the proportion of working people involved has increased eighteen times. Given the rather low base line for such comparisons, this indeed may not amount to very much in real time. But Lane points out what is anyway missing in such a situation. The political influence of the Soviet worker is categorically limited:

> He participates in improving production and he is closer to the administration both socially and politically than the worker in a

capitalist society. But he does not actively shape the overriding values of his society, which are largely determined by the ruling political elite.[7]

In fact, he or she does not even participate in improving production in any meaningful way: control over even this limited domain is successfully undermined by the political structure. Ostensibly, the most powerful of low-level control structures would be the party committees and cells. Lewin has discussed the roots of their impotence. First, he concurs with Lane:

> At best [the criticisms of the ordinary party cell member] could be directed officially only against marginal phenomena, because the party has asked for criticism only to expose defects in the implementation of plans, not in the plans themselves, so that such criticism may be turned exclusively against nonpolitical officials. The party simultaneously has erected barriers against more effective and broader criticism.[8]

But even the second-order tasks of monitoring implementation of policy are rendered unachievable:

> On paper, [the party cells] are supposed 'to supervise the administrations' and to mobilize party members and the masses for the implementation of plans. However, it is quite obvious that they are not in a position to 'supervise' because, in fact, they are asked simultaneously to support the administrations they are supposed to 'supervise', to strengthen their authority, and to help them fulfil those plans by disciplining the workers. And this happens to be their real task.[9]

These points hardly amount to a revelation, and doubtless Corrigan and his co-thinkers could embrace these points as supporting their critique of Soviet political processes. But such a response is hardly legitimate. Corrigan, Ramsay and Sayer would attribute these deficiencies to contingent causes deriving from the illegitimate political power of the ruling élite. On the contrary, the power of that élite must be seen as deriving from the ability of the institutional form of the Soviet regime to render democratic processes impossible.

Our authors identify political participation with a right to partake in the monitoring of administrative processes. In this manner they simply replicate Lenin's fatal conflation of the political and administrative domain and the reduction of the former to the latter. It is then a simple step to perceive in officially sanctioned processes of participation in administration a genuine process of political will-formation. If a distinction can be recognized within this model, it will be one of degree. A discussion of the problems in meeting the quotas for the production of pig iron can therefore be supplemented by adding to the agenda of the meeting an item on the priorities of the plan, the inadequacies of the government, or whatever the members feel inclined to discuss. This is only prevented by the political determination of the rulers not to allow it.

On the contrary, it must be stressed that the difference between politics and administration is most fundamentally a matter of available *sites*. Administration is a process that exists *internal* to a particular institution, be it factory, office, college, regional planning authority, or whatever. The political forms that Corrigan *et al.* refer to *are* internal structures: they are the offspring of institutions already present and formed. The issues that the worker is empowered to discuss are consequently determined in advance by sheer contingency: it depends upon which institution they happen to find themselves working in. Thus the pig-iron worker cannot discuss what is happening in the cutlery factory across the road, as he suffers from a lack of rights to do so reinforced by a lack of knowledge and information to make such a discussion possible. The most basic processes even of administrative monitoring may be rendered impossible by this. But if *administrative* control is eviscerated by the division into separate institutions, what of *political* control? A politics can be defined as the consideration of a particular problem in the light of all the other social institutions, factors, forces, interests and problems extant in society; or, conversely, the consideration of the general direction of society in the light of adequate information about the relevant component parts of the organism. Above all, of course, it involves the ability to judge and select those elements of information, those forces and factors, which are considered relevant to the issue under discussion. Such a right is not denied simply by the absence of a free press, although that perhaps constitutes a necessary component of the control mechanism. It is denied by the entrapment of politics in disparate and isolated institutions. A politics that is registered within separate institutions and which lacks any mode of articulation beyond the hypostatized and frozen boundaries of those positive institutions is not a public politics. And a politics that is not sited in a public domain, and which is not empowered to transcend the institutions of the status quo, is one that lacks the most basic means of reflection on the status quo. Politics can only, therefore, be a reflection *of* the status quo, not a reflection *on* it. A reflection *of* a phenomenon is simply a mirror image of it, a reflection on it is a critical process.

The Soviet state does, of course, include institutions which overcome the limitations of the single factory or authority. These are the public political structures, notably the soviet structure itself. A supreme soviet formally fits my prescription of institutions possessing the locational ability to obtain a unified overview of a reality that, for the lower-level structures, is fragmented. From this therefore may derive a genuine political process. But this does not happen, and not only because the supreme soviet may be elected by a deformed political process which ensures that its members will be those most uncritical of the status quo. Again, it is a matter of institutions. Official institutions are part of the status quo; therefore their definition of reality *coincides* with the status quo. They are denied a critical access to the existing arrangements because they lack a stance from which to grasp the whole, or elements of it, as something *other* than themselves. At best, therefore, they are condemned to an 'immanent' critique, which must concentrate on details of discrepancies between plan and performance. Political institutions which can genuinely bring to bear a critical edge on the current situation must, therefore, be allowed to claim a distance between itself and *what is*. Such a distance can only be embodied in a public sphere separate from the official structures, a public sphere which is constituted by *voluntary* associations. If official bodies can only replicate the official reality – and this is a structural fact, not a contingent situation derived from the attitudes of the rulers – any differing reality that will provide the foundation for a genuine criticism of official reality must lie outside the control of that reality. Citizens must be entitled to form associations articulating their alternative reality – otherwise called a political party and programme – in a space between the fragmented ignorance of the workplace and the unified positivity of the governmental authority. In fact, not only is this a fundamental precondition for safeguarding any form of popular and democratic power, it is, as I have already suggested, an inescapable condition for sensible administration. Indeed, Piccone's concept of 'artificial negativity', which will be more fully discussed later, suggests that if criticism does not exist, then governments will have to invent it if they are to fulfil their function. Otherwise they are blind, and the problems of the contemporary

Soviet government, the gross costs and wastages it produces in managing only very inadequately to administer and steer the Soviet economy, are examples enough.

We thus experience once again the effects of the hegemony of Lenin's constitutional discourse. The collapse of politics into administration is repeated in the Corrigan–Ramsay–Sayer thesis. Their assertion that 'there is less place for a separate polity' in socialist society expresses a signal failure to transcend the crudities of Lenin's thesis; indeed, it dignifies it. In the light of the terrorism of this concept, it cannot be repeated too often that without a genuine process of discursive will-formation, there is no politics that merits the name, and there is no democracy that is not a travesty of the meaning the concept holds. And such a process of will-formation can only take place in a polity that is composed of voluntary associations of individuals who are legally constituted as trans-situational citizens, entitled to a framework of legally safeguarded institutions wherein a public sphere may form reinforced and sustained by informal and myriad modes of communication and publicity. To argue for anything else would seem to be a new version of the *trahison des clercs*.

The purpose of this latter discussion has been twofold: first, to indicate some points of refutation of the Corrigan analysis, and thus strengthen the case for the treatment of the political and constitutional sphere as not reducible to determinations of another domain; second, it is an instructive example of how such theories can be not simply wrong, but can themselves conspire in that which they genuinely seek to oppose – the authoritarian state. It is an example of how the discourse we are examining manages to police itself. The discourse instructs that liberal democracy might be no worse, but it can certainly never be any better, than the political institutions born of the discourse. Like Oedipus, the discourse blinds itself so it may not see the offences that it has unwittingly committed. The discourse will entertain no difference between the 'really existing' freedom and the 'really existing' authoritarianism. Certain things cannot be thought of, certain phenomena will not be legitimized as 'facts'. How else can we explain this enormous lapse at the heart of a serious work of emancipatory theory written in 1978?

Corrigan and Sayer have made an effort to confront the degeneration of Soviet democracy. It is ultimately a sorry effort because, despite their intentions, they fail in their efforts to reject Leninism. Their model of politics remains polluted with Lenin's heritage at the most fundamental level. They are not the first to make such an attempt and register such a failure. Radical critiques that have directed their fire against both the dictatorship in the Soviet Union and problems of politics in the west have been crippled by this same unconscious Leninist burden. At least a part of this hegemony is not attributable only to the power and simplicity of Lenin's theory; it is also due to a serious failure to grasp the distinctness of the model of the modern state constructed by Weber, and attempts to subordinate Weber's model to a Leninist logic. Only if we truly appreciate what sets Weber's model profoundly apart from Lenin's model will we be able to define the true nature of the 'problem of bureaucracy' in the Soviet Union.

## AFTER WEBER, AFTER LENIN

Weber's definition of the tendencies of bureaucracies to escape and nullify democratic control proved an indispensable and influential source for subsequent theories of the contemporary state. The period after his death was dominated by the rise of state systems whose main integument appeared to be an exceptionally powerful bureaucracy. The most extreme and brutal examples of this phenomenon may now be seen to have possessed a more temporary character than analysts at the time contemplated. But the examples that still exist, while certainly less randomly brutal, are characterized, after the dismantling of the apparatuses of mass extermination, by an apparently undiminished role for the bureaucracy.

The existence of bureaucracy as a common feature of modernized societies provided the opportunity for the school of critical theorists to identify a commonality between contemporary state systems. It also allowed such writers to minimize important distinctions between state regimes. It is, possibly, an example of the 'barbarism' of the transcendent critique that elides vital features and differences. I will argue that the theory of the authoritarian state as developed by the most influential body of Frankfurt theorists – Horkheimer, Adorno and Marcuse – commits this unacceptable elision, and this is made possible by their reading of Weber. Weber became a central figure in their writings to an extent greater than any contemporary or subsequent Marxian school, and ultimately Weber's complex concept of 'rationalization' was transfigured into the ground for a universal critique of the 'dialectic of enlightenment'. It is my contention that this development was based upon a reading of Weber that may be seriously challenged. It was a reading polluted by Leninism. While the Frankfurt theorists certainly rejected Lenin at a conscious level, this rejection perhaps involved only the transparent and public face of Leninism, particularly the concept of the party. There remains at the core of their thinking, if not the fundamental themes of Lenin, an acceptance of the same traditional themes that make *The State and Revolution* such a dangerous document.

Horkheimer's 1940 article on 'The authoritarian state' was one of the first attempts to suggest that the three major state regimes that dominated in Europe were variants of a common model. The fascist state, the totalitarian socialist regime and the remaining liberal democratic states differed only in their position along a broadly similar line of development. All three state forms seemed to have many features in common: the manipulation of the masses, the demise of genuine democratic processes, the expansion of bureaucratic power, the technologization of social life and culture, the aggressive extension of the prerogatives of the state. But this argument amounted to a theoretical conflation that violated the actual distinctiveness of the three state regimes in reality.

References to the 'authoritarian state' occur in Frankfurt writings from some five years before Horkheimer's article, but exclusively refer to German fascism. Initially, the Nazi regime was represented as the naked terroristic dictatorship of monopoly capital, the final and barbaric stage of capitalist society. Such an analysis was not dissimilar to that of the official Comintern position. But Horkheimer, rapidly moving away from the orthodoxies of Marxian political economy, in 1940 identified the organizing principle of the new epoch of domination as technology and its consequences on culture and understanding, rather than on the imperatives of capital and its needs for coercion and open force. In this light, the German version was an imperfect and prototypical attempt at a form of domination much better represented by the Soviet Union. The crudeness and internal conflicts that characterized the process of domination in Germany stood in stark contrast to the relatively more efficient ordering of matters that prevailed in the Soviet Union. The threat to the future of humanity now derived, at least to some (and to an increasing) extent, not from the commodity economy, but from the political plan and the state that promulgated and guarded it. Thus: 'The most fully developed kind of authoritarian state, which has freed itself from any dependence on private capital, is integral *Etatism*, or state socialism.'[10]

This reassessment of the German and Russian regimes made possible a different analysis of the liberal democratic state form, one that was bound to be markedly pessimistic. Horkheimer was well aware that the difference between living in a fascist or 'reformist' state was of considerable importance to the individual; but from the standpoint of human emancipation, all contemporary regimes were almost equally ominous. Bureaucratic domination existed, or was imminent in each regime, and those where freedom was the most distant prospect were not necessarily those where domination was most terroristic. Horkheimer suggested that little distinction remained between the openly authoritarian regimes and the liberal democracies. He gave a scathing description of the relationships of domination that existed in Weimar Germany, between the political and bureaucratic élites and the masses. This relationship was replicated within the workers' movement, which 'negatively reflects the situation it is attacking'.[11] Capitalism had evolved into its monopoly form. The institutions of the liberal state were increasingly evacuated of real content, and ultimately became a mere façade for the introduction of the irrational authority of the fascist regime. For Marcuse, there was an organic process involved: 'we can say that it is liberalism that ''produces'' the total-authoritarian state out of itself, as its own consummation at a more advanced stage of development.'[12]

Jay reports Horkheimer's own argument as stressing 'the end of the liberal mediations, economic, political or legal, that had previously forestalled the realization of the domination implicit in capitalism'.[13] Thus while the transition to totalitarianism may not yet have been effected in the western democracies, it was argued that the continued existence of liberal institutions signified little in terms of real democracy and, anyway, the actual disappearance of these institutions was probably imminent.

For our purposes, it is this estimation of the institutions of liberal democracy that is important. The 1940 article is seminal in the development of the Frankfurt theorists, or more precisely, in the careers of Horkheimer, Adorno and Marcuse. Others, particularly Pollock and Neumann, at the time regarded these institutions with less pessimism, with consequences that we shall see. But for the most renowned of the Frankfurt writers, this original pessimistic estimate, the identification of liberal democracy as a society cast in the same mode of bureaucratic domination as Nazism and Stalinism, was fateful. Technological dominion by a bureaucratic apparatus as the generic quality of both democratic and authoritarian regimes mapped out the path to the argument of the 'dialectic of Enlightenment', wherein European rationality inevitably produced a society of total and hermetic domination. The most influential version of this thesis was ultimately expressed in Marcuse's analysis of 'one-dimensionality'. The combination of mass consumption, government regulation and the culture industry had finally transformed an outmoded entrepreneurial capitalism into a totally administered society characterized by a simultaneous process of atomization and homogenization of the populace. In 1965 Marcuse explained:

> the tendencies that linked the liberal past with its totalitarian abolition. This abolition was not restricted at all to the totalitarian states and since then has become reality in many democracies (and especially in the most developed one). . . . Today total administration is necessary, and the means are at hand: mass gratification, market research, industrial psychology, computer mathematics, and the so-called science of human relations. These take care of the non-terroristic, democratic, spontaneous-automatic harmonization of individual and socially necessary needs and wants, of autonomy and heteronomy. They assure the free election of individuals and policies necessary for this system to continue to exist and grow.[14]

Then, in a startling phrase, he summed up the paradox and the pessimism of this world as the 'frantic expansion of totalitarian mass democracy'.[15]

The thesis of the totally administered society was briefly a persuasive one. But the events of the 1960s, in which Marcuse's ideas themselves played no small part, served to undermine its very viability. This was the period of large-scale popular movements of protest which effected, or at least contributed to, political change by utilizing a combination of conventional and innovatory political channels. Aware of this, Piccone, has attempted to amend the theory from a position basically sympathetic to Marcuse. He holds the thesis to be valid, but only for a distinctly limited historical period: a transitional period between classical capitalism and contemporary capitalism. The drive towards one-dimensionality was, he argues, a necessary part of the introduction of a state-regulated capitalism. Without such massively increased intervention by the state, the conditions of existence of capitalist society could not be secured: its rampant crisis mechanism would have brought about the conditions for widespread social dislocation; the position of the subaltern classes in their non-integrated state would have made them available to oppositional political doctrines. But the process of bureaucratic extension must, he argues, have its limits. The shift from entrepreneurial capitalism to the New Deal may be necessary, but so is the shift from the 'New Deal society' to a subsequent arrangement. An administrative process that has absorbed the whole of society will be bereft of the critical inputs which are necessary if it is to fulfil successfully its function of rationally steering the society.

The administrators must therefore provide 'artificial negativity'. In order to avoid the consequences of administration without informative and critical input from outside the apparatus, the apparatus is driven to create opposition to itself. This could be a revealing line of research: there are certainly many examples of contemporary administrations providing funds and personnel with which citizens may be encouraged to criticize and point out the inadequacies of policy decisions and implementation. This is particularly relevant in attempts to maintain the integration into the body politic of the more marginal and anomic groups of contemporary society. In connection with discrete problems of modern administration, 'artificial negativity' is an evocative thesis. But is it really adequate as a 'grand theory' of the current state of western society? Obviously, if artificial negativity is to be an 'important' theory, it must explain important things. And so it does. For example, it can explain the Vietnam war, and, more importantly, the ending of that war. Piccone derides the way in which

> the US 'defeat' is still celebrated in conventional New Left nostalgia as the greatest achievement of the student movement and the successful mass mobilization that it provoked. But what was the Vietnam War other than the extension of the logic of transition [i.e. of the totally administered society] *after* that logic had become historically obsolete?[16]

Thus those who actually fought against the war deceive themselves if they believe they played a significant political role in that conjuncture. For Piccone, the reality is either that the war was ended when the 'progressive' sector of the capitalist class won out against the 'backward' sector or, at most, the anti-war movement was created and manipulated to a specific end by the capitalists who realized that a united Vietnam would be easy to exploit via the terms of trade, whatever the government in power.

The same logic applies to the removal of Nixon over Watergate, the reduction of the powers and apparatus of the CIA and 'strong state', and the civil rights movement. The revealing aspect of this analysis is what it says about the one-dimensionality thesis itself. One possible explanation of these events that Piccone cannot discuss – even seems unaware of – is that they had something to do with the existence of a constitutional state, fundamental democratic freedoms and a functioning public sphere of debate and dissent. Piccone seems to retain the traditional Marxian dismissal of these concepts as not only bourgeois, but vacuous and in reality non-existent. He is bound to do this by the one-dimensionality thesis: if this regime actually existed for a period, and if dissent must now be manufactured by the ruling class, it follows that at some point these elements of democracy disappeared – if they ever had any real existence.

As a mode of historical explanation, the thesis of 'artificial negativity' reveals itself as rather absurd in its crudity. In a weird Hegelian inversion, it presents the 'capitalist class', or at least one section of it, as a version of the 'subject–object identical', manipulating political movements to its own desired end, and doing so successfully. In a model of disturbing simplicity, it reduces all the complexities of the political sphere, even the already simplified version expounded in some Marxian versions of political science, to the manoeuvrings of an all-powerful ruling group. It is a condign fate for Horkheimer and Marcuse's original theory. Piccone has the intelligence to realize the inadequacy of the Marcusian vision of the contemporary scene. His discomfiture arises from his attempt to redeem aspects of that model which are irredeemable, because they are based on a simple, but profound, misunderstanding. This is the misappropriation of Weber's theory of bureaucracy that entered into the theories of the authoritarian state in the 1930s.

The developments that Piccone attempts to explain in his theory of artificial negativity are evidence of the fact that the liberal democracies have not, and did not, enter the state of total administration. Once this fact is grasped Piccone's tortuous sub-Hegelian schemes are redundant. But both Marcuse and Piccone are forced to such resorts by the misuse they make of Weber. In fact, a reinterpretation of Weber is the pivot upon which Marcuse's argument shifts. In 1941 Marcuse was still analysing bureaucracy in liberal democracy in a positive manner which echoes certain of Weber's themes:

> In the democratic countries, the growth of private bureaucracy can be balanced by the strengthening of the public bureaucracy. . . . In

the age of mass society the power of the public bureaucracy can be the weapon which protects the people from the encroachment of special interests upon the general welfare. As long as the will of the people can effectively assert itself, the public bureaucracy can be a lever of democratization.[17]

But by 1964 Marcuse's reading of the Weberian model is crucially different. Contemporary industrial society tends towards the absolute power of the bureaucracy:

the connection between capitalism, rationality, and domination in the work of Max Weber [is that] . . . the specifically Western idea of reason realizes itself in a system of material and intellectual culture . . . that develops to the full in industrial capitalism and this system tends towards a specific type of domination which becomes the fate of the contemporary period: total bureaucracy.[18]

Piccone's discussion of 'steering problems' offers a convincing refutation of the possibility of a totally administered society. But he falls into error by trying to maintain that *for a time* this represented an accurate description of the tendency of western society. To do this, he believes that *he* must correct *Weber*.

Contrary to the Weberian vision of a constantly rationalizing and bureaucratizing process of capitalist development, bureaucratization becomes counter-productive when it successfully penetrates what it seeks to rationalize. What makes its fragmenting formal mechanisms successful is the lingering resistance of that yet-unrationalized specificity which it constantly destroys.[19]

Piccone here conflates Weber with Marcuse. Marcuse may indeed have taken from Weber a terminally pessimistic vision of social development; but that vision is not necessarily Weber's. The delicate and crucial distinction is made by Salvador Giner who insists that Weber 'refused to identify "rule by officials" and administrators with political power'. Giner thus dismisses the view of 'contemporary society *as* bureaucracy' as an invention that had nothing to do with Weber. He stresses the *conditionality* of Weber's view of the bureaucratic threat. Moreover

he was at pains to explore the many mechanisms through which the excessive power of bureaucracies is, or can be, curtailed, such as political democracy, collegiality of decisions, decentralization, and the separation of powers.[20]

Weber did not need to explain in detail *why* bureaucracy could not take over the whole of society, as Piccone attempts to do. The reason for this is simply that the possibility was unlikely to occur to him. This is not due to naivety or lack of insight into the horrendous state formations that the future held in store. It is due to the fact that the bureaucracy that he was describing and analysing did not, in reality, contain that possibility. In the event of the disappearance of the 'checking' mechanisms on bureaucracy that Giner refers to, the consequence is *not* a society ruled by the norms of bureaucratic rationality, but something quite different, where formal rationality all but collapses under the pressure of illegitimate value considerations. Such an argument involves an aspect of Weber's analysis that appears to escape the Frankfurt theorists. Surprisingly enough we shall once again, even here, encounter the corrupting influence of Lenin's model of the radical democratic state.

It has been established that bureaucracy contains problems and threats. But the political domain also contains problems and threats. If the discussion of these is less developed in Weber's writings, this is doubtless attributable to his experience of Wilhelmine Germany, where an excessively powerful bureaucracy treated an inadequate and powerless parliament with scant regard.[21] But we can nevertheless construct from his writings a theory of political dangers relevant to the issues under discussion. Mass democracy contains one great danger: the predominance of emotional over rational elements in the process of political decision-making. This is not meant to imply a pejorative view of the capacities of the citizenry. The political realm has to deal with questions to which no answers have so far been found that have the status of absolute truth and can command the assent of an entire populace. Politics, therefore, is fundamentally the contest of conflicting value orientations. The answers to these fundamental issues can never be derived and formulated in the language of rationality and calculability that is the proud possession of the administrators. The struggle against the 'bureaucratization of the world' is presumably a struggle to retain for the citizenry the right to debate and decide issues according to standards other than that that guides the administrators: instrumental efficiency. Now, if a political domain is considered desirable, it makes no sense to assume that such a domain will always produce the 'right', i.e. ethically acceptable, value orientations. Politics is the name of the field defined by the absence of such certainties. As Habermas summed up Weber's basic thesis on this domain: 'In the last analysis political action cannot rationally justify its own premises.'[22]

Thus while many of the forms of thought – value orientations – which a political sphere contains may be repugnant, and demand refutation and vehement opposition, those who would combat bureaucratism must accept that the political sphere they seek to defend will contain a multiplicity of ideas, approaches and perspectives. It is not possible to achieve the same standards of certainty as obtain in the administrative realm. The only exception to this lies in the possibility of discovering an ethics which is irrefutably grounded in an apodictic science, one that reveals the pristine essence of society, humanity and history. In the light of contemporary experiences such a possibility is at least distant, if not unlikely. And, be it understood, such a discovery would truly mean the end of politics and the advent of the age of total bureaucracy; for there would be nothing left to discuss.

What, then, is the precise nature of the danger that emanates from the political sphere? It is that it may seek to colonize the administrative sphere. This is no new phenomenon; it is in fact the very situation that the establishment of bureaucratic organization sought to supersede, a situation wherein administrative decisions are taken on the basis of grace, favour, influence, prejudice and even corruption. The extent of this problem will become apparent in a discussion of the Soviet Union. What will also become clear is that the necessary division of labour, the necessary balance and equilibrium between the two domains of administration and politics must be carefully prescribed. This task cannot be ignored by clinging to either of the naive assumptions that underlie the theories that construe excessive bureaucratization as the only danger, that ignore the complexities of the political field that is supposed to act as panacea to this threat. It is as naive to assume that bureaucracy can and will be banished from the face of society, leaving nothing but a political sphere bathing in limpid clarity and mutual enlightenment, as to assume that politics can be sufficiently rationalized to make the relationship between the two domains a perfect fit, devoid of conflicts and permeated by fraternal deference. This, of course, *is* precisely the naive assumption of the model constructed by Lenin in the pages of *The State and Revolution*. It is also the assumption upon which Horkheimer based his critique of state regimes in 'The authoritarian state' in 1940. This, the first article to include the Soviet Union unequivocally in the collection of authoritarian regimes, expresses a faith in the regime of workers' councils. Horkheimer's touchstone, therefore, is still the possibility of the transcendental class subject of traditional Marxism. His critique of the Weimar republic derived its sweeping character from the actual absence of this subject. Neither the tiny oppositional sects nor the mass social democratic and communist parties offered any hope of the emancipated society.[23] But here Horkheimer drew no conclusions about the viability of the project of emancipation; on the contrary, the Marxian subject is still present, and provides the foundation for a conception of the post-revolutionary state that, while allusive (in keeping with Horkheimer's style), expresses the same assumptions as Lenin:

> After the old positions of power have been dissolved, society will either govern its affairs on the basis of free arguments, or else exploitation will continue . . . the future form of collective life has a chance to endure not because it will rest upon a more refined constitution but because domination is exhausting itself in state capitalism . . . in a new society, a constitution will be of no more importance than train schedules and traffic regulations are now.[24]

It should perhaps be remembered that train schedules are promises that the relevant authorities frequently fail to fulfil, and that traffic regulations are often treated by the citizenry with a fair degree of selectivity or indifference. This does not seem to be a promising metaphor for the political processes of the future society.

It is clear that Horkheimer still shared a great deal of ground with traditional Marxist theory; in particular he still believed in the emancipatory potential of Marxism. This led him to surmise that the Soviet Union, while being the most efficient example of the authoritarian state, was also the one most prone to overthrow in an emancipatory direction. This was due to the fact that the legitimating ideology of the ruling group was Marxism itself. As Arato has pointed out, this derived from an 'inadequate analysis of Soviet conditions and of the nature of Soviet Marxism as a pseudo-science of legitimation'.[25] Horkheimer's dubious assessment of the nature of Marxian ideology was presumably a major cause of his weakness for the traditional council-type solutions to the problems of politics and administration.

In contrast to the theories of absolute bureaucratization, Weber's far more modest model of the bureaucracy is relevant to, and revealing of, the fundamental nature of the 'authoritarian state'. I have referred to the less pessimistic attitude to the institutions of the liberal state that was adopted by Neumann and Pollock. These theorists stress the juridical – legal protection of civil rights and the survival of some forms of popular political participation under 'late' capitalism. Pollock announced the advent of a new socio-economic formation termed 'state-capitalism', which was applicable in a generic form, just as was Horkheimer's, to the varied regimes of advanced capitalism. But he maintained a distinction between the totalitarian and democratic forms, the democratic form enjoying a profound superiority:

> Under a democratic form of state capitalism, the state has the same controlling functions but is itself controlled by the people. It is based upon institutions which prevent the bureaucracy from transforming its administrative position into an instrument of power and thus laying the basis for the transshaping of the democratic system into a totalitarian one.[26]

Pollock's recognition of the still profound difference between authoritarian regimes and the liberal democratic state led him to a series of questions which he could only pose speculatively. But these questions, it may be suggested, have a vibrancy and relevance forty years later, which (for all their profound insights) are lacking in the political writings of Horkheimer and Marcuse:

> What measures are necessary to guarantee control of the state by the majority of people instead of by a small minority? What ways and means can be devised to prevent the abuse of the enormous power vested in the state, industrial, and party bureaucracy under state capitalism? How can the loss of economic liberty be rendered compatible with the maintenance of political liberty? How can the disintegrative motive forces of today be replaced by integrative ones? How will the roots from which insurmountable social antagonisms develop be eliminated so that there will not arise a political alliance between dissentient partial interests and the bureaucracy aiming to dominate the majority?[27]

It is precisely these problems, and developments of them, that have provided the complex of issues that Habermas' work has sought to investigate. The period of European totalitarianism has, at least for now, receded into the historical past, and taken with it the viability of the inevitable grand generalizations and horrific prognostications. We may consider Habermas' work as an example of the fruit to be gathered from Weber's basic model; a contrast to the barrenness of the Leninist heritage. The starting point must surely be a realization that it is false to present the dangers embodied in the modern state as consisting only of the tendency of the bureaucracy to conquer the rest of society. That such dangers exist, and constitute an ominous threat to civilized society, is hardly worth repeating. But if the cure is not to be worse than, or identical to, the disease, the other dangerous tendency we have described must be appreciated. The theorists of absolute bureaucracy are too extreme: the problem is the existence of any bureaucracy and the only answer is zero bureaucracy. Weber's crucial insight consisted in understanding that, while the political sphere acts as a restraint on the administrative, the administration is also necessary to defuse the dangerous tendencies of the politicians (a term which may mean the *whole* of the citizenry).

Habermas offers a typology of problems that Weber's model points to in contemporary society; he has also opened a discussion that gives Weber's distinctions their true weight, by insisting on a fundamental distinction concerning the nature of politics and administration. This latter theme occurs in the first chapter of his *Theory and Practice*, first published in 1971. Here he defends the assumptions of the classical doctrine of politics, with its origins in Aristotle. This doctrine asserted a distinction between forms of human knowledge. One form is that of *techne*, 'the skilful production of artifacts and the expert mastery of objectified tasks'; politics is the field constituted by a different type of knowledge.

Aristotle emphasises that politics, and practical philosophy in general, cannot be compared in its claim to knowledge with a rigorous science, with the apodictic *episteme*. For its subject matter, the Just and the Excellent, in its context of a variable and contingent praxis, lacks ontological constancy as well as logical necessity. The capacity of practical philosophy is *phronesis*, a prudent understanding of the situation, and on this the tradition of classical politics has continued to base itself.[28]

Habermas contrasts the classical doctrine of politics with attempts to define a science of politics, initiated in the work of Hobbes and Machiavelli. From Hobbes emerges a quite new set of principles: first, it is deemed possible to devise a scientifically grounded social philosophy whose assertions will be valid independently of time, place and circumstances; second, the translation of this knowledge into practice is a technical problem – prudence can be replaced by calculation; third, human behaviour is now considered to be the province of science, which will recommend the necessary conditions and institutions that will ensure that humans behave in a 'calculable' manner. Politics is separated from morality; if the task of preparing individuals for life in the community was previously that of the teacher and moralist, it now becomes the job definition of the social engineer and administrator.

We have here, therefore, in this modern political science a fundamental confusion and conflation: the technical is presumed to fulfil the responsibilities of the 'practical'. That in contemporary parlance there appears to be little, if any, distinction between the two terms is evidence of the dominion that 'science' has established over social life and thought.[29]

The consequent tendency to reduce all questions of 'action' to issues of technical control and manipulation clearly underlies the threat of bureaucracy. Habermas grounds this threat separately and more fundamentally than in the bureaucratic power complex itself. The problem arises from the hegemony over contemporary thought exercised by science, its methods and its practitioners. In the light of this, Habermas can then provide us with his models of possible relations between 'expertise and political practice'. He describes first the 'decisionistic' model, the pure form of Weber's theory, whereby there exists a strict division of labour between experts and politicians, the former pursuing by means of rational calculation the ends prescribed by the latter. These ends themselves are not subject to the dictates of administrative rationality. But for Habermas this situation leaves much to be desired: 'Rationality in the choice of means accompanies avowed irrationality in orientation to values, goals and needs.'[30]

While politics certainly has, and must retain, its own modalities of thought that are quite distinct from those of administration, it is difficult for Habermas to accept that these must continue to be without grounding in 'rationality'. In the last section of *Legitimation Crisis* Habermas acknowledges the contradiction and difficulty in which he finds himself. A 'partiality for reason' is a partisan position which cannot itself be made the object of rational will-formation that depends upon the assumption of reason. He is forced to an admission of his 'irrational' starting point: a *passion* for 'old European human dignity'.[31]

Nevertheless a clear distinction exists between the 'decisionistic' model and the more contemporary 'technocratic' one. Technical and intellectual developments have made an alternative possible:

Systems analysis and especially decision theory do not merely make new technologies available, thus improving traditional instruments;

they also rationalize choice as such by means of calculated strategies and automatic decision procedures.[32]

The technocratic model is that where the politician becomes dependent on the expert for definition of aims and ends, as well as means. The extension of rational techniques and calculations into the options available in the social world itself (Weber's 'disenchantment' writ large), and the ability to prognosticate the long-term consequences of the selection of any set of goals, means 'the politician in the technical state is left with nothing but a fictitious decision-making power'.[33]

As I have already indicated, Habermas suggests neither that this state of affairs is inevitable, nor that it can resolve the problems it is designed to tackle. These new methods still cannot impinge upon the fundamental problem-complex from which political decisions ultimately derive – value systems. In the light of his belief in the inadequacy, both descriptively and, of course, normatively, of both the decisionistic and the technocratic modes, he suggests a model that may counter the weakness of both. This is the 'pragmatistic' model, wherein he attempts to replace the relationship of domination of expert to politician by one of 'critical interaction'. His argument benefits from the fact that this is *not* a purely speculative model.

> Despite the technocratic view, experts have not become sovereign over politicians subjected to the demands of the facts and left with a purely fictitious power of decision. Nor, despite the implications of the decisionistic model, does the politician retain a preserve outside of the necessarily rationalised areas of practice in which practical problems are decided upon as ever by acts of the will. Rather, reciprocal communication seems possible and necessary.[34]

The formulation is arguably optimistic. The pragmatistic model is at least on one level a response and reply by Habermas to those visions of a 'totally administered' society that were articulated by Horkheimer, Adorno and Marcuse. He both rejects the possibility of the development they predicted and manages to indicate that such a rejection opens up equally fruitful approaches to the problems that do undeniably exist. But, operating in the Weberian mode, Habermas has clearly constructed only ideal types; he has not described anything that in reality yet exists. He will, therefore, be aware that just because neither the decisionistic nor the technocratic models in reality have occurred it must not be assumed that the pragmatistic model prevails.

The degree of decisionism and/or technocratism which is necessary if a democratic project is to be thwarted is not an absolute. These tendencies need not be present in gigantic and publicly transparent form; contemporary experience offers daily examples of their frustrating the possibility of a genuine democratic society. In his later work, Habermas has demonstrated the difficulty involved in defining the conditions that would make possible a model of politics and administration based upon 'free communication between equals'. But that difficulty is a necessary difficulty, one that is contained in the reality of the problem, and it magisterially corrects the themes of Lenin, Horkheimer and others, which reduce the problem to *removing* simple barriers to the democratic control of administration. Rather, a remarkable job of philosophical, cultural and institutional *construction* is involved.[35]

## WEBER AND LENIN: THE PROBLEM OF THE RULE OF LAW

The Weberian model cannot describe the state regime of the Soviet Union, although it will help to explain it. The Soviet Union cannot be read through Weber's fundamental categories or through the typology that Habermas has derived from them. It is neither of the two extremes that might evolve from the regime Weber described: political power devolving into the hands of the apparatus or administrative process corrupted by political interference. The puzzling thing is that it appears to display the symptoms of an extreme case of both diseases. At one and the same time it is an all-powerful, rigid and highly structured administration unconstrained by normal modes of political control; *and* a totally politicized structure wherein norms, laws, regulations and procedures may be overturned at a moment's notice by political decree. Perhaps Serge's Comrade Tulayev is the victim of the former, Koestler's Rubashev of the latter. Yet both are victims of the same instrument at the same hour of its power. How may this be explained? Does not the reality here point to inadequacies in Weber's model, inasmuch as it appears to be unable to bring its explanatory categories to bear?

The authority of Weber's model is in fact restored by a distinction that is crucial to my argument. This distinction has been indicated above: Weber never constructed a model of totalitarian bureaucratic society because *his* bureaucracy contained no possibility of achieving total power and consummating the expropriation of the political domain. He recognized regrettable costs, the costs of modernity, and he recognized possible corruptions. But every system that contains human beings is open to corruption, and perhaps Weber's willingness to reconcile himself to the bureaucratic age came from the appreciation that these corruptions took the form of possibilities, not inherent qualities in fixed quantities. Countervailing tendencies could limit these possibilities, but only so long as it was possible to maintain the two domains of politics and administration as distinct and separate.

Thus Weber's bureaucratic society is not a totalitarian one. Although totalitarian regimes depend upon a vast bureaucratic apparatus, any similarity this suggests with the society that Weber was analysing is superficial. What emerges from a proper understanding of Weber's model is the momentous aspect wherein the two regimes have nothing in common. This is what Weber defines as 'the rule of law'. The existence of the rule of law is the primary precondition for the existence of the modern state: an administrative and legal order that is subject to change by legislation and an administrative apparatus that conducts official business in accordance with legislative regulation. The rest of Weber's model is built upon this simple assumption; and if this assumption does not apply, all Weber's comments on politicians and bureaucrats, on norms and authority, on domains and responsibilities, on citizens and officials, are simply irrelevant. They are tools too sophisticated to apply to the brute structure of a totalitarian regime: it is naive to expect them to have any relevance. It is like trying to understand the workings of a bicycle by reading the workshop manual for a car. A categorically different object is under discussion.

There are certain situations where the rule of law cannot exist. Clearly, the rule of law cannot be assumed in a society undergoing revolutionary reconstruction. As Bendix put it: 'Where norms can be changed at a moment's notice, the rule of law is destroyed.'[36] Revolutionary regimes, by the very act of the seizure of power, dismiss the existing structure of law and its processes; and they are unlikely to restore that old structure once the new regime is secure. The norms embodied in that old system of law will have been a primary motivation for the revolutionary initiative itself: revolution is a statement that existing procedures of enacting and changing legislation have been found ineffective or inadequate. The new regime must perforce construct its own legal assumptions anew, in line with its ideological preconceptions. This reconstruction is at very least a time-consuming and complex process. A multitude of contradictory interpretations of the newly dominant ideology will for some time obtain, until the features of the new culture are firmly established. Competing versions will abound, both publicly and privately. The political struggle of the Bolsheviks against all other political tendencies, from liberals to anarchists, is the evidence of this public struggle. No less important, although certainly less apparent, will be the conflict between the new public norms and the assumptions upon which the everyday private lives of much of the population will continue to be ordered.

Consequently, the law becomes a more overtly political instrument. Law may follow in the trail of new social arrangements, often to confirm them, but perhaps as often to contradict them, as with the decree on 'one-man management' which opposed the popular syndicalist control that to some degree existed. Additionally, the law becomes an instrument by which attempts are made to undermine and destroy old social relationships, and thus clearly come into conflict with majority norms, as in the prolonged conflict between the Soviet government and the peasantry. Law, therefore, in a revolutionary regime, may be very far from being based upon a consensual acceptance, let alone an understanding, of the norms that lie behind it as far as large sections of the population are concerned. Even if it may be asserted that consultation would in fact reveal a coincidence of norms between the government and the majority of the populace, the process of enactment of such norms is problematic. Revolutionary governments legislate by decree not by debate. A vast new legal edifice must be established in a brief time-span; all the greater is the task if the new regime is distinguished from the old by its belief in modernization, a process which, I have already indicated, produces a huge increase in the areas of society that are considered as the legitimate sites of government intervention. The sheer magnitude of the tasks allows little room for the deliberative delays of due process. The habits consequently inculcated into administrative officials will be such as to aggrandize their powers considerably.

All these are perhaps inevitable costs of situations where the crisis of a social formation forces revolutionary change. It would be foolish to suggest that such situations do not occur, and that the problems posed by them can be avoided. But if the process of change inevitably undermines and banishes the rule of law, the question remains as to the possibilities of, and the conditions for, a return to a regime of the rule of law once the immediately transitional situation is passed. How is the ruling party, for whom the law has become an instrument in its own possession, to return to a situation where its members are once again subordinate to that law? This problem greatly exercised previous revolutionary actors. All revolutions are made in the name of some kind of freedom, and a common core of these various definitions of freedom is the freedom from arbitrary rule. The problem for the makers of constitutions is how such a freedom may be established out of an act which is itself arbitrary and necessarily represssive, which had observed no laws and has exercised violence against 'legitimate' rulers. The new laws cannot be written before the new law-making body of the revolutionary regime is constituted. The authority of that body cannot therefore derive from the law; but if it does not possess this necessary authority, how can the laws stand above man? Rousseau described the dilemma thus: 'The great problem in politics, which I compare to the problem of squaring the circle in geometry . . . [is]: How to find a form of government which puts the law above man.'[37]

Apart from any possible corruption, therefore, which a revolutionary government might suffer (reluctance to relinquish the power, and the fruits of power), there is a genuine conceptual problem. How are those who have placed themselves above the law to subordinate themselves to the law? The legitimations that previously applied can no longer satisfy. An appeal to a transcendental authority, or to the authority of tradition and custom are clearly not available to revolutionaries who have proceeded against precisely those legitimations. The concept of the 'general will', a more appropriate foundation, reveals itself, if attempts to determine that will are genuinely made, as, in Arendt's words, 'built on quicksand':

> The constitutional history of France, where even during the revolution constitution followed on constitution while those in power were unable to enforce any of the revolutionary decrees [indicates] . . . that the so-called will of a multitude (if this is to be more than a legal fiction) is ever-changing by definition.[38]

In the absence of any alternative firm foundation, there exists simply the constant temptation – and often demand – for some individual to embody the general will and impose its interpretations upon the rest of the society: 'Napoleon Bonaparte was only the first in a long series of national statesmen who, to the applause of a whole nation, could declare: 'I am the *pouvoir constituent*.'[39]

An appeal to the authority of the revolution contains no solution to this problem. The revolution can only legitimize the power of those who made it, of those of its heirs who are considered to be the most legitimate claimants to its tradition. The authority of the revolution legitimizes exclusive power, not the transfer of power between competing parties in the consequent regime. Those who were not instrumental in making the revolution, or more precisely in leading it, are de facto deprived of the credentials it bestows. If the appeal is to the authority of the revolution, the Mensheviks have no right to dispute policy with the Bolsheviks in the new Soviet Union.

The American revolutionaries managed to avoid these consequences, by virtue of a remarkable stroke of good fortune. Thomas Jefferson pointed to it in his explanation of how America was able to maintain the republican form of government when the French revolutionaries lost it. Republican government in France failed, he argued, because 'the party of *"un et indivisible"* had prevailed'. There existed no other organs of authority to which the people might have turned to combat the dissolution of democratic forms.

> But with us, sixteen out of seventeen states rising in mass, under regular organisation, and legal commanders, united in object and action by their Congress . . . present such obstacle to a usurper as forever to stifle ambition in the first conception of that object.[40]

The point is not simply that power was decentralized, but that legitimate authority lay at this level, and any central power could only derive its right to rule from the local institutions. But even this does not fully account for the survival of democracy in revolutionary America. The local institutions embodied the *continuity* of the rule of law. Authority, not least the authority of the men who drafted the Declaration of Independence and the Constitution, derived from the complex of bodies that pre-existed the Revolution – the districts, townships and counties. And their authority derived from the 'constitution' which the *Mayflower* colonists agreed among themselves for their own security in the 'state of nature' that awaited them. The American Revolution was made in the name of established legal conventions, and not against them; the Revolution was against what were interpreted as attempts to impose a tyranny upon a previously free society.[41] Few creators of modern states have been able to draw upon such clear and incontrovertible lineages of legitimacy, deriving from a 'free contract' arrived at in a territory previously without government. But the example is relevant for those who would attempt similar tasks in less favourable conditions.

For it may be that neither the problems that the Russian revolutionaries were attempting to solve, *nor* the fundamental assumptions with which they approached these problems, were profoundly different from those of the American revolutionaries. Here, of course, I am minimizing the differences that are often held to separate and distinguish 'bourgeois' revolutions from 'proletarian' ones. I am particularly concerned to set aside arguments that would attribute to the thinkers of the American Revolution no other motive than that of establishing a new class power, the power of the indigenous bourgeoisie, in its own right. Similarly, I am concerned to avoid attribution to the Bolsheviks of fundamental motivations in specific class terms: the determination to establish either the class power of the proletariat or, more deviously, the power of a 'new class', – bureaucracy, state bourgeoisie, intelligentsia, or whatever. Instead, it is worth suggesting that both bodies of revolutionaries partook of a fundamental ethical aim, and drew in significant measure upon a common intellectual tradition.

I want to present two sets of themes that our revolutionaries appear to possess in common. First, that involved in Jefferson's concept of 'self-evidence' and the Marxian concept of its own status as a science; second, the possible congruences between Lenin's concept of the commune-state and the American concept of 'public happiness'. On the first theme, I have previously commented on the manner in which the Bolsheviks 'constructed' a 'general will'. The attribution of a scientific status to Marxism provided the Bolsheviks with a ready-made and almost automatic method of excluding various forces from the political process, and relegating political *problems* to the status of conflicts between those who knew the truth and those who, out of ignorance, malice or self-interest, refused to acknowledge that truth. But in this context the words of the American Declaration of Independence are evocative: 'We hold these truths to be self-evident.' It was upon the assumption of self-evidence for certain rights that the case against British tyranny was built, and the Revolution made.

Jefferson's choice of words is crucial, because it is an assertion of John Locke's epistemology of self-evidence against the doctrine of innate ideas. The concept of innate ideas, it was held, was a secure buttress for 'dictators'. It was necessary to admit the use of reason into the process of the judgement of political institutions, for the use of reason would persuade everyone of the precepts upon which democratic government was based. It was therefore self-evident that all men were created equal, entitled to inalienable rights including life, liberty and the pursuit of happiness, that governments were instituted to secure these rights, and that citizens had the right to overthrow such governments as failed to discharge satisfactorily their obligations.

But the political consequences of such philosophical assumptions may prove problematic. Has every citizen the right, simply by claiming to be moved by reason, to reject the legitimacy of the government if he or she so wishes? It was necessary for the sake of political stability to introduce certain distinctions:

> When we speak of a tyrant that may lawfully be dethroned by the people, we do not mean by the word *people*, the vile populace or rabble of the country, nor the cabal of a small number of factious persons, but the greater and more judicious part of the subjects, of all ranks.[42]

Locke's arguments were therefore called on to stress that reason was a faculty, and one which it was entirely possible that people might fail, or refuse, to use. There are those

> whose opportunities of knowledge and inquiry are commonly as narrow as their fortunes; and their understandings are but little instructed, when all their whole time and pains is laid out to still the croaking of their own bellies, or the cries of their children.

This may appear to be an élitist attempt to exclude the labouring classes from the democratic political process, but Locke does not confine himself to such classes. There are those, morally inferior, persons who have the opportunity to use reason, but lack the will:

> Their hot pursuit of pleasure, or constant drudgery in business, engages some men's thoughts elsewhere: laziness and oscitancy in general, or a particular aversion for books, study and meditation, keep others from any serious thoughts at all; and some out of fear that an impartial inquiry would not favour those opinions which best suit their prejudices, lives and designs, content themselves, without examination, to take on trust what they find convenient and in fashion.[43]

It is thus clear that the assumptions of the Americans appear to contain implications that we could consider dangerously undemocratic. For those who are not capable of using, or who refuse to use, reason not only have a very dubious claim to participate in a democratic process founded on reason, but their constant pollution of the public life with the politics of unreason might threaten the survival of the republic itself. Surely, we are not far from Lenin? The latter quote from Locke could refer equally to Lenin's bourgeoisie, impelled either by moral degeneration, or 'class situation', or class interest, to deny the truths of Marxism; and how reminiscent of Lenin's complaints about the low cultural level of the masses is Locke's description of the labouring poor! In this crucial, overriding sense, then, both Jefferson and Lenin were children of the Age of Reason: claiming their authority on the basis of reason, and then driven to use reason to halt the corrosive undermining of their own positions that reason, once loose, may effect. Without pursuing the comparison any further, we may simply suggest for consideration the effect of the following in producing the very different results of the two revolutions. The tasks that the American governments were subsequently to take upon themselves were, of course, minimal: the American populace lived in a state agreed by all as one already of 'prosperity', and it was a long time before industrialization became the central objective of revolutionary governments. Therefore the American revolutionaries were not immediately confronted with a class or bloc resistant to the 'self-evident' rationality of an interventionist government programme. The new state was in fact little more than a loose association of agrarian states. Jefferson's political postulates were predicated upon precisely such an economy and polity, and their continued validity depended upon the continuation of such an arrangement.

The uncompromising radicalism of his democratic-rationalist stance was doubtless compromised in reality. At the time of the revolutionary victory voters constituted only 3.6 per cent of the population,[44] and such restrictions continued well into the era of Jacksonian democracy several decades later. This certainly guaranteed that the potentially dangerous and irrational popular will was markedly moderated. Further, Jefferson's distaste for centralized power could be suspended when deemed necessary, as in his unilateral securing of the Louisiana Purchase. Nevertheless there is little doubt that his adherence to the general democratic principle was more consistently maintained than has since been the case with egalitarian revolutionaries in power. He seems to have kept his faith in the people to the end, placing ever greater emphasis and confidence in the power of education and the provision of a public educational system.[45] This continuing faith is surely a reflection of the cultural roots and resources upon which American democratic radicalism drew. Their acknowledgement of their European intellectual inheritance, their awareness of constructing the 'Empire of Liberty' as an essentially European experiment, seems to have provided a context which the Russians, with their rejection of 'bourgeois ideology', so sadly lacked. More precisely, inasmuch as they were working within a tradition of avowedly *moral*, not scientific, philosophy, which did not claim to conquer and systematize the whole of human knowledge, or effect a fundamental rupture with all that had been previously thought, the imperious claims of reason were balanced by inheritances from a Christian tradition. Locke himself declined to write a handbook of ethics based upon his concept of reason because he considered these to be present in the New Testament, and thus already available, through faith, to the unenlightened. Further, the Americans were probably far more concerned than later imitators to justify intellectually the form of government they had created, and at least in his later career Jefferson was prepared to admit the existence of a 'moral sense' that pre-existed the use of reason, although it was still the inescapable duty of reason to judge and verify these pre-rational responses. The existence of a 'moral sense' will admit to the political process those whom clumsiness in the field of reason might have excluded.[46]

Arguably we might be able to find a further parallel between this eighteenth-century concept of moral sense and Lenin's concept of the 'proletariat'. The attempt to introduce a 'proletarian' counterweight to the burgeoning bureaucracy via Rabkrin, and similar measures, suggests Lenin's continuing acceptance of a proletarian moral sense. That is, he believed in an essential faculty of a sociological group which depended not upon its ability to absorb Marxism but, rather, makes it possible for the proletariat, or its best elements, to absorb and understand Marxism and avoid the corruptions of power. But Jefferson's 'moral sense' was a capacity with which people are endowed by a creator; Lenin's, being dependent upon an exclusive sociology, was rather more attenuated. Indeed, far more than Jefferson, Lenin lacked confidence in both the willingness to reason and the innate moral capacities of the people, and that could not be without consequences.

But if Jefferson's principles articulated in the Declaration of Independence were those upon which a revolution against tyranny could be made with a fair guarantee of an acceptable outcome, they were not in themselves the principles upon which a new nation could be built. And if the nation could not be built, the very concept of self-government embodied in the concept of independence would be ephemeral indeed. There was a tension here between Jefferson's principles and the course that had to be taken to ensure the existence of the nation.

The efforts most notably associated with Alexander Hamilton were devoted towards the construction of such a *national* system wedded to a *national* consciousness, efforts which Jefferson himself condemned, before the obligations of the supreme national office fell to him, as 'monarchical', and a betrayal of the revolution. As secretary to the Treasury in the administrations of Washington and Adams, Hamilton attempted to establish a national bank and mint, and also to foster considerable government intervention in the economy in order to develop a native manufacturing base.[47] An independent nation dependent for its industrial and technical needs upon a foreign power was a contradiction in terms. Industrialization therefore had to be attempted, even if in terms that today we might regard as leisurely. This had to be accompanied by those tendencies toward centralization and administration that Weber identified as the corollary of modernization.

To some degree at least Hamilton's politics were a response to the weakness at the heart of the Jeffersonian concept of the constitution. An insistence upon the local roots of political legitimacy does not aid the formation of a genuine nation. At worst it can lead to the fracturing of the new polity along regional and ethnic grounds, as in so many new twentieth-century nations. Thus Jefferson's constitutional guarantee of liberty was not yet a representational theory that could reconcile the rights of the individual with the needs of the modern state. The constant threat of 'nullification' of disagreeable laws, up to and including the possibility of secession, injected an ambiguity into the very heart of the American project, an ambiguity that was to reach sad fruition a century later. Nevertheless, Jefferson was at least consistent. If he was not particularly disposed towards the modern state, neither was he enamoured of modernity itself. He was in fact an 'enthusiastic supporter of the physiocratic doctrine that agriculture was the only source of true wealth',[48] and he believed in a small-scale and localized society based upon an agrarian economy, an appropriate basis for his constitutional theory.

The experience of modernity thus far suggests that the only way in which the rights of individuals and minorities to dissent may be reconciled with the integrity and continuity of state and society is through *party*. The modern political party may be ideological, or opportunist, or charismatic; it may possess a clear class constituency or it may express shifting blocs and alliances – clearly the detail is of infinite variety. But it is essentially characterized by its compatibility with the state in modernity: there is an essential creative affinity – as well as tension – between them. Because the modern political party takes as its arena precisely the territory of the nation state: it does not place that fundamental in question. And – here the echoes of the discussion of Lenin are piquant – it seeks precisely to take command of that state itself, and neither to abolish it nor to dismember it. Further, its source of legitimacy is neither an ideology (*pace* Lenin) nor an individual constituted prior to that state and nation (*pace* Jefferson). Just as the contemporary *episteme* creates the human subject, so the modern state creates the citizen.

The modern post-revolutionary state falls under the shadow of two potential natural disasters, two directions in which it is *most likely* that politics will develop. On the one hand centralized and irremovable revolutionary government, basing itself upon the legitimation of the revolutionary act; on the other, dissolution along regional and ethnic lines. In modern experience, of course, the two conspire to reinforce each other. Both these tendencies were vividly present in the early years of the American republic, and perhaps the most important – and remarkable – development in the whole revolutionary experience was the emergence of a party system which, whatever the countervailing tendencies, sufficed to preserve the essential spirit of the revolution. Lipset is right to insist upon the novelty and historic significance of this event:

> The defeat of the Federalists in the elections of 1800 represented the *first occasion in modern politics in which an incumbent political party suffered an electoral defeat and simply turned over power to its opponents*.[49]

This development was by no means inscribed in the initial intentions and documents of the revolution, not least because it was a concept of considerable novelty. Indeed, prior to this event we may detect some fascinating, if uncomfortable, parallels with the years after 1917.

In the immediate post-war years the Union was held together by the role of Washington as charismatic leader, around whom apparently developed a cult quite comparable to the Leninolatry of the 1920s.[50] Washington's first administration included both Jefferson and Hamilton so that 'all important differences of opinion could be expressed within the government'.[51] Hamilton organized the Federalists as the 'first party', the 'government party', to ensure and mobilize popular support for government policies. This did not at all imply the necessity and legitimacy of creating other, opposition, parties. When Jefferson withdrew from the administration to form such a party the Alien and

Sedition Acts seemed to follow almost naturally, and the subsequent 'trials were travesties of justice dominated by judges who saw treason behind every expression of Republican sentiments'.[52] As in so many Marxist regimes and ex-colonial states, opposition was considered by the government not simply as an unacceptable challenge to their power and privileges. It was a genuine failure of understanding – such activities simply did not make sense: 'The conclusion almost forced upon the reader of . . . hundreds . . . of Federalist condemnations is that *the two party system is immoral.*'[53]

The party system is immoral in the post-revolutionary years because it is a concept born ahead of its time, but necessarily so. It pre-echoes and pre-figures the complex articulation of liberty and authority that defines the modern democratic state. It does not express its own times, but the future. How can a child so prematurely born expect to survive to enter into its estate in some future time? Yet how can revolution give birth to anything other than a betrayal of its founding aspirations, a miscarriage of its conception in the liberty of the individual, if this concept and principle be not established, against all the odds, during the infancy of the new regime?

Why this strange but profoundly legitimate child of the revolution that ushers in modernity survived and flourished in America yet died stillborn in Russia is one of the questions which earlier parts of this argument may help to answer. Doubtless there are further depths which remain to be explored. But this part of the argument does seem to suggest that, in the period of transition from revolution to democracy, it is an incalculable benefit and safeguard that some elements and sources of traditional legitimate authority continue to exist as a counter to the totalizing ambitions of the revolutionary mood. For a further striking parallel in the projects of Jefferson and Lenin may be suggested.

It was very far from the mind of both Lenin and Jefferson simply to remove a set of specific grievances that a tyrannical government imposed upon the people. It was not their aim merely to free people to live their lives as they might once have done, without a tyrannical government. Arendt argues that it was not simply the colonists' intention to regain liberties which were, or had been, possessed by native Englishmen, and which were denied them due to their status as colonists.[54] That was no longer enough. The claim to the 'right to happiness' was, for the Americans, not simply a right to private happiness, the happiness of the subject secure in his domestic and professional pursuits, untrammelled by arbitrary interference from unpredictable government. It was also, and most significantly, a claim to a new 'public happiness'. This claim derived from the assumption that the right to participate in the affairs of government was a central element of the highest happiness at which men might aim. Participation in public affairs was no longer, as in the past, a burden that some must bear in order that others might pursue unhindered their private happiness. Where critics might ascribe the happiness that the American legislators derived from their work simply to an 'inordinate passion for power', those men would reply that their enjoyment merely confirmed that such activities would afford the same reward to all and any who engaged in them. Thus the entitlement of all citizens to participate in the public realm was a central motivating theme for the Americans.

It is clear that Lenin conceived of the politics of the new society in terms similar to Jefferson's. He also was not content that the new state should simply avoid the abuses of the old and allow the citizens a life free from material deprivation and political abuse. That, again, was his argument with the Social Democrats. He also wanted a state which would itself express and encapsulate the new happiness of the people: the happiness that derives from running their own lives, from taking to themselves decisions that had previously, for good *or* ill, been made for them.

Perhaps it is possible to speak of this aspect of the American Revolution being, in a sense, 'betrayed', just as were Lenin's aspirations for the new Russian state. Arendt points out that Jefferson failed to articulate clearly in the Declaration the concept of public happiness, as distinct from 'private happiness'. The two are, arguably, conflated in the term 'the pursuit of happiness'. For Arendt, the rapidity with which the specific concept of 'public happiness' was forgotten

> and the term used and understood without its original qualifying adjective may well be the standard by which to measure, in America no less than in France, the loss of the original meaning and the oblivion of the spirit that had been manifest in the Revolution.[55]

For the concept of the pursuit of happiness, in its attenuated form of the pursuit of *private* happiness, can be seen as the basis for a culture of aggressive accumulation of personal wealth, of the elevation of material happiness at the expense of public good, of the worship of the technology that promises the satisfaction – and the constant expansion – of those desires that may go under the name of private happiness. It can consequently be seen as one root of the transformation of public life from the field of highest happiness – through sagely exercising responsibility with the approbation of others – into the instrument for the further accumulation of personal wealth – and 'happiness'. Marcuse's moral critique of contemporary American society is therefore one with which the American revolutionaries might wholeheartedly agree.

I would not want to pursue much further the parallels I have suggested between Lenin and Jefferson, although clearly the considerations that they prompt go much further than the points I have tentatively suggested. But the strikingly similar ideas that the American and the Russian experiences contain suggest how relevant is the experience of the former to the sad story of the latter, a relevance that has certainly not been fully explored. Beyond that, it may for my purposes be sufficient simply to underline the importance of the area wherein, I have suggested, the assumptions and the experiences of the two revolutions were markedly, and consciously, dissimilar – that of the rule of law.

## THE PARTY PROBLEM

It is common in critiques of the Soviet state to attribute its deficiencies to the authoritarian structure of the Bolshevik party from its earliest pre-revolutionary days. Its intolerance, its exclusivity, its hierarchical structure, its concentration of effective power at the top can all be detected in the Soviet Union not long after the seizure of power. This apparent similarity suggests a process of organic growth as the authoritarian party creates the authoritarian state. My argument would not seek to deny this, but rather to relegate it to a subordinate status as an explanatory schema. A concentration on the responsibility of the party allows the responsibility of the constitution to escape unexamined. Indeed, the absence of the party from the pages of *The State and Revolution* had provided an argument for the innocence of that text, by implying to its ideas a viability and practicality that was simply corrupted or abolished by the democratic centralist organization. In contrast, I would suggest that the regrettable features of the Bolshevik party were not a world apart from features that all political parties tend to display; the fact that these features came to define the lineaments of the Russian state, whereas elsewhere they appear to have been kept under control, is due to Lenin's concept of state form, not his concept of party.

The Leninist party is accused of two ominous qualities. Internally, it has an excessively rigid and centralist character, denoted by the term 'democratic centralism'; and in its relations with the external political world, it claims a status of privilege over other political tendencies inasmuch as its politics claim to be 'scientific'. The consequences of both these assumptions may then be identified in the subsequent authoritarian regime.

Essentially, democratic centralism was intended 'to make the local organisations the principle organisational units of the Party in fact and not merely in name, and to see to it that all the higher-standing bodies are elected, accountable, and subject to recall'.[56] In this it differs hardly at all from the manner in which the internal life of political parties is normally organized except in one respect. The *differentia specifica* of democratic centralism lay in its definition of conditions under which *no* democratic norms would be allowed to prevail:

> In the heat of the battle, when the proletarian army is straining every nerve, no criticism whatever can be permitted in its ranks. But before the call for action is issued, there should be the broadest and freest discussion and appraisal of the resolution, of its arguments and its various propositions.[57]

The question acutely posed is therefore, who shall issue the 'call for action' which will terminate discussion? Who is to decide what shall constitute such an 'action' and for how long shall its authority be deemed to have sway? Lenin proposed the simple answer: the party congress, the highest and most representative authority of the party. But if the 'action' situation ever came to prevail over a number of years, as it quite publicly did in the desperate post-revolutionary situation, the party congress will be composed of members elected under conditions from which full democratic discussion has long since been excluded. The party congress, under such conditions, contains no guarantee of expression of the arguments of the membership.

The assumption of a 'scientific' status for the decisions of the Leninist party suggests that in its relations with other political parties it will pursue a quite unique course. This assumption establishes that political differences with the party may not be considered as differences of opinion, but as error. This clearly legitimizes the dismissal and suppression of oppositional and critical political tendencies, and explains the course of events from the suppression of the Constituent Assembly in November 1917 to the eventual disappearance of all other parties, and then to the suppression of all political differences within the single surviving party.

The internal and external threats to democracy contained in the Leninist party are thus clearly culpable in the subsequent developments of the dictatorship. But they can be only part of the explanation, and for this reason my argument does not place a great deal of emphasis on the implications of Lenin's thoughts on the party. Parties, after all, are voluntary institutions, and have the right to determine how they shall order their internal life; no one is obliged to join. Further, if 'democratic centralism' is overtly ominous in its implications for the political life of a party, it may be that this hardly represents a more fundamental violation of the principles of free association and control than the situation that actually obtains within political parties that have not taken the pains to make their assumptions so explicit. The ability of political élites to determine the nature and course of debate, to minimize the effectiveness of their internal opponents, to perpetuate their own rule and ideology, are familiar elements of the critique of oligarchical tendencies of mass parties. The power of such oligarchies may well be all the greater for being informal and unwritten.

Michels summarized his analysis of such tendencies:

> if we leave out of consideration the tendency of the leaders to organise themselves and to consolidate their interests, and if we leave also out of consideration the gratitude of the led toward the leaders, and the general immobility and passivity of the masses, we are led to conclude that the principle cause of oligarchy in the democratic parties is to be found in the technical indispensability of leadership.[58]

Thus the simple existence of 'democratic centralism' is unconvincing as an explanation for the decline of democracy in the Soviet Union.

Similarly, it may be argued that every political party has the right to formulate its own ideology, and will necessarily assume a clear and rational superiority for its own ideas over those of its opponents. The idea of civilized exchange of opinions is always to some degree at odds with the passions and interests involved in the issues constituting the field of politics. The Leninists were not the first to fall to the temptation of sabotaging or, where possible, suppressing their political opponents.

Bolshevism was, therefore, composed very largely of methods of internal organization, and attitudes toward the external world, that favoured an absolutist outcome. Doubtless, a political party would do well to do without these features if at all possible. But since political combat is very often about fiercely held views, it would be difficult to establish a set of prescriptions that would guarantee the absence of such features. Whether or not these features are allowed to express themselves to the extent of constructing the authoritarian state will therefore depend upon whether there are institutions within the *society* that can balance and limit such tendencies. The problem of the Bolshevik dictatorship is ultimately a question of the *constitution* of the state.

Constitutions are rules for limiting the powers which any institution may aggregate to itself within a complex of institutions. The problem of the simple state of Lenin's model, simply put, is that the fewer institutions there are that make up the body politic, the greater the proportion of the total sum of power that will be lodged in each institution. If these institutions are reduced to one, or to a set of institutions that are not significantly separated, power is unitary, not distributed. This, then, is the negation of the field of democratic politics.

## CONCLUSION: THE GUILT OF 'THE STATE AND REVOLUTION'

The problem of bureaucracy is thus only seriously confronted when its deepest roots are discovered. It is possible to control a bureaucracy only when its prerogatives and limits are defined by the process of legislation. In the absence of that it will either write its own laws and amplify its own powers, or it will be victim of unrestrained political authority, performing its functions according to diktat, and consequently under pressure of haste, whim, expediency and corruption. Since the absence of the rule of law plunges the administration into a sea of arbitrariness, there is no reason why it should not do both.

A bureaucratic problem does not, therefore, only emerge when popular power is usurped by a ruling minority, as in the Bolshevik coup. In reality, there may be little difference between the situation of party dictatorship and that of the popular power of Lenin's commune-state as far as their consequences on the problem of bureaucracy are concerned. Both illegitimately invade the domain of the administrative decision and distort its proceedings with a pervasive set of value orientations. The distinction between the two domains collapses, and there ensues an unhealthy and chaotic osmosis whereby each domain comes to absorb approaches appropriate only to the other. Thus the 'political' institutions of the Soviet state – the factory committees, the party cells – take on the culture of administrative apparatuses, forced to accept the limited powers and rights of knowledge and discussion more appropriate to the administration. And the bureaucracy becomes a Byzantine labyrinth of interest and intrigue.

I am, therefore, suggesting that there is a conflation of politics and administration in *The State and Revolution*. Such a conflation must herald a disastrous cross-pollution of the two domains, and this is what underlies the enormous steering problems of Soviet society. The mechanism of social operations become inpenetrable and devoid of any possibility of control.

The arguments in chapters 2 and 3, therefore, lead to a central suggestion, which may counter the collection of naive and distant interpretations of Lenin's text which were discussed in a previous chapter. The common thread of all those interpretations was the essentially *innocent* nature of Lenin's text. That is, the text is innocent of the subsequent destruction of democracy under the Bolsheviks. The text is a utopian document that could not be implemented in the harsh objective conditions; the text is an ambiguous document that contained the acceptable and the unacceptable – the Soviet as well as the terror; the text is a tactical work which really should not be asked to measure up to the actual strategic problems that faced the new governments; the text is part of an argument with the Social Democrats of Paris and Berlin, not a serious contribution to political theory; or, the text is the repository of genuine emancipatory politics, betrayed by the dull positivity of historical conditions or the ambitions of political careerists; and so on. My argument would suggest, instead, that the text, in all its moments – libertarian and authoritarian – is guilty of subsequent developments: that is, the features of the authoritarian Soviet regime are present within every line and concept of the text. And it is not just a question of *similarity* between what was written and what later happened: the *cultural* effect of *The State and Revolution* can be suggested as the *causal link* between the text and subsequent events.

The central absence in Lenin's politics is that of a theory of political institutions. All political functions are collapsed into one institution, the soviet, and even that institution itself will know no division of labour within itself according to different functions. Lenin's state form is one-dimensional. It allows for no distances, no spaces, no appeals, no checks, no balances, no processes, no delays, no interrogations and, above all, no distribution of power. All are ruthlessly and deliberately excluded, as precisely the articulations of the disease of corruption and mystification. The new state form will be transparent, monological and unilinear. It is, in sum, a gigantic gamble; the gamble is that it will be possible to set about constructing this state in 'the best of all possible worlds'. The odds against the gamble are astronomic. It does not simply demand the absence of the peculiarly unhelpful conditions of post-1917 Russia – although those conditions themselves have for a long time conspired to suggest the essential innocence of the model. It also demands a situation devoid of all political conflicts, of all economic problems, of all social contradictions, of all inadequate, selfish or simply human emotions and motivations, of all singularity, of all negativity. It demands, in short, for Lenin's political structures to work, that there be an absence of politics.[59]

But the 'crime' of Lenin's text is not that it did not work: it is that it did. The 'libertarian' Lenin bears equal responsibility for the Gulag with the 'authoritarian' Lenin. Lenin's theory of the state rigorously outlawed all and any version of those political institutions and relationships that can make the triumph of the Gulag less likely. In their place, *The State and Revolution* put a concept of the state that already, in August 1917, was monolithic, authoritarian, single-willed and uncheckable. It matters not what Lenin's intentions were. The extent of Lenin's responsibility is not defined by his intentions, but by his implications. Lenin's text was responsible for things that Lenin, perhaps, never conceived. The issue is not what the author intended, but what the text dictated. The text created a discourse – a field of ideas within which subsequent thinking had to take place, outside of which thought was not merely illegal, but impossible, a non-sense. The Cheka, the Politburo, the Institute of Marxism–Leninism were hardly needed to police the borders of that discourse: a discourse has no need of border guards because the discourse is a *world view*. It colonizes the whole planet of thought and leaves no enclaves from which resistance may be mounted. Only the passage of time can subvert such a discourse; reason can do nothing.

**NOTES**

1 L. Colletti, 'Bernstein and the Marxism of the Second International', *From Rousseau to Lenin*, London, 1972, 65.
2 U. Santamaria and A. Manville, 'Lenin and the transition', *Telos*, 27 (1976), 79–96.
3 P. Corrigan, H. Ramsay and D. Sayer, *Socialist Construction and Marxist Theory*, London, 1978, 26.
4 ibid., 45, 46.
5 ibid., 46.
6 P. Corrigan, H. Ramsay and D. Sayer, 'Bolshevism and the USSR', *New Left Review*, 125 (1981), 58.
7 D. Lane, 'Soviet industrial

workers: lack of a legitimation crisis?', in B. Denitch (ed.), *Legitimation of Regimes*, New York, 1979, 190.

8 M. Lewin, *Political Undercurrents in Soviet Economic Debates*, London, 1975, 278.

9 ibid., 279, 280.

10 M. Horkheimer, 'The authoritarian state', in A. Arato and E. Gebhardt, *The Essential Frankfurt School Reader*, Oxford, 1978, 101. The precise translation used here, however, is taken from D. Howard, *The Marxian Legacy*, London, 1977, 110, as it seems to express the idea more clearly. The full 'dialectic of enlightenment' thesis is presented in T. Adorno and M. Horkheimer, *Dialectic of Enlightenment*, New York, 1972.

11 Horkheimer, 'The authoritarian state', 99.

12 H. Marcuse, 'The struggle against liberalism in the totalitarian view of the state' (1934), *Negations*, London, 1972, 19.

13 M. Jay, *The Dialectical Imagination*, London, 1973, 155.

14 Marcuse, *Negations*, xii, xii.

15 ibid., xvii.

16 P. Piccone, 'The crisis of one-dimensionality', *Telos*, 35 (1978), 47. See also P. Piccone, 'The changing function of critical theory', *New German Critique*, 12 (Fall 1977), 29–30; T. Luke, 'Culture and politics in the age of artificial negativity', *Telos*, 35 (1978), 55–72. There is, I believe, a deal of truth in Piccone's suggestions about *what* happened and *why* concerning the ending of the Vietnam war.

It would indeed be naive to attribute it simply to the irresistible force of the National Liberation Front, or the anti-war movement, or both. There clearly occurred a changing appreciation of America's international role and obligations among élites in the United States. Peter Berger provided a sophisticated and detailed account of this process in his article 'The greening of American foreign policy' (1976), included in his *Facing up to Modernity*, London, 1979. Another argument about the stimulus to and rationale of the Vietnam intervention in terms of the consequences of liberalism and Wilsonian internationalism, which casts a different but equally interesting light upon the question, may be found in S. E. K. Ambrose, *The Rise To Globalism*, London, 1980, particularly chapters 10, 11 and 12. The insupportable part of Piccone's argument concerns the *how*, as the subsequent argument should make clear.

17 Marcuse, 'Some social implications of modern technology' (1941), in Arato and Gebhardt, op. cit., 155.

18 Marcuse, 'Industrialization and capitalism in the work of Max Weber', *Negations*, 203.

19 Piccone, 'The crisis of one-dimensionality', 46.

20 S. Giner, *Mass Society*, London, 1976, 209.

21 In 1917 Weber criticized the politics of post-Bismarckian Germany for the way in which the cult of the recent charismatic

leader suppressed the possibility of genuine development of vigorous parties in a meaningful parliament: '[Bismarck] left behind him a nation *without any political sophistication*. . . . Above all he left behind him a nation *without any political will of its own*, accustomed to the idea that the great statesman at the helm would make all the necessary political decisions. . . . *A completely powerless parliament* was the purely negative result of his tremendous prestige.' Weber, *Economy and Society*, 2, Berkeley, 1978, Appendix 2, 'Parliament and government in a reconstructed Germany,' 1392 (emphasis in the original).

22 J. Habermas, *Towards a Rational Society*, London, 1971, 63.

23 Horkheimer, 'The authoritarian state', 98.

24 ibid., 104, 105.

25 Arato, 'Political sociology and the critique of politics', in Arato and Gebhardt, op. cit., 19.

26 F. Pollock, 'State capitalism: its possibilities and limitations' (1941), in Arato and Gebhardt, op. cit., 73.

27 ibid., 93.

28 J. Habermas, *Theory and Practice*, London, 1974, 42. The most elegant, persuasive and accessible defence of the classical doctrine of politics and its contemporary relevance is Bernard Crick's *In Defence of Politics*, London, 1982. In contrast to this approach, which would seek to define politics as a limited – if crucial – human activity whose organizing principle must be tolerance, we can only shudder at the consequences of the principle now being popularized: that 'the personal is the political'. If it is anything, that which is political is open to free and unrestrained investigation and debate. It is a mark of the times that well-intentioned people can now seek to complete the system of totalitarianism by policing the bedroom. Doubtless it is the case that if we subscribe to certain values about how we should treat people in general, there is an imperative that we should seek to act according to our principles in our personal lives. But that is an *ethical* question, not a political one, and the defence of that distinction is at least one of the barricades I would still willingly man.

29 R. J. Bernstein, *The Restructuring of Social and Political Theory*, Oxford, 1976, 187. This provides a very clear account of Habermas' ideas.

30 J. Habermas, *Towards a Rational Society*, London, 1971, 63.

31 J. Habermas, *Legitimation Crisis*, London, 1976, 142, 143.

32 J. Habermas, *Towards a Rational Society*, London, 1971, 63.

33 ibid., 64.

34 ibid., 67.

35 Habermas' later investigations are published in *Communication and the Evolution of Society*, London, 1979. Variously useful discussions of Habermas' work occur in T. McCarthy, *The Critical Thought of Jürgen Habermas*, London, 1978; J. Sensat, *Habermas and Marxism*, New York, 1979;

D. Held and J. Thompson,
*Habermas: Critical Debates*,
London, 1982; G. Kortian,
*Metacritique*, Cambridge, 1980;
R. Bubner, *Modern German
Philosophy*, Cambridge, 1981;
R. Keat, *The Politics of Social
Theory*, Oxford, 1981; D. Held,
*Introduction to Critical Theory*,
London, 1980. Karl-Otto Apel's
work is at points parallel and
complementary to Habermas'
concerns and, especially in 'The
a priori of the communication
community and the foundations
of ethics', *Towards a Transfor-
mation of Philosophy*, London,
1980, is very stimulating.

36  R. Bendix, *Max Weber: an Intellectual Portrait*, London, 1966,
466.

37  Quoted in H. Arendt, *On Revolution*, London, 1964, 183.

38  ibid., 163.

39  ibid.

40  T. Jefferson, *Letter to Destutt de
Tracy* (1811), in *The Portable
Thomas Jefferson*, London, 1977,
524.

41  Arendt, op. cit., 165.

42  This is a quotation by John
Adams from the work of a French
*philosophe*, J. Barbeyrac, cited in
M. White, *The Philosophy of the
American Revolution*, Oxford,
1978, 49.

43  John Locke, *Essay Concerning
Human Understanding*, book
IV, chapter XX, sections, 2,
6, cited in White, op. cit.,
55.

44  A. Mason and R. Leach, *In Quest
Of Freedom: American Political
Thought and Practice*, New
York, 1959, 231.

45  ibid., 205 – 8.

46  White, op. cit., chapter 3,
*passim*.

47  S. M. Lipset, *The First New
Nation*, New York, 1963,
52 – 68; Mason and Leach, op.
cit., 172 – 9.

48  Lipset, op. cit., 53.

49  ibid., 50 (emphasis in the
original).

50  ibid., 18 – 23, *passim*. For an
entertaining picture of the
'monarchical' Washington, as
well as a cynical account of the
actors in the American constitutional drama, Gore Vidal's
historical novel *Burr* is a diverting
alternative view. If, in this
account, Hamilton emerges as
the 'Stalin' of the American
Revolution, the protegé of Washington's 'Lenin' and the
opponent of Jefferson's
'Trotsky', one might briefly –
albeit fancifully – relish the
piquancy of Stalin falling to the
assassin's blow, in the duel with
Aaron Burr, Trotsky having
already succeeded to the reins of
power!

51  ibid., 42.

52  R. Hofstadter, W. Miller and
D. Aaron, *The American
Republic*, New York, 1959, 331,
cited in Lipset, op. cit., 45.

53  M. Smelser, 'The Federalist
period as an Age of Passion',
*American Quarterly*, 10 (1958),
395, cited in Lipset, op. cit., 43.

54  Arendt, *op. cit.*, chapter 3, 'The
pursuit of happiness', 115 – 40.

55  ibid., 132.

56  Liebman, *Leninism under Lenin*,
London, 1975, 51.

57  ibid.

58  R. Michels, *Political Parties*, New
York, 1959, 400. It does not, of

course, follow from the existence of these regrettable, and perhaps inevitable, features of modern party life that it is possible or desirable to dispense with political parties. Weber, who was well aware of these problems, criticized those who offered ostensibly more wholesome and healthy alternatives. In an argument clearly relevant to the previous discussion of the inadequacies of the soviet form, he points out the consequences of 'proposals to displace . . . parliaments based on universal . . . suffrage by electoral bodies of an occupational nature' ('Parliament and government in a reconstructed Germany', 1396). It must at least assume a degree of stability of occupational, economic and social function incompatible with a dynamic economy. Further, party would at least continue to exist under another name, only in this case party would no longer constitute collections of citizens attempting to offer answers to general problems of national direction, but narrow economically defined interest groups, their programmes constantly vitiated by rampant and naked *self*-interest.

Parliament would become a mere market place for compromises between purely economic interests, without any political orientation to overall interests. Any public control over the administration would be vitiated since the decisive moves and compromises of the interested groups would be made behind the closed doors of the nonpublic associations and would be even less controllable than before . . . a 'representative' body of this kind would be the least proper place imaginable for the solution of political problems according to truly political criteria. (ibid., 1397)

And all this would increase the ability of the bureaucracy to reinforce its own power by playing off opposed economic groups through 'log-rolling' and 'patronage'.

59  Murray Bookchin offers an incisive and stimulating account of some of the problems of political representation in the Marxist tradition and modern society in 'Beyond neo-Marxism', *Telos*, 36 (1978), 5 – 28.

# FOUR  **THE TEXT AND ITS CONTEXT**

## A MICROSCOPIC UNIVERSE

In chapter 1, I discussed the judgements of Lenin's texts that historians have attempted, and one of the qualities that could be seen in their comments was a certain air of surprise. That is, *The State and Revolution* was something of an 'absurd' or 'impossible' text in the light of Lenin's extremely practical politics. At best, this absurdity could be reconciled to reality by attributing its writing to devious, or even dishonest, motives.

Doubtless, there *is* a contradiction; such accounts of the text are not wrong in insisting on absurdity. If politicians may be criticized for their failures to fulfil the promises they make, there is no more outrageous example of 'bad faith' than the state that Lenin constructed after 1917. In the preceding chapter I have attempted to show, however, that the connection between the text and Lenin's subsequent activities is more intimate, and more rational, and more inevitable, than such criticisms would allow. I propose now to consider the problem from another angle: having established the relationship between the text and the state that subsequently emerged in Russia, I will investigate the relationship between the text and Lenin. That is, I want to map Lenin's path to *The State and Revolution*. I do not intend a comprehensive intellectual biography; it will be more useful to highlight and focus on four domains, or four stages in Lenin's path, that were influential in determining the destination of his intellectual journey. These four domains may be, loosely, termed those of Lenin's cosmology, Lenin's concept of parliamentarism, Lenin's culture, and Lenin's theory of political motivation.

## LENIN'S COSMOLOGY

Much has been written in recent years to the effect that Marx's project was essentially scientific. Althusser prefaced his influential essay on 'Marxism and humanism' with what he regards as a paradigmatic quotation from one of Marx's last writings: 'My analytical method does not start from man but from the economically given social period.'[1] In other words, Marxism is not a humanism.

Althusser seeks to establish a straightforward opposition between the Marx who started from 'man', and the Marx who conceived man as a result of an 'economically given social period'. Accordingly, the early Marx consecutively adopted two assumptions that were undermined by the same philosophical error. The common error was humanism, the suggestion that there existed a human 'essence' or 'nature', and that history was an account of the effectiveness of such essential themes. Marx's first version of this was 'liberal-rationalist', a theme derived directly from the Enlightenment. This was later displaced by the concept of 'communialist' humanism, wherein such a human essence could only be expressed in 'universal human relations, with men and with his objects'. Here Marx's philosophy is already politics, a practical politics of social revolution. But for Althusser this was by no means the true scientific Marx. That could only appear when the concept of man was abandoned and this unacceptable humanism was replaced at the centre of philosophy and politics by a different subject: the social formation constituted by the specific articulations of forces of production and relations of production, an ensemble which produces, not man, but simply different specific levels of human practice.[2]

It may indeed be possible to construct a Marxism that is purely such a science of social formations. But the problems that Althusser experiences in identifying the writings of Marx that are truly free of non-scientific (in other words, Hegelian) influences indicate that the assumptions that Marx held about his own work are rather different. If we are to understand Marxism sociologically (rather than understand Marxist sociology) we must attempt to define the impulses behind it. To ignore the origins of Marx's work is to fail to grasp its specific intent, and consequently to be left bereft of its significance within European culture, and its impact upon contemporary society. The early writings and the humanism that Althusser rejects illuminate Marx as a child of the Enlightenment, and in particular of that period of the Enlightenment wherein reason was revealed as being not without profound costs; in this the work of Kant was of great importance. While Marx pays little or no attention to Kant's writings, it is clear that he was involved in working out an alternative to the answer which Hegel offered to the Kantian problem. This problem was how to resolve the impact of Kant's thought on the integrity of man. It has been said that Kant found man whole and left him internally shattered, the victim of the acutest of antinomies:

> the opposition between thought, reason and morality on one side, and desire and sensibility on the other; the opposition between the fullest self-conscious freedom on one side, and life in the community on the other; the opposition between self-consciousness and communion with nature; and beyond this the separation of finite subjectivity from the infinite life that flowed through nature.[3]

Appropriately translated, this amounts to a summary of the problems of modernity that have become a central concern of sociologists and political philosophers over the past century. It expresses the costs of 'rationalization', the roots of 'anomie' and, of course, Marx's most powerful and evocative theme of alienation, the feeling of a lack of completeness and sufficiency surrounding one's being in the world. For industrial man, Kant evoked potent themes, and, whatever the claims of Althusser and his school, it is indisputable that Marxism would have had little significance in the world as a politics did it not address itself centrally to these themes. A philosophy that can offer answers to the contemporary problem of being in the world of modernity will find adherents where a science of the development of social formations will remain forever lonely; it is perhaps no surprise that Althusser accepted that he and his fellow scientists of Marxism would remain a distinct élite in his future society.

It has been said of Hegel that 'His ideal, like that of most of his contemporaries, was that of the *recreation of a whole man in an integrated cohesive, political community*',[4] and Marx may clearly be said to have adopted this as the essential purpose of his work. Perhaps it would not be too much to suggest that Lenin in his own way was driven by such impulses. Hegel and Marx, of course, differed from later social critics of 'dehumanization' such as Weber and Durkheim by their willingness to embrace the project of discovering a comprehensive solution to the problem. But it is here that a philosophical assumption may become a political threat.

I refer to the threat inherent in what Adorno calls 'identity theory'. That is the assumption of an identical structure of mind and matter, the actuality or the possibility of the identity of concept and object. After Kant, it was hardly possible to maintain previous naive assumptions to the effect that such identity already existed; but similarly, after Kant, few were happy to reconcile themselves to a universe which emphatically escaped the possibility of human control, and which rendered inevitable the acute existential problems already referred to. Thus identity was not rejected; rather its achievement became a historical project as opposed to a pre-existing feature of an ordered universe. In Hegel this issued in the concept of the Absolute Idea, translated, in history, as the modern state: 'the free individual must ultimately come to see himself as the vehicle of universal reason; and when the state comes to full development as the embodiment of this reason, the two are reconciled.'[5]

For Marx, clearly, identity would become possible by the act of proletarian revolution, when the universal class, the proletariat, became identical with the object, with society and history, and rendered it transparent and rational. This would constitute the 'end of prehistory', that is, the resolution of all those conflicts and torments that arise from a situation where man is confronted by society as something unknown and uncontrolled. Lukacs' later 'subject–object identical' succinctly summed up this project.[6]

What are the dangers of the search for identity? Adorno described the philosophical threat involved:

> Whenever something that is to be conceived flees from identity with the concept, the concept will be forced to take exaggerated steps to

prevent any doubts of the unassailable validity, solidity, and acribia of the thought product from stirring. Great philosophy was accompanied by a paranoid zeal to tolerate nothing else, and to pursue everything else with all the cunning of reason, while the other kept retreating farther and farther from the pursuit. The slightest remnant of non-identity sufficed to deny an identity conceived as total.[7]

If the search for identity changes from being a philosophical project to describe the world into a political project to change the world, its consequences can be terrifying: 'exaggerated steps' and 'paranoid zeal' will be acted out in history. That which is pursued will be men, not just things. Thus the identity project makes permissible the treatment of human beings in a hitherto unprecedented manner. All singularity must be absorbed into unity; all singularity constitutes, not a mere opposition, but a mortal threat from an unreconciled and unabsorbed Other. Such an Other will have few defences: it is illogical, meaningless and ultimately ephemeral. As Adorno concluded: 'Auschwitz confirmed the philosopheme of pure identity as death. . . . Genocide is absolute integration.'[8]

Lenin, of course, was actually philosophically anachronistic. Sartre condemned 'Lenin's unthinkable pre-critical philosophical thought',[9] demonstrated by his commitment to an eighteenth-century version of mechanical and reflectionist materialism. Perhaps his belated appreciation of Hegel during the war years produced an epistemology more in keeping with the projects of Hegel and Marx; there is little specific evidence for this. Nevertheless, Lenin was a philosopher of identity, in the following sense.

It is arguable that Leninism is an original doctrine, not merely a technology of power, because it provided the necessary reworking of the identity project in the light of the problems that seemed to undermine Marx's version. The simple problem was the apparent inability or reluctance of the proletariat to act as the self-conscious agency of revolution. This profound absence in reality ruptured the classical simplicity of Marx's doctrine. There were several possible reactions to this absence. The Lukacsian project could proceed no further after its enunciation in 1922: it was simply incapable of embracing the contemporary reality,[10] and consequently produced a utopian and leftist brand of political tactics which could not construct a tactical domain of any viability. The Bolsheviks had already overcome this problem by accepting the displacement of class by party. The 'immanent class-consciousness' thesis

found its theoretical elision and practical subversion in Lenin's introduction of the concept of the party – the interventionist, manoeuvring, tactic-seeking party. This had to result in the implicit interment
of the concept of the proletariat as the transcendental subject of history.

Bolshevism accepted this displacement of class by party as historical
subject. This resulted in the body of strategies and practices subsequently known as Stalinism, which internalized politics as manoeuvre
and manipulation in a manner foreign – and indeed morally repugnant – to classical Marxist theory. There were still those who rejected
the ethical implications of such a choice of party over class, and opted
for the alternate pole of class-as-subject. The 'left communists' and
'council communists' who did so had to accept the consequences:
'utopian' politics and historical 'irrelevance'.[11] Others came to accept,
at least implicitly, the absence of a revolutionary subject, and on such a
basis were able to develop sophisticated analyses of classes, individuals
and ideas in capitalist society. Such was the career of the Frankfurt
school. Trotskyism, whose career was to be as unrewarding as that of the
left communists, simply refused the twentieth century. The moral
strength (which accounts for its attractiveness among certain sub-
cultures), but political weakness, of Trotskyism resided in its refusal to
recognize the chasm between sociological actuality and Marxian theory
that opened up some time early in this century. Trotskyism insistently
believed in the need to build parties, but the theory constantly attempted
to displace agency from party to proletariat. Here, a spirit of liberation
still exists, yet history becomes a source of embarrassment. Parties constantly manage to substitute for the proletariat, as the working class
demonstrates its inability to progress without the party. Trotsky's
politics thus became impoverished beyond seriousness, a product of
sheer incomprehension – on the one hand, theories of betrayal and
treachery; on the other, organizational fetishism offering to the proletariat simplistic analyses and exhortations to action.

The twin paradoxes of the collapse of Marx's theory of agency are
then these: mass parties that, fundamentally, do not believe the masses
have any right, or role, to play in their own liberation; and tiny collec-
tivities that ground themselves in mass self-emancipation but remain
desperately devoid of mass support.

All of Lenin's actions were ultimately motivated by a ruthless and
unsparing search for the agency that would overcome the apparently
irreconcilable diffuseness of the experience of the human subject. In
1902 his argument in *What Is To Be Done?* indicates the first assertion

of the inadequacy of the proletariat for this task, and the elevated role of the party that results. But he could be swayed. The 1905 revolution, displaying the spontaneous combativity of the Russian people, resulted in a greater appreciation of the working class, and brought him to moderate his views about how easily workers could be allowed to join and control the party. The decline of the revolutionary wave sees Lenin in the subsequent years obsessively monitoring the purity of the party once again. The impact of the war, which will be considered in detail later, was disorientating. Working-class support for the war was attributable to the betrayal of the parties of western Europe. This necessitated the further purification of the 'international' party by consummating the split with the 'opportunists'. But that experience, along with the none too impressive performance of the Bolshevik party before Lenin's return in April and the astounding activities of the Russian working class, must also have brought the possibility of class-as-subject once again to priority in Lenin's mind. The absence of the party from the pages of *The State and Revolution* is at least partly attributable to this.

Thus the problems of the philosophy of identity may have a bearing upon the legacy of Lenin. This specific historical legacy for the Russian people consisted of, first, the rise to power of an absolute dictator and, second, the horrendous loss of life associated with, or consequent upon, this. Part of this may perhaps be attributed to regrettable necessities of the industrialization process or the demands of state survival in hostile conditions. But much of the violent history of the Soviet Union seems to defy explanation in rational terms. Once the dictatorship of the party was consolidated in the early 1920s, there seems to be a remarkable disparity between the potential of any putative opposition (whether they were internal party groups, anti-Bolshevik political remnants or hostile social classes) and the degree of violence and energy expended against them. Perhaps, therefore, the rise to power of the absolute dictator can be partially explained by the constant displacement of the transcendental subject of history: from class to party to central committee to, finally, general secretary, as each potential subject consecutively demonstrated its inadequacy to the task assigned to it by history. And perhaps the violence against all real or potential opposition can be understood by realizing that those who fell victim to the terror machine were identifiable as elements of an unreconciled Other, a standing outrage to the claims and sensibilities of the imperialism of identity theory.

Such considerations may in fact be brought to bear upon Lenin him-self, his role and his historical fate (and consequently upon the remark-able hegemony that Lenin's *ideas* established within the culture of the Soviet Union). Marx's original project possibly contained *in nuce* the seeds of its later power of enchantment. This is the ability to reconcile the irreconcilable. The axiom about philosophers now having the task of changing the world is also a statement that philosophers now possess that very power. It is the possibility of creating a body of thought that removes the separation between 'is' and 'ought', and establishes a doc-trine that combines a science and an ethic. The world can be known, and that known world will be revealed as expressing the highest ideals of the human spirit. But within this 'possibility', Lenin is unique. Despite Marx's aspirations, his role was to be little different from the one commonly reserved for the philosopher and intellectual: to com-ment on and criticize from the sidelines those actually engaged in the practical tasks of movements and states. This is not to condemn Marx: the communist philosopher – politician is a unique animal in history. Within the communist movement as it has developed since Marx's time the difficulty of combining the two roles is demonstrated by the scarcity of those who could truly claim to have done so. The division of party labour into 'theoreticians' and 'functionaries' is one that has been replicated throughout Marxian parties and regimes.

Thus the philosophical and political writings of those who have aspired to such a dual role – Stalin, Brezhnev, Ho Chi Minh, Kim Il Sung – while assiduously published and propagated by the state regimes they themselves constructed, are devoid of real content or intellectual significance. The functionary mode came easily to cancel other possibilities. The reverse of this coin are those people who in the Russia of the 1920s found that their insistence on 'theoretical' debate as the foundations for state policy contributed in no small measure to their rapid elimination from practical politics. Bukharin is a case in point, but far more illustrative is Trotsky.

Trotsky appears to be the supreme example of the man of action capable of reflecting profoundly on his every political deed and state-ment: a man with a highly intellectual cast of mind, cultured and philosophically rigorous, who at the same time achieved a role in state affairs equalled by few. But the truth is that Trotsky was hardly a success when confronted with the practical tasks of *politics*: that is, of reaching administrative decisions capable of encompassing and rec-onciling contradictory influences, pressures and demands, in situations bounded by scarce resources and the demands of the moment. His moments of real power bear this out. Trotsky emerged into the mainstream of history on two occasions. The first was his chairmanship of the St Petersburg soviet in 1905. This experience, however, has little to do with the problem under discussion. It was not an administrative post: the soviet was rather a theatre for grandiose and heroic gestures, an exercise in the true romanticism of the powerless, and Trotsky in his accounts of the experiences revels in precisely those dramatic gestures.[12]

The second occasion was when he was finally entrusted with the problems of state in the post-1917 government. He resolved the problems that he encountered with a singular lack of subtlety. As Lenin diplomatically suggested in his *Testament*, Trotsky's actual state practice was 'excessively administrative' in character. His baptism of fire was the Brest-Litovsk negotiations, where he pursued a policy of 'no-war, no-peace' in anticipation of the spread of the revolution, a policy that earned him the strictures of Lenin and further advances by the German armies (an 'ethical' position). It appears to have been an educational experience. This brief romanticism was subsequently replaced by a determination to pursue the most ruthless form of practical politics: the purely administrative mode displaced any more sophisticated political confections. He had no compunction about executing deserters from the Red Army *pour encourager les autres*; he scorned those who advocated a new 'revolutionary' form of military strategy and organization, and insisted on the superiority of conventional warfare and disciplined and hierarchical formations; he could see no better solution to the problem of relations between the trade unions and the state than to turn the unions into the arms of the state under the slogan of the 'militarization of labour'; and his role in the suppression of the Kronstadt revolt is well known. Trotsky collapsed into the administrative mode with a vengeance, and rejected all criticisms as the vapourings of woolly-minded liberals (his 'scientific' mode).

This brief, and ultimately embarrassing, experience of the realities of power soon gave way to his role as inner-party critic. He could return to his books, his references, his superb arguments and debating skills. Now he was the theorist and dissector of other people's mistakes – that is, their failure to apply Marxist philosophy rigorously to the affairs of state. And, not surprisingly, as his distance from the levers of power grew, as his responsibilities diminished, so grew the theological cast of his criticisms and the utopian flavour of his solutions.

The list of those who managed to retain the leadership of party and state while justifying their actions with a recourse to Marxian doctrine is therefore limited to two: Lenin and Mao Tse-Tung. The latter is, however, somewhat different from Lenin; perhaps he is so distanced from the original roots of Marxian philosophy and social theory that it is valueless to discuss him as a Marxist. It was, after all, Mao's lifetime project to achieve the 'sinofication of Marxism'.[13] Lenin's project was never the Russification of Marxism; he had too much contempt for Russian culture to dream of the idea. His project was the westernization of Russia, through the most western of doctrines, classical Marxism. He believed that, at most, he was doing no more than creating a 'sub-set' of classical Marxism to take into account the needs of transforming a semi-feudal society into the image of that studied by Marx.

Lenin, therefore, achieved the symbiosis of science and ethics with unique success, embodied in his own person. He made the revolution according to the scientific mode, and that revolution was 'good'. His person is therefore the paradigmatic character of the twentieth-century lust for identity. His ability to sustain, to live, to reconcile, the tension between revolutionary élan and humanist vision, on the one hand, and the brute necessities of success and power, on the other, transformed him from a political leader into something truly unique. Those who bemoan the creation of a 'cult of Lenin' after his death[14] fail to realize the inevitability of such a process.

According to the culture he had created, he was not simply the great and respected leader of the revolution, but a figure of transcendental significance, a person who had broken through the crude limitations of human character to become the living embodiment of the identical subject – object. How, then, could one do less than worship him, and the successor who claimed his mantle?

## LENIN'S PARLIAMENT

In mapping the discourse that gave rise to *The State and Revolution* an obvious step is to attempt to trace the origins and evolution of the themes in Lenin's earlier writings. Such an examination will in fact prove disappointing and yield little in the way of an explicit genealogy for the ideas of 1917. Indeed, despite the fact that the problem of parliament and the role of socialist parliamentarians had been considered in all its nuances within the European movement, particularly in the German party, there is in Lenin a practical absence of any considerations of a fundamental nature: his discussion is exclusively in the domain of tactics towards particular institutions at particular moments. What comments there are cannot easily be brought to bear upon Lenin's later definitive statement on the issues.

The socialist movement in nineteenth-century Europe did not conceive democracy, in general, and parliamentary institutions, in particular, as ends in themselves. Their concern was the complex of issues that emerged in the wake of the paradigmatic revolution against autocratic power, the French Revolution. The 'social problem' remained, and indeed was perhaps for the first time revealed as a problem of a different order and depth, inaccessible to the purely political and constitutional innovations that radical movements had so far achieved. An awareness of the social problem thus constitutes equality as an unsolved problem within political democracy and transforms constitutional achievements into a means as well as an end.

Colletti proposes as Marx's most perceptive account of parliamentary democracy his discussion of the French Constitution of 1848. This analysis is notable for its recognition of the ambiguity of that short-lived institution:

> The comprehensive contradiction of this constitution, however, consists in the following: the classes whose slavery it is to perpetuate, proletariat, peasantry, petty-bourgeoisie, it puts in possession of political power through universal suffrage. And from the class whose old social power it sanctions, the bourgeoisie, it withdraws the political guarantees of this power. It forces the rule of the bourgeoisie into democratic conditions, which at every moment help the hostile classes to victory and jeopardise the very foundations of bourgeois society. From the one it demands that they should not go forward from political to social emancipation; from the others that they should not go back from social to political restoration.[15]

Colletti uses this formulation to counter what he considers to be two major misinterpretations of the constitutional state. One sees political equality as a mere 'trap' and the other sees the representative state as a genuine expression of the 'general interest'. Against these 'sectarian' and 'revisionist' positions, Colletti asserts an interpretation that refuses to *pre-judge* the institutions of democracy themselves. For him, they have a certain quality of neutrality: they are the 'best terrain', upon which the dimensions of the social problem and the struggle to resolve it may be revealed.[16]

But clearly we are here still talking the language of tactics. There is no serious consideration of the problem of democratic institutions *per se* and how these may best be constructed to achieve the maximum of popular power in a non-authoritarian form. On this problem, as in the rest of the Marxian tradition, there is only a practical silence.

Engels certainly, in his 1894 introduction to *The Class Struggles in France*, is famous for taking a more than positive attitude towards the parliamentary and electoral experience of the German Social-Democratic Party. But this statement itself is fraught with dangers of interpretation, since Rosenberg had argued that it was incomplete due to reasons of censorship.[17]

The politicians of the Second International were, of course, forced to take a more precise position, aptly summed up by Kautsky in 1892:

> The bourgeoisie, with all sorts of talents at its command, has hitherto been able to manipulate parliaments to its own purpose. Therefore, small capitalists and farmers have in large numbers lost all faith in legislative action. . . . The proletariat is, however, more favourably situated in regard to parliamentary activity. . . . Whenever the proletariat engages in parliamentary activity as a self-conscious class, parliamentarism begins to change its character. It ceases to be a mere tool in the hands of the bourgeoisie. . . . It is the most powerful lever that can be utilized to raise the proletariat out of its economic, social, and moral degradation.[18]

Kautsky's estimate of parliamentary activity carries a positive message, intended as it was to justify the work of the party. But it is interesting that the attitude to parliament expressed there is more manipulative, more tactical and less categorical than Marx's comments on the constitution. Marx's comments did not contain the suggestion that, under certain circumstances, the constitution would be a 'mere tool in the hands of the bourgeoisie'. On the contrary, the constitution itself set limits on the freedom of both parties to manipulate the political sphere as freely as they might wish. Kautsky sees the constitutional form as perhaps solely determined by the character with which it is invested by particular social forces. He does not foresee any possibility that the progress he notes might ever be reversed; but he does perhaps open a door for quite a reverse and negative estimate of the parliamentary form to be made by other people, under other circumstances.

Kautsky's attitude was of course never itself acceptable to the more radical elements of the socialist tradition. They rejected parliament as both a genuine democratic form and as any aid to the struggle for social emancipation. This conception was to gain weight after 1914 as a result of the fury and frustration felt by radicals at the outbreak of war. The clear inability of parties and parliaments to control and subdue the tendencies that brought war for no very clear reasons could be at least partially laid at the door of parliaments – they were complicit in the disaster. A putative instrument for the rational and dignified control of human affairs was apparently revealed as impotent. The more radical a body of politics is, the greater the belief in the innate susceptibility of human affairs to rationalist discourses and practices. It was not, therefore, surprising that the failure of parliament to effect this control was blamed on certain inherent inadequacies of that system.

The indeterminate nature of all these positions would have denied to Lenin any coherent and authoritative tradition upon which he might have based his thoughts on democracy in the Russian context. But his early estimate of parliamentary structures in the United States and Switzerland was not noticeably negative,[19] and his strategy for Russia certainly included the need for parliamentary developments in the European style. Writing in 1895, he asserted that 'the struggle of the working class for its emancipation is a political struggle, and its first aim is to achieve political liberty.'[20] Political liberty is here defined as consisting of the convening of a constituent assembly under universal suffrage, and the standard freedoms of assembly, the press, etc. These were required because 'the worker needs the achievement of the general democratic demands only to clear the road to victory over the people's chief enemy . . . capital'.[21]

Both Lenin and Kautsky defined the positive role of parliamentarism as educational as well as legislative. Kautsky argued that electoral activity was a means of bringing political confidence to the working class: 'This very participation of the proletariat proves to be the most effective means of shaking up the hitherto indifferent divisions of the proletariat and giving them hope and confidence.'[22] For Lenin, the educational experience is didactic rather than mobilizing: 'It is far more advantageous to the workers for the bourgeoisie to *openly* influence policy than, as it is the case now, to exert a *concealed* influence.'[23]

But Lenin is not discussing parliaments and democracy as a substantive issue; the above is an argument he derives from the need to seek allies against the autocracy. The 'democratic' struggle is one in which the proletariat can have an interest because it is a campaign in which it can ally with other social forces; the benefits of the democratic achievements themselves are secondary. Kautsky has the same feelings about the way in which democracy can clarify the processes of ruling-class power, but in his argument it is in parliamentary activity that the proletariat can counter the activities of the bourgeoisie, not just observe them:

> Great capitalists can influence rulers and legislators directly, but the workers can do so only through parliamentary activity. . . . By electing representatives to parliament, therefore, the working class can exercise an influence over governmental powers.[24]

There are, therefore, nuances here which might indicate the seeds of the later violent disagreement between the two men on the issues of democratic institutions. But the texts will probably not bear that weight of significance. The significance of the positions of both writers in the 1890s is probably what they held in common, not what separated them. Lenin's estimate was bound to be less positive than Kautsky's, given that Kautsky's party enjoyed the benefits of parliamentary activity at the time, whereas the Russians had no such institutions and the bourgeoisie took a pusillanimous attitude towards creating them. What both men had in common was an almost inevitable tendency to relegate the problem of democracy to the sidelines, a domain assessed in terms of its *usefulness* for the purpose of social emancipation. Certainly, for Kautsky, democracy had already been to an extent achieved, whereas for Lenin the issue of democracy was a minor issue in the sordid reality of Tsarist Russia. But it would be tendentious to construe any of this as indicating significant *differences* between the two theorists.

For Lenin, the Duma did not help matters. He argued against a boycott, because it was necessary to 'explain to the people the impossibility of achieving political freedom by parliamentary means as long as the real power remains in the hands of the Tsarist government', and to show the people 'the utter uselessness of the Duma as a means of achieving the demands of the proletariat and revolutionary petty-bourgeoisie, especially the peasantry'.[25]

He could hardly be faulted for this. The Duma itself lacked meaningful powers; it was subordinate to an appointed second chamber, and had no prerogative at all over the key areas of state finance and military affairs. It was not seriously representative. The first electoral law ensured unequal representation of the social classes. Some 90,000 workers, on one hand, and 2000 landowners, on the other, each enjoyed the representation of one deputy. Worker representation was organized, like the soviets, on the basis of factories, and due to the fact that factories employing less than fifty workers were excluded from the franchise, along with building workers, casual labourers and artisans, some 63 per cent of the urban male working population had no vote. None the less, the results proved less than satisfactory to the regime, and 'From the outset the Duma clearly expressed all the forces disrupting Russian life.'[26] The electoral system was consequently readjusted until it produced a Duma that the regime felt it could live with.

Nevertheless, Lenin did not make the mistake of identifying the existing Duma with parliamentary institutions in general. The Duma was not taken to serve as a model of genuine constitutional forms. Lenin compared the Duma with what was possible under such genuine structures. The parliamentary form was not condemned, a priori, to be nothing more than a 'talking shop' serving to 'fool' and 'distract' the people. It could, indeed, be an institution that controlled the affairs of state. The problem of 'constitutional illusions' concerned only a situation where the parliament did not live up to its claims and responsibilities.

When a constitutional system has become firmly established, when, for a certain period, the constitutional struggle becomes the main form of the class struggle and of the political struggle generally, the task of dispelling constitutional illusions is not the special task of the Social Democrats, not the task of the moment. Why? Because at such times affairs in constitutional states are administered *in the very way* that parliament decides. By constitutional illusions we mean deceptive faith in a constitution. Constitutional illusions prevail when a constitution seems to exist, but actually does not: in other words, when affairs of state are not administered *in the way* parliament decides. When actual political life diverges from its reflection in the parliamentary struggle, then, and only then, does the task of combating constitutional illusions become the task of the advanced revolutionary class, the proletariat. The liberal bourgeois, dreading the extra-parliamentary struggle, spread constitutional illusions even when parliaments are impotent. The anarchists flatly reject participation in parliament under all circumstances. Social Democrats stand for utilising the parliamentary struggle, for exposing 'parliamentary cretinism', that is, the belief that parliamentary struggle is the sole or under all circumstances the main form of the political struggle.[27]

It is certainly instructive to compare this formulation with Lenin's final attitude towards parliaments in the years after the Revolution. In *Left-Wing Communism* Lenin takes up the same debate, and his argument appears to be with the same schools of thought. The social democrats spread constitutional illusions; the anarchists, who bear the main weight of the pamphlet's strictures, argue an abstentionist position. But Lenin's position will in fact have changed. In 1905 Lenin clearly entertained the notion that parliaments can be just what they claim to be, that 'affairs in constitutional states are administered *in the very way* that parliament decides.' In 1920 he sees the anarchists to be essentially right in their negative estimate of parliaments, and sees the virtue of participating to be a tactical one: facilitating the destruction of constitutional illusions. There is no possibility that parliament is other than a front or a sham, by its very nature expressly denied the ability to control the affairs of a state.

Clearly Lenin's views on this issue in these years were rather incoherent and unimportant, dictated more by time and audience than real reflection. Certainly there is nothing in his characterization of parliament that will determine a rejection of parliamentary forms within the socialist state. Similarly, however, he reveals no strong attachments to the idea and the institution that will place any particular barrier in the way of a passionate commitment to an alternative form. It is all far too vague and temporary to allow any more definite lineage to be established. What *is* perhaps interesting is the fact that Lenin's view of the soviet as a governmental form was hardly more positive than his view of parliaments. It may come as a surprise to realize that the Mensheviks adopted a far more positive attitude towards the soviets than did Lenin. Martov in particular viewed the widest establishment of local organs of self-government as crucial, at least to the revolutionary process itself. This reflected Martov's long-standing suspicion of any Bolshevik-type conception of organizing revolution from above, already made public in the 1903 argument over the form and role of the party. For him, the first objective was 'the formation of revolutionary committees in this or that town, this or that region, for the sole purpose of helping spread the rising and the disorganisation of the government'.[28]

The Menshevik conception of the soviets could also have a clearly constructive role. In response to the government's first toying with the ideas of limited representative institutions, Martov rejected any idea of boycott; but he combined participation in whatever institution the autocracy devised with a more radical idea which would claim representation for those excluded by the electoral law. What he called 'people's agitational committees' would be formed, ostensibly to mobilize participation in the official elections, but:

> At the same time the committees strive to create, apart from the legal representation, an illegal representative organ which at a certain moment could appear before the country as a temporary organ of the people's will. The committees would call the population to elect their representatives by universal vote, these representatives would at a given moment meet in one town and proclaim themselves a constituent assembly.[29]

The sympathy for, and responsiveness to, the possibilities of the new organization which is obvious in Martov is quite absent from Lenin. Lenin was not guilty of the extremes of suspicion with which his supporters regarded the soviets. Convinced of the virtues of organization and suspicious of spontaneous movements outside the control of party, they were tempted to boycott them altogether; or else were seduced by the idea of turning them into a section of the Bolshevik party by compelling them to accept the Bolshevik programme and the authority of the Bolshevik central committee. Lenin himself argued that the question of party and soviets was not either/or, but both. But the institution had little role in terms of administration as opposed to disruption. Lenin did not conceive of the soviets' role as anything but temporary: the real weakness of the soviet was not its possible politics – he had enough confidence in his own to be able to disregard that – but in its structure: 'This reservation was due to the weakness that Lenin saw in the Soviet organisation, in particular its excessively dispersed character, the lack of a central authority.'[30]

What is clearly absent from Lenin, even more than from the Menshevik account, is any conception of the soviets as the actual institutional structure of a post-revolutionary state. But arguably there was no reason for Lenin to consider this problem, given that the coming post-revolutionary state in Russia could not be a *socialist* one. As the physiognomy of the post-Tsarist society would be determined not by a proletarian policy, but by some appropriate combination of class forces, it was extremely unlikely that the definition of the state form would be a task that would fall to the Bolsheviks. Lenin's thoughts are inevitably structured from the point of view of the proletariat as a less than hegemonic and indeed possibly subordinate class in the coming society. Lenin's responsibility was thus to a specific class interest, not to society as a whole.

It would seem, therefore, that Lenin's pre-1914 attitude to both sides of the problem of state forms – to parliaments and to soviets – amounted to little more than disinterest. Prior to the catastrophe of the 'split in socialism' there is no indication of any reason in Marxian principles *or* in contemporary revolutionary experience to reject one and elevate the other, and establish the distinction as a fundamental of revolutionary ideology. What was to become the essential core of twentieth-century revolutionary theory derived *ab initio* from Lenin's response to the disaster he considered had been visited upon his movement in 1914. This is not to suggest that the whole theoretical reconstruction that followed is no more than another moment in Lenin's permanent career of personal and political disputation. It obviously grew into more than that. But it does confirm the total nature of that reconstruction: Lenin could derive from his prior political thinking practically nothing that might guide him in this reconstruction. He was forced back on those fragments of knowledge and understanding that might be termed his own culture.

## LENIN'S CULTURE

At one point in his book on the problem of 'beginnings', Edward W. Said discusses the acute problem posed for the reader by Milton's *Paradise Lost*. Discussing the passage where the angel Raphael informs Adam of the events in heaven, he points out that:

> The truth is at about five removes from the reader. First suppressed in night, suppressed once again by Raphael (who as an angel knows more than Adam), suppressed still further because Adam after all is the original man from whose priority we have all fallen, suppressed another time by Milton's use of English to convey the conversation in Eden, and finally suppressed by a poetic discourse to which we can relate only after a mediated act (of reading a seventeenth century epic) – the Truth is actually absent. Words stand for words which stand for other words.[31]

This is a vivid expression of the problems of textual analysis I have already discussed. It also highlights the problems inherent in Lenin's reformulation of Marxism that produced *The State and Revolution*. The text represents an attempt to reveal the 'truth' of the political process called parliamentarianism. Lenin certainly operated with a clear belief in the existence and accessibility of this truth, even if such a concept seems increasingly inappropriate to researchers in the human disciplines. Yet, if we do not share Lenin's confidence in the existence of such unquestionable truth, we cannot operate without a belief in the possibility of discriminating between the relative merits of competing explanations of social phenomena. We must simply be aware of the historical and contingent nature of the adequacy of such truths. Here, we must try to judge the *probability* of Lenin's reformulation attaining an adequate insight into his object of study. This can be approached by analysing the *removes* that separated Lenin from his object, and the *suppressions* that these involved.

It is well known that the outbreak of war in 1914 was a moment of profound rupture in Lenin's life and politics. It occasioned a reformulation of his politics of a most fundamental kind. To estimate how likely this project was to be successful, it is worth considering the resources that Lenin had at his disposal for the task.

The events of August 1914 were a doubly debilitating blow for Lenin. Not only had events taken a startling and horrific new turn; his socialist colleagues, mentors and leaders in the Second International had committed a gross act of 'betrayal'. He was bereft of both his political and personal moorings. Here was an undisputedly Marxist leadership which had gone back on its most fundamental word; which had transformed what had appeared to be sincere and strongly held principles into basest verbiage; which 'knew the truth' and deliberately buried it. It was a stunning shock for Lenin because it amounted to, not least, a personal betrayal. Not surprising, then, that he thought the report of the German Socialists' vote for war credits the work of police provocateurs. In his first writings after the terrible truth became clear he spoke of his 'most bitter disappointment'.

Lenin was thus thrown back on his own resources, and these were meagre. His view of the world had always been structured through a series of suppressions. He had strictly disciplined his thought to exclude contamination from anything other than the Marxian tradition: Russian culture had long been dismissed as unworthy of much consideration, characterized, for Lenin, by that most devastating of handicaps, 'backwardness'. Russian culture had produced the contemporary mess of Russian society, and certainly could not contain a solution to that mess. But Lenin was no more comfortable with a foreign culture. The culture of Europe was 'their culture', the culture of the bourgeoisie. The European tradition was anathema. Marx inherited a cosmopolitan European education, and was able to draw on the whole tradition of classical Enlightenment culture to focus on a problem. He could, at will, refer to Heraclitus, to Shakespeare, to Hegel, to any of the streams and shallows of European thought.

Lenin was quite different. We know for certain that he had not read Shakespeare, Byron, Molière or Schiller. Dostoevsky was 'rubbish'; he had respect only for the populist novel in the tradition of Chernyshevsky. 'A contemporary of Max Weber, of Freud, of English logic and German critical philosophy, he knew nothing of any of them.'[32] Even more surprising is his confessed ignorance until the war years of Hegel. A survey of his writings is a revealing activity: the meagreness of his references confirms the philistinism of his intellectual formation.

Consequently Lenin had, throughout his career, depended upon a knowledge of the world that was massively attenuated. It was the knowledge produced by Marx as transmitted through the parties and theoreticians of the Second International. And despite any pretensions of the Marxian tradition to an encyclopedic understanding of history and society, its legacy to Lenin was similarly stilted. Marx and Engels' discussions of specific and concrete social institutions was concerned almost exclusively with moments of rupture, destruction and reconstruction in European history – the years 1789, 1848 and 1871 being the recurrent foci. Lenin was transmitted no knowledge at all of the realities of stability, of the complex networks of institutions and practices which constituted the body of western society.

Therefore in all his agonizings and reconstructions subsequent to the split in the International, he was manoeuvring within a universe of intellectual possibilities whose dimensions were microscopic. If his intellectual resources were limited so long as he had confidence in the thinkers of the Second International, it, at least, had a certain intellectual rigour. After 1914, his confidence shattered, he resembles nothing so much as the incredible shrinking man.

If we focus on the specific problem of the critique of parliamentary democracy, a further handicap is revealed. Lenin's critique was crippled by its own situation in historical time. Perhaps he here only partook of a common human failing to pass judgement on historical developments before they have attained maturity. But his critique was attempted at a time when the world was practically devoid of examples of parliaments that could, even formally, be called genuinely representative of the citizenry and untrammelled by the old class power. According to Therborn,[33] the first democracy without qualifications on suffrage was established in New Zealand in 1907, and Denmark and Norway in

1915. These were the only institutions that predated Lenin's remarks of 1917 (although it must be conceded that male franchise did obtain in certain countries several years earlier – e.g. in France in 1884, in Norway in 1898). Clearly these facts amount to extenuating circumstances for Lenin's argument; although the subsequent spread of full formal democracy within and outside Europe underlines the paradox of *The State and Revolution*.

Thus it can be said that, in a literal sense, *Lenin did not know what he was talking about*. The 'suppressions' embedded in his own thought are sufficient to render improbable any access to an adequate account of the object he was studying. First, the 'truth' is indeed 'suppressed in night', the night of history not yet made, the night of the unknowable future. The second suppression is the assumption that the parliamentary form in fact has no future; the third suppression derives from the lack of any personal experience of a culture that contained such embryonic versions of the institution as *did* exist; the fourth suppression is the estimation of this lack as inconsequential; the fifth, the adherence to an understanding of parliament derived only from its relevance to the *social* question; the next, the assumption that the only meaningful discourse on that relevance was that of the theoreticians of the Second International; the next, the acceptance as legitimate of only those elements of that discourse that fell indisputably within the nostrums of Marx and Engels; the next, Lenin's own entirely hypostatized appropriation of Marx and Engels, derived from his own personal incapacity to estimate the degree of coincidence between the classical analysis and the object it surveyed, due to the final suppression: his own near-absolute lack of any intellectual or cultural resources from which to judge that privileged discourse. Truly, 'Words stand for words, which stand for other words. . . .'

Despite his assumption that he had cleansed his thought of unacceptable pollutions, Lenin could, no more than any of us, escape his culture. He found no Archimedean point from which to survey reality with a true and pristine objectivity. In fact, he ensured the reverse. His refusal to open himself to the multitude of cultural and intellectual influences that Europe offered resulted in his falling far more abjectly under the sway of the influences that had formed him at an unconscious level. In a way then, Lenin never escaped his own childhood socialization. Intellectual maturity, it may be suggested, is achieved by a process of critical selection; the child becomes an adult by appreciating and critically reviewing the manner in which he is a cultural product,

and his intellectual *independence* begins from the point of that realization. But, in contrast, an outright and enraged rejection of one's own
culture is a 'childish' act: the act of an adolescent unable to come to
terms with the complexity that is himself. It is an attempt to constitute
oneself as a *tabula rasa*. Needless to say, not only is such an attempt
impossible, but the assumption that it is possible leads shallow thinkers
very easily to convince themselves that they have achieved it. And thus
the continuing power that native culture continues to exercise over the
individual remains uninterrogated and unchallenged. This is a power
to which Lenin clearly fell victim.

*The State and Revolution* has been treated as a western artefact in
this argument. And it certainly is that, in its classical roots, and in its
continuing spectral presence in western political thought and culture.
But we may, nevertheless, discover specific conditions for its production not in Europe, but in Russia, and deriving from an entirely
different history and tradition. This was a tradition to which Lenin was
an unconscious but remarkably faithful heir. I shall here seek only to
evoke those elements of the Russian intellectual and cultural tradition
whose echoes we may find in the pages of Lenin's utopian text.

What were the characteristics of the Russian intelligentsia of which
Lenin was an indubitable, if resentful, heir? There seems to be a consensus about two features in particular: the espousal of a loyalty to a
vaguely defined and often imaginary national uniqueness; and an
openness to European intellectual innovations which was, however,
marked by a profound absence of discrimination or rigour. As a result,
the Russian intelligentsia were dangerously vulnerable to totalizing and
utopian projects.

There is no need to relate the details of Russian social structure in the
nineteenth century.[34] The patrimonial system of rule had for centuries
claimed for the autocracy the rights of both the ruler and the owner of
the realm. Such was the overwhelming weight of the state within the
society that the development of those classes whose interests were those
of modernity was blighted or crushed. As a result the intelligentsia
began its life far more socially isolated than had been the case in
Europe. Besançon places the emergence of this group from 1850
onwards, the product of a national organized system of education
under total state control. In this, as in so many other developments,
from Catherine the Great's introduction of political debate in the
eighteenth century to Zubatov's surprisingly successful police-sponsored
unions, the autocracy was the initiator of so much that elsewhere were

independent and organic results of economic and social development. The Russian intelligentsia failed to find a natural, congenial and, above all, successful ally in a rising bourgeoisie. Instead from the first it experienced an acute rootlessness due to the 'incapacity of civil society to impose on the young its own values and *raison d'être*'.[35] Rather, its formative experiences evoked distrust of potential allies who constantly succumbed to fruitless compromises with the autocracy.

Here we have, therefore, a sort of 'free-floating' intelligentsia, that is, one that remained without ties or connections to any particular interest group. This represented a genuine opportunity for a messianic ideology to seek a hegemonic social role. The classic modernizing revolutions of Europe were intended, despite the more ambitious of the ideologies they inspired, to satisfy the aspirations of specific rising interest groups. The political programmes of such groups always, therefore, had elements of a realist and 'minimalist' practicality about them, as did their subsequent actions. But, as Pipes points out, 'in Russia the struggle for political liberty was waged from the beginning exactly in the manner that Burke felt it ought never to be waged: in the name of abstract ideals'.[36] The radical intelligentsia were given by history full licence to elaborate an ideology of the most maximalist character. It is true that the validity of this maximalism was called into question when economic and social developments around the turn of the century indicated that political development in Russia might take the more normal course of the emergence of competing social classes. The crisis in Marxism, which sought to replace the more eschatological cast of revolutionary strategy with a process of integration into developing civil society and a 'long march through the institutions', was evidence of this. But the impact of populism and terrorism, and the success of Bolshevism, indicate that a large number were resilient enough to resist these temptations.

While a mass intelligentsia was a product of the second half of the nineteenth century, this group inherited a culture of political speculation from the prior generation. The freedom to think and write had arrived under the tutelage of Catherine the Great (1762–96). While the popular philosophy of the time was European rationalism, and the political ideas those of American constitutionalism, the appeal of these ideas faded in the wake of the Decembrist failure, and the radicals turned to a different source, that of German idealist philosophy. Schelling was introduced into Russia in the 1820s, Hegel in the 1830s. Their philosophies effected an immediate conquest, and held overt sway

until forced into retreat by materialism in the second half of the
century. But their imprint was never eradicated nor escaped.

The principle import of Hegelianism was the way in which its critique
of modernity – the problem of alienation – linked up with the search
for a national identity. It enabled intellectuals to translate Russian
'backwardness' into evidence of a historic role. This was what became
known as Slavophilism. It argued that the communal spirit formed the
essential feature of the Russian national character and provided the
basis of all Russian institutions, in contrast to the atomized individualism which permeated the west. It derived from the mystical and
euphoric nature of the Orthodox Church, which had resisted the
rationalism that had poisoned both Catholicism and Protestantism,
and found its expression in the peasant community, and the peasant's
intuitive and affective culture.

It was of course the case that many of the assumptions of Slavophilism were illusory. The peasant commune, in particular, had no very
ancient roots, provided little economic security, and was no effective
mechanism for preventing economic and social differentiation and
securing an integrated community.

But naive though the picture the intellectuals held might have been,
it coincided in a vague way with what they could assume were the
peasants' *aspirations*, as they had been expressed. There was undoubtedly a peasant revolutionary tradition, which lay in the revolt of
the seventeenth and eighteenth centuries, from Bolotnikov to Pugachev.
The long-lasting myths of 'return' that they engendered were permeated with dramatic beliefs proclaiming the imminent arrival of a
messiah who would bring to an end the suffering of ages and establish a
golden dawn of abundance and tranquillity that would last for ever.[37]

The disappointments of political activity among the peasantry would
not necessarily destroy the fundamental images with which the revolutionaries operated. In a universe of ideals structured by a poorly
understood Hegelianism, there was no difficulty in believing in an
'invisible people', a hidden kernel or essence trapped within the
irrational appearances of everyday life. Once an ideology appeared that
could offer a political technology for extracting the one from the other,
the myth of the communalist people could be transformed into a project of social engineering.

In Europe, the mood that led from Kant to Hegel was engendered by
the faltering confidence of its rationalist precursors. It was one moment
in the intense, rigorous and serious philosophical debate which had

been a permanent feature of European culture since Descartes. But perhaps the most striking feature of the Russian reception of the European philosophical debate is its lack of seriousness. There was only a brief flirtation with the rationalist mind before the enthusiasm for Hegel swept all before it. The absence of a rigorous native intellectual tradition meant that any critical and creative acceptance was displaced by intoxicated speculation based upon ill-digested nostrums. Modern commentators concur on the essential *superficiality* of the treatment given to these, and subsequent, intellectual imports into Russia.[38] From Hegel, the Russians derived only a belief in a naive historical teleology, a superficial and indiscriminate critique of western intellectual and social development, and an essentialism which *ab initio* defied all need for empirical verification. All this became the grounding for the mission of this radical intelligentsia: to act as midwives to the mission of ancient Russia itself, which was to give the world the example of a society which declined to follow the erroneous path of western rationalism and liberalism, but instead reconstituted an integrated human psyche within the organic society. The national roots of Lenin's project for the commune-state begin to appear.

From the 1850s, the old radicalism was overlaid by the adoption of a scientific or positivist philosophy, and its proponents declared a definitive rupture with the beliefs of the previous generation. But this 'materialist' revolution suffered from the same lack of caution, subtlety and creativity. The Russians adopted the crudest form of mechanical materialism, whereby the whole world could be reduced to basic physical or chemical processes. Pipes points out how they remained in blissful ignorance of the philosophical crisis that assailed this simplistic scientism in the form of the neo-Kantian criticisms of mechanistic science. Feuerbach and the materialists of the early nineteenth century remained the idols in this religion of uncomplicated materialism.[39]

But the radicals could now subscribe to a belief in the possibility of an absolute rupture with the specifics of history and environment, and the creation of a 'new man' from the primal socio-biological material. This was emphatically not the new man of the Enlightenment vision of rationality. This was one who would reject the false sirens of western individualism in favour of voluntary submergence in the collective. The emergence of social and individual differentiation, which was both the prize and the penalty of the western path, was to be avoided; as were, therefore, the institutions which expressed this diversity. Thus it would appear that the 'materialist revolution' in Russian social thought was not allowed to penetrate to the level of fundamental anthropology. The same mystical essence – appearance polarity was now simply reinforced by the possibility of a new *practicality*. The Hegelian generation had been hard put to define a practical programme for themselves, let alone find a means by which it might be carried out. The new radicals, however, could derive from their iconoclastic scientism a diversity of strategy and tactics. They were no longer bound by what history had produced, and condemned to be the passive òbservers of an unfolding historical process. They could, by spreading ideas, or by practical grassroots activity, or by exemplary and provocative violence, dictate the course of political development. Their ability to reduce the complex intellectual innovations of Europe to the simplest of axioms produced an unbounded confidence in their own potential.

We can in this story already discover the essential elements on which Lenin's model could be built. The maximalist rejection of 'practical' politics and institutions; the dramatic eschatology which grounded the concept of the new man, for whom politics as social diversity and conflict would be alien; the positive image of the peasant commune as model; the unique 'Russian' – naturally translated by Lenin into 'proletarian' – essence that would make this viable, are all themes we have already encountered in the discussion of *The State and Revolution*. These are the creative images out of which the future could be conjured. Miasmic and simple-minded they may well be, but it is important to remember how dramatically they could be confirmed by the negative experience of the Russian reality. It is hardly surprising that Lenin's estimation of the problems of bureaucracy, politics and the state differed so widely from the European themes articulated by Weber. His bureaucracy, his state machine, entirely lacked the elements which were the central organizing principles of the modern state. His state was characterized by corruption, inefficiency, irregularity of procedures, particular interest, secrecy, arbitrariness and all the other sins which Weber insisted it was the task of the modern state to eradicate, not to sustain. It was Lenin's tragedy that he could not see that what he was articulating was not a theory of the modern state, but a critique of the primeval and obsolescent Russian example.

I have in previous chapters placed some emphasis upon Lenin's failure to grasp the truth, among others, of two aspects of the modern state: first, that of the rule of law, and second, that of the precise nature and role of the bureaucracy. These failures may now be attributed to some extent to the fact that in autocratic Russia phenomena existed which went by the same name, but bore no resemblance to the European examples.

We may recall the essence of Lenin's unremitting hostility to the modern state. There was, he asserted, only one possible relationship between the people and the state, and that was one of bitter conflict. The state existed only to maintain the monopoly of power and wealth held by the privileged, and it was consequently a machine of 'monstrous oppression'. Whence derived this powerful, appalling image? For it clearly did not fit in such unequivocal form either with the experience of western Europe or with the mainstream of political thought that derived from and commented upon that experience.

In Lenin's experience there existed no possible connection between the state and freedom, there was only a profound antagonism. Yet the European experience was different. There the connection between the state and freedom was law. In Europe, the rise of the modern state was bound up with the construction of a legal system designed to fill the vacuum left in the regulation of social relationships by the disappearance of the feudal networks of rights and obligations. Thus a legal system provided a system of security for the citizen which ensured a regularity of both public and private behaviour. The persuasive virtue of such a system was not whether the laws were 'good' or 'bad', i.e. whether they favoured the privileged or otherwise, but that they provided a stable framework within which life might be lived. It was often the disruption of this stability due to the flouting of laws by traditionalist monarchs which aroused the revolutionary fury of the seventeenth, eighteenth and nineteenth centuries.

It took no great feat of perception to see that if a legal system was something to be valued, then its necessary concomitant was the existence of the modern state, of which it was but a part. Courts needed agencies to make the laws; they clearly also needed agencies of policing and punishment to render them meaningful. Herein arises the ambiguity of the European experience of the state which escaped Lenin, as it escaped most of his compatriots and predecessors. Ulam comments on the philosophy of the man who was possibly the first Russian revolutionary: 'Pestel may be excused for not realizing, in 1820, the necessary link between freedom and the government of laws.'[40] But those who followed were to be no more perceptive; and perhaps for a good reason.

At least until 1864, no concept of independent justice existed in Russia. Crimes committed by one person against another, or by a public official against a citizen, were no matters of public concern. A legal code was first issued in 1649, but rapidly became irrelevant, and had anyway little to offer for the redress of private grievance. Under Nicholas I a new code was issued, but to little effect, since the actual practices of justice were so dubious. The government initiated legal actions only when the state itself, or one of its agents, had been offended. Private individuals were left to their own resources, and usually simply bought justice – or, more accurately, a decision in their favour – by payments to the court secretary. No one was, anyway, very sure about what laws they should be obeying, since laws and decrees were promulgated in an entirely haphazard fashion, requiring only the approval of the Tsar, and new laws were in fact often kept secret from the citizens.

Alexander II's attempts to transform Russia into a state grounded in law were consequently ill-fated. For his attempts appear to have met with a cynicism on the part of public opinion which condemned his efforts to failure. When the government attempted to try terrorists as ordinary rather than political criminals before the newly established juries, the accused were often acquitted despite the undisputed – and often proudly admitted – evidence against them. Citizens rendered judgements based not on the merits of a case, but on their abhorrence for the regime of the gendarmes and their sympathy for the idealistic defendants. The regime that had for so long confronted even its most sophisticated and moderate critics with a legal system that was political and biased to its very core was unable to convince them that here was a system to be run according to different principles. The citizens simply responded by using the new system as a vehicle for their *own* politics. In consequence the government reverted to its old methods of administrative justice, a step which of course confirmed liberal public opinion in its original estimation of the government's initiative. Therefore it was quite understandable that the concept of the rule of law should fail to find any place in Lenin's thought, even though such a failure is a further indication of his regrettable intellectual limitations.

His image of the nature of bureaucracy is similarly home-grown. We can clearly establish the origins of his near obsession with bureaucratic corruption, and his characterization of civil servants as unprincipled seekers after cash, in the Russian system of 'feeding'. For centuries, Russian public servants had been expected to 'feed themselves from official business'. That is they were paid no salary, but were expected to provide for themselves out of monies raised within the district under their administration. It was their sole obligation to send to Moscow a fixed sum of revenue, and their standard of living then depended upon the degree to which they were able to supplement this sum for their own purposes. Clearly, the system provided licence for corruption of the widest kind. Honest public officials were only to be found in the centre, staffing the ministerial offices, an innovation imported from Germany, and greatly appreciated by the imperial regime. Anywhere outside Moscow and one or two other urban centres, it was commonly accepted that civil servants were not just corruptible, but that public administration was synonymous with corruption. In terms of the images the leading Bolsheviks held of the state machine, then, it is perhaps significant that Lenin lived in provincial Russia until the age of twenty-three. He was born in Simbirsk, a provincial town on the Volga, briefly attended Kazan University, moved with his family to Samara, spent another equally brief period at St Petersburg University in 1891 and returned to Samara to practise law before moving more permanently to St Petersburg in 1893. Bukharin, by contrast, was a Muscovite, and spent only four years of his life in Russia outside that great city. Lenin, presumably, would have been acquainted with only the most tawdry aspects of the imperial state, while Bukharin would have known an animal of an entirely different, and more modern, species. Thus Weber might make sense to Bukharin, but never could to Lenin.

## LENIN'S THEORY OF POLITICAL MOTIVATION

It was from this background that Lenin was forced to attempt a reconstruction of his understanding of the world. The reconstruction he achieved was considerable, inasmuch as it resulted in a world view that was entirely coherent and consistently revolutionary. It was a rather less impressive achievement in terms of its complexity or subtlety and, indeed, its adequacy. It comprised three basic organizing principles: imperialism, the labour aristocracy and the soviet. Imperialism was the problem, the labour aristocracy was the basis of the continued existence of the problem, and the soviet form encapsulated Lenin's new answer. Concisely, the development of capitalism into imperialism had provided the bourgeoisie in the metropolitan countries with the opportunity to undermine the proletarian progress to revolutionary politics that had previously been considered inevitable. The labour aristocracy was a section of the proletariat that had been detached from its true class allegiance, and consequently become enmeshed in the fabric and institutions of bourgeois society. Thus, the bourgeois state, in both its administrative and political forms, had become the core of the process whereby the organizations of the proletariat were delivered up to imperialist politics. Lenin hinted at a fairly sophisticated model of this relationship when he coined the term 'Lloyd-Georgeism'[41] to describe the impact of social reform upon the labour movement. This analytical avenue, however, remained emphatically underdeveloped, and in its place is an argument of a much simpler nature. Reformist politics were, in this argument, not a mass political phenomenon; they were confined to the labour aristocracy.

This reduction is perhaps surprising, and certainly not necessary for Lenin's project of salvaging revolutionary politics. Lenin could have argued – as we have seen Colletti argue – that the institutional forms of parliamentarism paralysed the revolutionary impulses of the proletariat by a combination of social atomization, manipulation and mystification. The soviet form could have been offered as the counter to all three processes. Such an argument would render redundant a concept of the labour aristocracy as specially significant in diverting the revolutionary process. There is no need to single out any distinct part of the working class as uniquely guilty of bearing, conspiring in or succumbing to the culture of social peace and parliamentary progress. But the organizing principle of Lenin's explanation for the split in socialism was not the rejection of parliamentarism, but the definition and critique of the labour aristocracy. It is possible to trace in the development of Lenin's analysis the gradual disappearance of the effects of peaceful decades, parliamentarism, legal organizations, etc., and their replacement by direct and crude material determinants effecting a small minority of the movement: crumbs, bribes, 'lucrative and soft jobs'.[42] Lenin thus chose to pursue a far simpler analysis which, paradoxically, involves a far more complex and weaker chain of explanation if the soviet form is to be justified.

In that analysis, the proletariat constitutes a 'silent majority', those who have simply not been heard from. But, if the masses do not appear to have succumbed to the charms of parliamentarism and social peace, it is hardly necessary to advocate the soviet form to counter such dangers. At this point in the argument, therefore, there exists no necessary or useful connection between Lenin's analysis of the split in socialism and the Soviet alternative. What I shall seek to do is suggest the necessary connection that in fact does exist. For it seems to me that the institutions of the commune-state that Lenin was to advocate in 1917 derive their viability from a theory of political motivation, and that this theory of motivation can be discovered as the fundamental assumption of the theory of the labour aristocracy.

We can find a concise and representative statement of the analysis in the 1920 Preface to *Imperialism, the Highest State of Capitalism*:

> Capital exports yield an income of eight to ten thousand million francs per annum, at pre-war prices and according to pre-war bourgeois statistics. Now, of course, they yield much more.
>
> Obviously, out of such enormous superprofits (since they are obtained over and above the profits which capitalists can squeeze out of the workers of their 'own' country) it is possible to *bribe* the labour leaders and the upper stratum of the labour aristocracy. And this is just what the capitalists of the 'advanced countries' are doing, they are bribing them in a thousand different ways, direct and indirect, overt and covert.
>
> This stratum of workers-turned-bourgeois, or the labour aristocracy who are quite philistine in their mode of life, in the size of their earnings and in their entire outlook, is the principal prop of the Second International, and in our days, the principal social (not military) prop of the bourgeoisie. For they are the real agents of the bourgeoisie in the working class movement, the labour lieutenants of the capitalist class, real vehicles of reformism and chauvinism.[43]

I shall not seek to present a comprehensive critique of the theories of imperialism and the labour aristocracy. Although it should be clear from what follows that I find both of them inadequate as explanatory categories, there already exists a varied literature to this effect, and to retell it would be redundant.[44] I shall seek only to register some points which may reveal the theory of political motivation produced by these concepts.

First, Lenin's concept of imperialism is one that cannot be seriously sustained by the arguments that he presented. In *Imperialism, the Highest Stage of Capitalism*, written in 1916, Lenin outlines the general features of the imperialist stage of capitalism, stressing what he considers to be the key factor – the export of capital from the metropolitan countries to the colonies or semi-colonies. In chapter 8 he considers the effects of this on the metropolitan nations. An extensive quote from Hobson advocates the idea that the western nations were becoming totally parasitic in their economic role, drawing all productive wealth from the Asian and African continents. The result,

Lenin suggests, will be the transformation of the proletariat into 'great tame masses of retainers, no longer engaged in the staple industries of agriculture and manufacture, but kept in the performance of personal or minor industrial services under the control of the new financial aristocracy'.[45] The condition of southern England is advanced as a foreshadow of what might come to pass. He then proceeds to offer evidence for Hobson's analysis. He seems to support the vision of the gradual disappearance of manufacturing capital from western Europe. But his evidence is rather bizarre: an increasing proportion of land in England is being taken out of cultivation and used for sport and the diversion of the rich; England spends annually £14 million on horse-racing and fox-hunting; the number of rentiers in England is about 1 million. The corollary of those tendencies is this: 'The percentage of the productively employed population to the total population is declining' – from 23 per cent in 1851 to 15 per cent in 1901. The surprising scale of these figures would have given anyone less committed to the thesis pause for thought. In fact Lenin is equating 'productively employed' with those 'employed in the basic industries', which by any economic theory is an insupportable device.[46]

Of course it is true that the economic structure of the country was undergoing change, but both Lenin and Hobson entirely misconstrued what was happening. An advanced stage of industrialization produces tendencies for the service sector to undergo expansion at the expense of the primary and secondary sectors. Together with the development of the service sector went the extension of the factory system into previously marginally involved sectors, and the transformation into a factory workforce of parts of the population whose situation was previously quite different. The decline in the numbers employed in domestic service and the reverse process of the increase in industrial employment of women, prefigured by developments in the First World War, are indicative of this. Note should also be taken of the growing industrialization of agriculture, and the growing productivity of labour *within* the manufacturing sector which must, on the one hand, produce a tendency for slow or negative growth in employment in that sector and, on the other, growing employment among those sectors needed to service the technical developments reflected by this rise in the productivity of labour.[47]

Lenin therefore constructed an entirely mythical sociological grouping under the category 'labour aristocracy' – 'great tame masses of retainers'. They lived off the 'crumbs' from the table of imperialism;

they were directly bribed out of superprofits. Lenin even gave a rough estimate of the size of this bribe,[48] although no attempt is made to define the method of distribution of this subvention. But what is clear is that Lenin nowhere considers this 'bribe' as passing through, or deriving from, the process of production in the metropolitan countries. High wages do not come from the worker's position in the production process; they are purely the dividend of parasitism. The labour aristocrats have become the 'coupon-clippers' of the working class. Clearly, such a mechanism can only have an utterly corrupting influence on those in receipt. Recipients of such an unearned and unjustified subsidy will surely fight to the death to defend the imperialism that provided it. The labour aristrocrat becomes akin to the Roman proletarian, whose existence was subsidized by the slave economy, unlike the non-aristocracy at whose expense society lives.[49] But what an absurd inversion of reality this constitutes, and its absurdity clashes more fundamentally with the assumptions of Marxian social theory than perhaps any other.

The higher-paid worker in Lenin's time achieved and maintained his position due to his skill – or rather to the short supply of that skill – or his organization, and usually by a very specific combination of both. It is puzzling that such a simple fact should escape Lenin's analysis, but two factors may account for this. The first, of course, is that Lenin's project excluded the realization: he was not seeking to explain the origin of the higher-paid worker, but simply to utilize it as a link in the chain of his explanation, proceeding from imperialism to the politics of the day. Second, there was little in Lenin's experience, or in his field of interest, to direct his attention to the simple explanation. *Imperialism, the Highest Stage of Capitalism* is a remarkably one-sided study of early-twentieth-century capitalism. It concentrates exclusively on methods of ownership and finance and excludes any consideration of the industrial process itself, i.e. *what* was being produced, and *how*. The remarkable changes in the techniques of production and the nature of finished products is entirely absent. One may wonder precisely what image Lenin possessed of the twentieth-century factory and those who worked there.

Thus, if we read *Imperialism* as at least in part directed to establishing the existence of a distinct social grouping which is essentially parasitic and unproductive, we have to register Lenin's attempt as a failure. He has failed to prove that such a group emerges as a consequence of economic development in an imperialist phase. As a result, he has further failed to demonstrate the existence of a social grouping which will be motivated to defend its native imperialism as a matter of automatic self-interest.

My second point concerns the assumptions which would be necessary to sustain the argument for this postulated social group. Lenin makes a silent but necessary assumption that the wages of members of the proletariat have a historic tendency to maintain, and always return to, a certain physical minimum. Otherwise there is nothing to explain in the particular condition of the labour aristocracy. This concept of an 'iron law of wages' is strangely resilient in the Marxian tradition. Bernstein made use of it as a stick with which to beat Marxism, and his criticisms were justified. He was castigating a belief that was widely held and articulated among the orthodox theoreticians of the movement. Kautsky included it in his popular explanation of the Erfurt programme in 1892: 'industrial development exhibits a tendency, most pleasing to the capitalist, to lower the necessities of the working man and to decrease his wages in proportion.'[50] It became a commonplace article of faith in the communist movement, in defiance of whatever evidence to the contrary might have suggested. It was possible fifty years later for Kuczynski to insist:

> conditions among the working class in Britain, on the average, did not improve during the second half of the nineteenth century. . . . Whenever we are able to point to improvements we are at the same time, unfortunately, obliged to point to deteriorations which over-compensate the improvements in the conditions of the working class during the last fifty or hundred years.[51]

The author, a Marxist historian, could only support this statement by suggesting a picture of British capitalism which left little room for the development of forces and techniques of production. Thus, in a discussion of productivity changes, he ascribed by far the greatest importance to the aspect of the 'increased intensity of labour per worker', i.e. the workers working harder, and only a minor significance to the revolutionizing of the techniques of production.[52]

It has been argued[53] that there is in fact no ambiguity on this issue in Marx's political economy. Nevertheless we can only note the frequent recurrence of this theme within the Marxian political movement. Such an assumption could clearly play an important political role at moments when employers have enforced reductions in wages and conditions in specific conjunctures. It enables a political argument to make the transition from the problem of the moment to the problem of the system. It is clearly a matter of some speculation how effective the theory of revolution remains when Marx's theory is substituted for the iron law of wages. When Colletti declares that

> It is the dependence which ties the workers to the will of the capitalist class, and not their absolute poverty . . . in other words, capitalist appropriation is not exclusively or primarily an appropriation of things, but rather an appropriation of subjectivity,[54]

a theory of revolutionary action becomes markedly more problematic.

The iron law of wages demands little empirical refutation. Rising living standards were common to the British working class in the latter part of the nineteenth century. There was undoubtedly a minority that was better off than most, but the differential was modest. It should also be noted that the existence of differentials was in no way unique to the imperialist stage of capitalism. In the light of the long-standing nature of the phenomenon, and the relatively minor material differentiation between the skilled and the unskilled, imperialist superprofits are an unnecessary import into the discussion. Far from the labour aristocracy being a creation of the bourgeoisie for political motives, made possible by their returns from the colonies, it is further arguable that such differentials underwent a tendency to diminish for some time before Lenin wrote his book.[55]

Third, whatever the economic facts, Lenin's appreciation of the politics of the higher-paid worker was an inversion of the truth. Clearly, ideas of respectability and conservatism could very easily flow from social stability and, more specifically, from the craftsman's elevated role in production. But very often situations of crisis or structural change produced among such people a fabric of consciousness that made them extremely and uniquely amenable to radical ideas. The experience of the communist parties after the war testifies to this. In most parties, workers from the skilled trades constituted the largest single elements of the membership, and if one considers the relatively small size of those groups in the working class as a whole, the attraction of communist politics for such people is clearly markedly stronger than among unskilled workers.[56] Nevertheless, for Lenin, the primary task of the communist parties after the war remained an 'immediate, systematic, comprehensive, and open struggle . . . against this stratum'.[57] The obverse of the dismissal of the 'top 10 per cent' was an exceedingly sanguine picture of what Lenin terms the 'revolutionary masses'. In

August 1914 he drew a sharp distinction between the opportunist leaders and the mass of the working class, insisting that it was 'imperative to appeal to the revolutionary consciousness of the working masses, who bear the entire burden of the war and are in most cases hostile to opportunism and chauvinism',[58] and in 1915 he declared: 'It is a falsehood for anybody . . . to say that the "masses" of proletarians have turned towards chauvinism: nowhere have the masses been asked.'[59] Clearly, such assertions had very little relation to the reality of the time. Thus Lenin's political sociology of the working classes of Western Europe, already theoretically dubious, can find no serious empirical support.

My fourth point concerns the effects of the weaknesses outlined above upon any more general theorization of the sociology of class and politics. It will be remembered that early in his career, Lenin advanced a particular version of the relationship between the two. He then asserted that, without the activity of political parties, the working class was incapable of developing a politics that escaped from what he called 'trade union consciousness'.[60] He had no reason to ascribe to the working class a mass politics that automatically reflected their class interests. Even later, during the 1905 revolution, his assertion that the working class was 'spontaneously social-democratic' was linked to the prior activities of political radicals within the labour movement, who had made the ideas available throughout the working class; and it should be noted that such a social democratic consciousness at that time probably for Lenin amounted to little more than a broad sympathy with the general aims of the overthrow of autocracy.[61] When he suggested the existence of a similar spontaneous political ideology among the masses after 1914, he was in fact suggesting the existence of ideas and sympathies considerably more sophisticated and rigorous: sympathy not merely for social reform, political democracy and social justice, but for specific attitudes towards conjunctural political issues of the day.

Lenin's thesis on 'trade union consciousness' was in itself not notably sophisticated, but it did contain the possibility of elaboration into a reasonably adequate statement of the culture of a subaltern class. It could, in other words, have been developed into a concept somewhat akin to Gramsci's idea of 'hegemony', wherein there is an appreciation of the complexity of the way in which society, class and culture constitute the network of meanings through which people see the world and experience their activities. As long as Lenin did not assume political consciousness to be an automatic reflection of class position, the opportunity remained for him to appreciate the political domain in all its diversity and complexity. But it must be pointed out that the 'trade union consciousness' theme itself was not even a simpler version of Gramsci's sophisticated sociology. In itself, it remained true to Lenin's reflectionist epistemology, for trade union consciousness is little more than a reflection of the specific factory situation in which the worker is placed: it does not allow room to take into account the far more important determinations that existed 'outside' the workplace: national culture, religion, socialization, authority patterns, etc. – not forgetting politics itself.

Nevertheless, Lenin remained for some time aware of sociological tendencies that produced in the working class a resistance to his politics. He referred to Engels' castigation of the 'bourgeois "respectability" which has grown deep into the bones of the workers'[62] in his discussion of England. In 1908 he suggested that the material locus of these tendencies lay in the 'small producers [who are] being cast into the ranks of the proletariat'[63] as capitalism develops. Two years later he made an attempt to define the causes of 'opportunism' in broader terms. The continued growth of the labour movement itself constantly introduced to its ranks those unschooled in its practices and ideology; the development of capitalism is uneven in pace and depth, recruiting to the labour movement many who were unable to make the break with the ideology of the enemy; the oppressive aspect of capitalist development – its degradation, its poverty – often counter-balanced the potential inscribed in the newly disciplined and organized workers; and the activities of the bourgeoisie itself must not be overlooked, as it had developed the tactic of conceding political rights and reforms which hampered the revolutionary development of the class.[64]

It is worth stressing at this point that even these relatively sophisticated definitions of the origins of political differences in the working class do not legitimize politics. That is, political ideas that are not sympathetic to Lenin's own are attributed to lags and lacunae in the movement of history; they remain, for Lenin, both incorrect and transitory. Even at this early stage, the possibility that political disagreements might simply testify to different value orientations or to conflicting political strategies is absent. Nevertheless, even such an approach provided for an understanding that was considerably more complex than what was to follow. Lenin was to come to deny the very existence of problematic political ideas within the bulk of the working class, and replace it with the idea of a clean ideological break between aristocracy and mass. His first reformulations of the problem after 1914 contain something of the old discussion. He referred to the results of 'the preceding peaceful period in the development of the labour movement . . . [which] taught the working class to utilise such important means of struggle as parliamentarism and all legal opportunities'.[65]

In these writings from 1914 and 1915 there is a dimension that is missing from later works. While attention is already directed to the importance of the labour aristocracy in this problem, their role is subordinate and not key in the analysis. But in his first major theoretical accounting with 'opportunism', *The Collapse of the Second International*, written in the middle of 1915, Lenin begins to confine the roots of this political practice to much more directly material factors than the 'peaceful decades'. The opportunist ideas of the labour aristocracy are no longer simply different from those of the mass of the proletariat in *degree* – perhaps due to their greater access to political expression and material improvement – but are directly counterposed to the rest of the class. A stratum of 'working men' has become 'bourgeoisified' during the period of economic growth and social stability, and consequently is isolated from the problems and ideas that permeate the lower masses. It is here that the breeding ground of chauvinist and opportunist ideas may be found.[66]

This is perhaps the first clear indication of the road that Lenin is to travel. The analysis has undergone what, even for Lenin, is a profound impoverishment. Almost ten years earlier he had already suggested a specific connection between 'opportunism' and the imperialist stage of capitalism, but he did not attempt to confine the effects of opportunism to a minority of the proletariat. He limited himself to the general suggestion that 'in certain countries [colonial profits provide] a material and economic basis for infecting the proletariat with colonial chauvinism'.[67] But the development of the theory from 1914 onwards is to narrow the causes of opportunism to imperialist superprofits, and the extent of opportunism to a labour aristocracy. Various descriptions of the infected stratum are given. Initially the description is confined to 'leaders' – parliamentarian, trade union, journalistic and other.[68] Then it is extended to 'Parliamentarians, officials of the legal labour unions, and other intellectuals . . . some sections of the better paid workers, office employees etc.'[69]

Lenin is dissatisfied with such a definition. It conflates two distinct categories, the 'labour aristocracy' and the 'labour bureaucracy'. He therefore attempts to define more precisely the sociology of this phenomenon. In later writings there are many attempts to identify the roots of opportunist politics in the labour aristocracy. What is this aristocracy? It variously includes 'the better paid workers', a 'petty-bourgeois "upper stratum" or aristocracy . . . of the working class', 'certain strata of the proletariat', 'near-proletarian elements', 'non-proletarian elements', a 'stratum of workers-turned-bourgeois . . . who are quite philistine in their mode of life, in the size of their earnings and their entire outlook', the 'upper stratum' that 'furnishes the bulk of the membership of the cooperatives, of trade unions, of sporting clubs and of the numerous religious sects', 'a section of the proletariat' that has 'become bourgeois', 'workers belonging to narrow craft unions', those infected by 'bourgeois respectability', etc.[70] A glance at these definitions reveals their remarkable variety – and consequently their conceptual vagueness. If Lenin were attempting to proceed from a general theory of the roots of opportunism to investigate the specificity of the phenomenon in various countries such oscillations would not be remarkable. Precise analyses would show differentiation according to national context. But this is not a precise analysis. These definitions are taken from attempts to state a *general* theory of opportunism. In this context such vagueness of definition points to problems in the theoretical schema itself.

Theoretically, we have reached a desperate pass. The sophisticated sociology offered by Marx has been reduced to a conceptually attenuated and empirically unsupportable *deus ex machina*, a scapegoat upon whom all the sins are heaped. The concept of the labour aristocracy is made to serve as the explanatory category for the problems of a world that has become in Lenin's mind simplified beyond reason. But does the demonstration of this have any consequences for the wider issues of political theory that have been discussed in previous chapters? My fifth point brings us to the consequences of the problems highlighted in this section.

It would seem that Lenin's reconstruction of revolutionary theory after 1914 is a remarkable failure. I have argued that in many respects he was simply *wrong*: wrong on the nature of imperialism; wrong on the economic trends in the capitalist nations; wrong on the roots of 'opportunism'; wrong in his definition and understanding of the 'labour aristocracy'; wrong on the politics of the 'masses'; wrong in his understanding of Marxian political economy; wrong in his appreciation of the changing role of the European state. Is not the whole enterprise, therefore, essentially valueless, and an examination of it redundant?

It is and it isn't. A reconstruction of Lenin's last problematic reveals the coherent structure of his world view. All that remains to be done is to allow the silent parts of that problematic to speak. The importance of the concept of the 'labour aristocracy' is that it articulates Lenin's theory of political motivation. He begins by constructing the *tabula rasa* of human consciousness. That is, the anathema is pronounced on all and any points of view, whether in natural science or in political theory, that differ from Lenin's own version of the Marxian world view. All such points of view are delegitimized *a priori*. They are not just 'wrong': that still casts the issue in terms of opinion. They are epiphenomenal and ephemeral. They are the products of specific and demonstrable *impurities* in the historical stream, and their transcience is ensured by the fact that history *moves*. It may be for this reason that Marxian politics has tended to enter a crisis when confronted with the development of cultures and institutions that legitimize difference.

Marx wrote in a period where there was consensus between the radical and the reactionary forces about the impossibility of a pluralistic and consensual politics. The reactionaries hid behind a battery of privilege, restrictions and exclusions even when allegedly in a democratic phase. The revolutionaries could not constitute democracy as an end in itself because its most positive role would be as midwife to the dismissal of their political enemies from the historical stage. The evolution of liberal democracy must thus occasion a horrendous confusion. The repeal of Bismarck's Anti-Socialist Law in 1890 was bound to produce a Bernstein by the end of the decade. The turn of the century in Russia replicated that crisis. Traditional characterizations of Russian society and economy between 1900 and 1914 as 'backward' have tended to exaggeration, as have the negative estimates of the policies of various 'reforming' ministries, notably of Witte and Stolypin. Political life was similarly subject to transformative impulses. Keep has suggested that this was the consequence of 1905. As a result of the relaxation of political repression, the radicals were confronted with a quite unfamiliar world of 'competitive open politics', in which much of their established thought and practice became simply irrelevant.[71] Some rethinking became a rather urgent task, to come to terms with the new context. In fact, the 'liberalizing' consequences of 1905 had deeper roots than the government's need to appease and manipulate. Society itself had changed in the preceding years, and was becoming more widely differentiated: culture, education, a liberal press all expanded rapidly, and, as a consequence, 'a Western-style political life was beginning to emerge'.[72]

It would be wrong to exaggerate these developments; but even in a modest form they introduced confusions into the Marxian camp. Russian social democracy had its Bernstein, in the form of Struve; the same tendencies launched Plekhanov on his slow journey towards 're-visionism'.[73] Even a minimal liberalization and democratization implies the possibility of evolution towards something more substantial. This must occasion fissures in any hermetic Marxian model of politics as the direct articulation of transparent class interests, a conflict between science and ideology, bodies of views buttressed by the whole armoury of uncompromising 'struggle'. Liberalization in fact undermines the central metaphor of Marxian politics, the 'class struggle'. How can a process saturated with the features of direct physical confrontation, mentally encapsulated in some image of brutal hand-to-hand combat, be reconciled to an image of ordered, genteel debate and negotiation? Such activities must be 'ploys' or instrumental and cynical tactics.

Lenin's first move is, therefore, to eradicate politics. The development of liberal democracy carries the awful possibility that disagreement over political policies, and negotiations over them, can become a legitimate activity. But to accept *that* is to accept that political positions are opinion, not fact; values, not science. Lenin must find this unacceptable – *his* ideas to be forced to 'compete' as an equal with those of liberalism, Struvism, Populism, constitutionalism? It is inconceivable. And the greatest embarrassment for Lenin is the politics of opposing tendencies within his own camp. The politics of the bourgeois and liberal parties can be attributed to uncomplicated class interests – whether they are being brutal in establishing dictatorships or conciliatory in introducing ameliorative and liberalizing measures. The apparent distance of any measure from obvious class interests is a matter of subtlety, nothing else. The politics of reformists, opportunists, Mensheviks, revisionists are another problem. They clearly betray a transparent class interest. A specific attribution must be found for this. But the only possible attribution is a version of the same interest. Politics is private self-interest made public. Thus Lenin's first move is to abolish any possible distance between the gross economic position of an individual and his motivations; to abolish any space for 'values', and consequently, disagreement over values. This first movement leads into the second: it is necessary only to construct a sub-set of *interests* for his political opponents in the working-class camp. This is the labour aristocracy, who have specific incomes and conditions to protect. We have already seen how the concept of motivation by self-interest permeates the pages of *The State and Revolution*. The theory of the labour aristocracy is Lenin's most consummate expression of this theory of political motivation. For crassness, vulgarity and inadequacy it perhaps has few competitors. But it achieves the necessary tasks. With this theory his Marxism is once again secured as science, not opinion. Its very success in this task will ensure its immunity from interrogation.

It is important to appreciate what Lenin has achieved by this simple sociological reduction. *He has ensured that politics is an ontological impossibility*. That is, there can be no genuine differences of *opinion* within political life. He has pushed to the limit the possibilities of economic reductionism that Marxism might contain. Each and every disagreement with Lenin's version of Marxist principle and policy can now be revealed as simply disguising the material self-interest of its proponents. Clearly, the advent of a society in which the economic grounds for conflict have been removed is also the advent of a society where there is no possibility of political disagreement and debate. Thus is grounded the theory of *The State and Revolution*, which promises the free society through institutions designed to cater for human beings who have no politics. And thus is founded the actuality of Bolshevik police-socialism, which implements those theories in a situation where human beings do, unfortunately, assert themselves politically.

## NOTES

1  L. Althusser, *For Marx*, London, 1977, 219.
2  ibid., 222–31.
3  C. Taylor, *Hegel and Modern Society*, Cambridge, 1979, 8, 9.
4  R. Plant, *Hegel*, London, 1973, 25.
5  Taylor, op. cit., 51.
6  G. Lukacs, *History and Class Consciousness*, London, 1971, *passim*.
7  T. Adorno, *Negative Dialectics*, London, 1973, 22.
8  ibid., 362.
9  Cited by Althusser in *Lenin and Philosophy*, London, 1971, 34.
10  For a discussion of this, see

A. Cutler, B. Hindess, P. Hirst and A. Hussain, *Marx's Capital and Capitalism Today*, 1, London, 1977, 189–95. For the reception given to Lukacs' ideas see P. Breines, 'Praxis and its theorists', *Telos*, 11 (Spring 1982), 67–103. For a more complex discussion of Lukacs' philosophical import, see L. Goldman, *Lukacs and Heidegger*, London, 1977. The impact of Korsch's writings at the time should not be underestimated, especially *Marxism and Philosophy*, London, 1972. Merleau-Ponty's *Adventures of the*

*Dialectic*, London, 1974, is an indispensable discussion of 'western Marxism'.

11 For an account of the activities of the left communists in Germany by a participant, see P. Mattick, 'Anti-Bolshevist communism in Germany', *Telos*, 26 (Winter 1975–6), 57–69, and *Anti-Bolshevik Communism*, London, 1978, *passim*.

12 L. Trotsky, *1905*, New York, 1971, 220–3 for example.

13 S. Schram, *Mao Tse Tung*, London, 1967, 'Conclusion', 313–16.

14 For example, M. Liebman, *Leninism under Lenin*, London, 1975, 433; V. Gerratana, 'Stalin, Lenin and Leninism', *New Left Review*, 103 (1977).

15 K. Marx, 'The class struggles in France', in the Pelican Marx Library, *Political Writings*, 2, London, 1973, 71.

16 L. Colletti, *From Rousseau to Lenin*, London, 1972, 108.

17 A. Rosenberg, *Democracy and Socialism*, Boston, 1965, 306.

18 K. Kautsky, *The Class Struggle*, New York, 1971, 187, 188. Some of these issues are touched on in J. Braunthal, *History of the International 1864–1914*, London, 1966.

19 Lenin, *Inflammable Material in World Politics* (1908), *Collected Works (CW)*, Moscow and London, 1960–70, vol. 15, 186.

20 Lenin, *Draft and Explanation of the Programme for the Social-Democratic Party* (1895), *CW*, 2, 96.

21 Lenin, *What the 'Friends of the People' Are* (1894), *CW*, 1, 291.

22 Kautsky, op. cit., 186.

23 Lenin, *Draft and Explanation of the Programme for the Social-Democratic Party*, 119.

24 Kautsky, op. cit., 186.

25 Lenin, *The Third Duma* (1907), *CW*, 13, 129.

26 L. Kochan, *Russia in Revolution*, London, 1967, 127.

27 Lenin, *Report on the Unity Congress of the RSDLP* (1906), *CW*, 10, 352, 353.

28 Cited in L. Getzler, *Martov*, Cambridge, 1967, 105.

29 ibid., 108.

30 Liebman, *Leninism under Lenin*, 98.

31 E. W. Said, *Beginnings*, Baltimore, 1979, 280.

32 A. Besançon, *The Intellectual Origins of Leninism*, Oxford, 1981, 192. For accounts of the 'cultural revolution' that passed Lenin by, see, for example, H. Stuart Hughes, *Consciousness and Society*, London, 1967; A. Janik and S. Toulmin, *Wittgenstein's Vienna*, New York, 1973; F. V. Grunfeld, *Prophets without Honour*, London, 1979; P. Gay, *Freud, Jews, and Other Germans*, Oxford, 1978.

33 G. Therborn, 'The rule of capital and the rise of democracy', *New Left Review*, 103 (1977), 11 and *passim*.

34 P. Anderson, *Lineages of the Absolutist State*, London, 1974, provides a concise and rigorous account.

35 Besançon, op. cit., 95.

36 R. Pipes, *Russia under the Old Regime*, London, 1974, 251.

37 P. Avrich, *Russian Rebels 1600–1800*, London, 1973, 257.

38 For example, Pipes, op. cit.,

chapter 10, *passim*; A. Ulam, *Lenin and the Bolsheviks*, London, 1966, chapter 2, *passim*.

39  Pipes, op. cit., 272.

40  Ulam, op. cit., 32.

41  Lloyd-Georgeism was 'a widely ramified, systematically managed well-equipped system of flattery, lies, fraud, juggling with fashionable and popular catchwords, and promising all manner of reforms and blessings to the workers' (Lenin, *Imperialism and the Split in Socialism* (1916), *CW*, 23, 117). This is still crude, but does at least approach the problem of a *mass* electoral politics.

42  ibid.

43  Lenin, Preface to the French and German editions, *Imperialism, the Highest Stage of Capitalism* (1920), *CW*, 22, 193, 194.

44  There is a large literature on the weaknesses of Lenin's theory of imperialism. The following are a sample: B. Warren, *Imperialism: Pioneer of Capitalism*, London, 1980; M. Barratt Brown, *After Imperialism*, London, 1970, 11–14; D. K. Fieldhouse, *Economics and Empire 1830–1914*, London, 1973, 38–62; Cutler, Hindess, Hirst and Hussain, op. cit., 1. On the labour aristocracy, the following works are relevant: E. J. Hobsbawm, 'Lenin and the labour aristocracy', *Monthly Review*, April 1970, 47–56, and 'The labour aristocracy in the 19th century', in his *Labouring Men*, London, 1964, 272–315; H. Pelling, 'The concept of the labour aristocracy', in his *Popular Politics and Society in Late Victorian Britain*, London, 1968, 37–61; R. Q. Gray, *The Labour Aristocracy in Victorian Edinburgh*, Oxford, 1976. J. Foster, *Class Struggle and the Industrial Revolution*, London, 1974, makes an original use of the concept, but the periodization he adopts distances his concept from that of Lenin – the connection with imperialism is dispensed with. Nevertheless, contributions to the debate opened by Foster often have relevance to Lenin's concepts as well, e.g. A. E. Musson, 'Class struggle and the labour aristocracy 1930–1960', *Social History*, 3 (October 1976), 335–6; G. Stedman Jones, 'Class struggle and the Industrial Revolution', *New Left Review*, 90, 35–69.

45  Lenin, *Imperialism, the Highest Stage of Capitalism*, 280.

46  ibid., 281, 282.

47  Between 1920 and 1938 the most resilient growth sectors in the UK in terms of numbers employed were distribution, insurance and banking (+36 per cent) and 'professional services' (+31 per cent); the reverse was true of sectors like manufacturing and mining. In power supply the increase was 57 per cent (S. Pollard, *The Development of the British Economy 1914–50*, London, 1962, 99). For a discussion of the impulses behind these changes, E. Mandel, *Late Capitalism*, London, 1975, chapter 12, is of interest. For a discussion of how London and south-east England developed in the twentieth century in a directly contrary direction to that

predicted by Hobson and Lenin, see Pollard, op. cit., 129, 130. Their image of 'post-industrial' London derives from a failure to appreciate that at the end of the nineteenth century they were still looking at an essentially *pre*-industrial London. The sociology of such a city is given in G. Stedman-Jones, *Outcast London*, London, 1971, *passim*.

48 '. . . a hundred million or so francs a year . . . [out of] super-profits most likely to amount to about a thousand million' (Lenin, *Imperialism and the Split in Socialism*, 115).

49 ibid., 107.

50 Kautsky, *The Class Struggle*, 24.

51 J. Kuczynski, *A Short History of Labour Conditions under Industrial Capitalism*, 1, London, 1972, 80, 190.

52 For a discussion of changing industrial techniques and products, see D. Landes, *The Unbound Prometheus*, Cambidge, 1969, *passim*, but especially chapter 5, 'Short breath and second wind'.

53 Colletti offers his disproof of Marx's support for an iron law of wages in 'Bernstein and the Marxism of the 2nd International', *From Rousseau to Lenin*, 101, 102. The presence of the law *may* be detected in the Marx of *The Communist Manifesto* (Marx and Engels, *Selected Works*, London, 1968, 43), but by the time of the *Grundrisse* Marx was arguing that the tendency for general living standards to rise under capitalism is 'an essential civilizing moment, and on which the historic

justification, but also the contemporary power, of capital rests' (Marx, *Grundrisse*, London, 1973, 287). A clear statement of the mature theory of wages is given in Marx, *Wages, Price and Profit*, in Marx and Engels, *Selected Works*, 226. Nevertheless, Rosa Luxemburg, for example, lent credence to a version of the iron law in R. Luxemburg, 'Reform or revolution?', *Rosa Luxemburg Speaks*, New York, 1970, 50, and Marx had to criticize its presence in the Gotha Programme of the German Social-Democratic Party. Marx, 'Critique of the Gotha Programme', in Marx and Engels, *Selected Works*, 328, 329.

54 Colletti, 'Bernstein', 102.

55 On rising living standards, see P. Mathias, *The First Industrial Nation*, London, 1969, 378 – 80, who suggests a rise in real wages for the average urban male worker of some 60 per cent or more between 1860 and 1900. On differentials at the turn of the century, see E. Hobsbawm, *Labouring Men*, London, 1964, 291 – 2, who argues that the skilled British worker received better wages than the unskilled in the ratio of between 1.2 : 1 and 2 : 1. This may be contrasted with a ratio of 17.6 : 1 obtaining between the wages of white and black labour in the South African gold-mining industry. Here a genuine labour aristocracy may be said to exist, where the white wage contains a surplus element over the actual calculated value of labour performed amounting

to 67 per cent of the total wage (R. Davies, 'The white working class in South Africa', *New Left Review*, 82, 50). On the long-standing character of differentials in the UK, Hobsbawm reports that in Macclesfield in 1793 artisans earned 3 shillings, labourers 1/8d; Portsmouth ship-wrights' wages between 1793 and 1823 averaged about double those of labourers (Hobsbawm, *Labouring Men*, 291, 292).

56  In the German communist party in 1927, skilled workers accounted for 40 per cent of the membership; unskilled 28 per cent; agricultural workers, inde-pendent craftsmen and commer-cial employees, the rest (F. Borkenau, *World Commu-nism*, 1962, 365). At the 1929 congress of the Communist Party of Great Britain, 69 per cent of the delegates were employed in coal, iron, steel, engineering or shipbuilding – the 'metals' that were the home of the skilled worker (K. Newton, *The Sociology of British Commu-nism*, 1969, 43). The skilled man was heavily represented in the early leadership of the British party: Murphy, Gallacher, Bell, Stewart, Peet, Mann and Inkpin were all engineers, Pollitt was a boiler-maker, Jackson a printer.

57  Lenin, *Theses on the Fundamen-tal Tasks of the 2nd Congress of the Communist International* (1920), *CW*, 31, 194.

58  Lenin, *The Tasks of Revolution-ary European Social Democracy in the European War* (1914), *CW*, 21, 18.

59  Lenin, *Opportunism, and the*

*Collapse of the Second Inter-national* (1915), *CW*, 21, 443.

60  Lenin, *What Is To Be Done?* (1902), *CW*, 5, 375.

61  Lenin, *New Tasks and New Forces* (1905), *CW*, 8, 211–20, articulates his tactical conceptions of the party question at the time. 'In the beginning we had to teach the workers the ABC, both in the literal and figurative senses. Now the standard of poli-tical literacy has risen so gigan-tically that we can and should concentrate all our efforts on the more direct Social-Democratic objectives aimed at giving an organised direction to the revo-lutionary stream' (ibid., 216).

62  Lenin, 'Preface to F. Sorge Corre-spondence' (1907) *CW*, 12, 375.

63  Lenin, *Marxism and Revisionism* (1908), *CW*, 15, 39.

64  Lenin, *Differences in the Euro-pean Labour Movement* (1910), *CW*, 16, 347–9.

65  Lenin, *Conference of the RSDLP Groups Abroad* (1915), *CW*, 21, 161.

66  Lenin, *The Collapse of the Second International* (1915), *CW*, 21, 241–4.

67  Lenin, *The International Socialist Congress in Stuttgart* (1907), *CW*, 13, 77.

68  Lenin, *Dead Chauvinism and Living Socialism* (1914), *CW*, 21, 98.

69  Lenin, *What Next?* (1915), *CW*, 21, 109.

70  ibid.; *The Collapse of the Second International*, 243, 250; *Opportunism, and the Collapse of the Second International*, 444; *What Next?*, 109; *Imperialism, the Highest Stage of Capitalism*,

1920 Preface, 194; ibid. (1916),
282, 284; *Imperialism and the
Split in Socialism*, 115, 120.
71  J. H. L. Keep, *The Debate
on Soviet Power*, Oxford, 1979,
18.

72  Besançon, *The Intellectual
Origins of Leninism*, 172, 173.
73  Plekhanov's progress is detailed
in S. H. Barron, *Plekhanov –
Father of Russian Marxism*,
Stanford, 1963.

# FIVE **THE TEXT AND ITS SECRET**

## A POLITICS FOR THE END OF TIME

Michael Foucault has expressed concern at the uses to which his work on internment may be put; in particular:

> A certain use which consists in saying 'Everyone has their own Gulag, the Gulag is here at our door, in our cities, our hospitals, our prisons, it's here in our heads'. I fear that under the pretext of a 'systematic denunciation' a sort of open-ended eclecticism will be installed.[1]

The temptation is obvious. The outstanding feature of the twentieth century appears to be a persistent violence against the human individual, either in overtly physical or in more subtle forms. The temptation is to ascribe all these to a common, supra-historical cause, in the hope of thereby making some sense out of it all, once and for all. But such an approach, however understandable, may ultimately only serve to obscure the crimes of the powerful.

Sociologists have certainly, if perhaps inadvertently, provided the appropriate concepts for such approaches. Secularization and democracy in de Tocqueville, rationalization in Weber, isolation and anomie in Durkheim, even, indeed, alienation in Marx, all contain the possibility of infinite extension until they may, separately or sometimes together, both explain our ills and convince us of an inescapable, inhuman destiny. I have pointed out previously the possibility of a less pessimistic interpretation of Weber, although it must be admitted that he himself was hardly a convinced optimist in these matters. Nevertheless, it is necessary to attempt whatever discrimination is possible between human ills and evils, and in the case of the Gulag, to refuse a 'universalising dissolution of the problem'[2] by asserting instead the specificity of historical events. This, for example, is the reservation that one feels impelled to register about the conclusions of the classical Frankfurt theories, wherein the 'frantic expansion of totalitarian mass democracy' becomes little different from the expansion of totalitarianism itself. Habermas' rejection of the totalizing thesis of the 'dialectic of enlightenment' in favour of an argument which accepts the necessity of the concepts of 'science' and 'progress', in their appropriate place, seems to be a necessary return to the exercise of such intellectual discrimination.

To the extent, therefore, that I have attempted to examine the roots of the Gulag in the previous chapters of this argument, I have done so in the spirit advocated by Foucault. Specifically, this means:

> Refusing to question the Gulag on the basis of the texts of Marx and Lenin or to ask oneself how, through what error, deviation, misunderstanding, or distortion of speculation or practice, their theory could have been betrayed to such a degree. On the contrary, it means questioning all these theoretical texts, however old, from the standpoint of the reality of the Gulag. Rather than searching in those texts for a condemnation in advance of the Gulag, it is a matter of asking what in those texts could have made the Gulag possible, what might even now continue to justify it, and what makes its intolerable truth still accepted today. The Gulag question must be posed not in terms of error (reduction of the problem to one of theory) but in terms of reality.[3]

My argument was not intended to explain the history of the twentieth century in terms of the consequences of one text, but to ask what in this one text could have 'made the Gulag possible'. And such an attempt must, in principle, remain a partial explanation. I have in passing acknowledged, and indeed made much use of, the contributions to such an understanding that is provided by the varying approaches of many different, and differing, analysts. But, despite all this, there is perhaps a need to move to a more general level of discussion.

For a problem remains: that is the continuing power and seductiveness of Lenin's themes in contemporary history, inasmuch as their prescriptions may still be advocated, and their consequences defended, at the cost of human suffering. And further, if the seductiveness of Leninism lies, as I have suggested, in the way in which the libertarian themes of *The State and Revolution* coincide with aspirations that may be found in many places and at many times, how is it that the dead positivity of authoritarianism proves so successful in conquering its opposite? Why was it that, whatever the presuppositions of Bolshevik theories, those aspirations were never powerful enough to say, at one of the many crucial points of Soviet history, 'Enough!'? It is, therefore, necessary to complete this argument by considering the nature and consequences of the desire for 'real freedom' that underlies Lenin's and, by implication, others' utopian and libertarian arguments.

It is in the work of Sartre that we may find the necessary depth to approach this question. Sartre lived in the political world defined by Merleau-Ponty's aphorism to the effect that 'it is impossible to be an anti-Communist and it is not possible to be a Communist'.[4] Merleau-Ponty was writing in 1947, and Sartre wrote the *Critique of Dialectical Reason* in 1960. Despite the difference in the two dates, they are both contained within a single political period, defined by the outcome of the Second World War and the development of the Cold War. At the same time, therefore, that both were conscious of the impossibility of not taking sides with the wartime communist resistance, and of not taking a similar side in a decisively bipolar world, there was too much in the experience of communist politics to make such a choice one that could easily be lived with. It would seem inevitable that Sartre would conclude that an existentialism that did not imply a specific political commitment was hardly adequate to the task of being in the world of post-war Europe. But there can be no doubt that the attempted reconciliation of existentialism and Marxism reached no final and satisfactory solution; in the light of Merleau-Ponty's assertion, it was impossible that such a resolution could be conjured out of abstract thought. The significance of the *Critique*, therefore, is that it attempts an investigation into the nature and possibility of freedom in a world that is recognized as almost inconceivably more complex and intractable to the dictates of thought than that of Lenin.

Thus the *Critique* is an attempt to define the nature and possibility of freedom. In this, Sartre is hardly unique; many before him have made the attempt. The difference of Sartre's attempt lies in the way in which his discussion honestly lays itself open to all the results of the twentieth century, and confronts the experience of freedom-becoming-authoritarianism. He does not take the easy path of counterposing his 'freedom' to the really existing varieties, thereby maintaining the purity of his model at the expense of saying nothing about the real world. His freedom is permeated with the awareness at every point of how close to unfreedom it lies, of how this threat is itself a condition of existence of that freedom. Sartre, therefore, honestly construes freedom as a gamble of the sort to which I have referred earlier.

The foundation of Sartre's argument is a fundamental phenomenology, that is, an attempt to structure a social theory around a concept of the individual that contains a minimum of assumptions. Where Marx assumes some version of ontology – according to interpretation, the necessity to labour, the necessity to co-operate, the necessity to objectify, etc. – Sartre is only prepared to accept such drives on the understanding that they are products of history – they do not precede the fact of being human in the world. Sartre will accept no such assumptions because of his insistence that the only essential quality of man is that of being free.

This stance will allow Sartre to attempt a definition of human freedom, and consequently of the nature of revolution, that escapes the one-dimensional logic and the naive optimism of the ontologically based traditional Marxian theories.

A phenomenology places the individual at the centre of the project of understanding. It signifies not simply that individuals are important in the scheme of things, but that the objects which appear to constitute the social world are expressions of human intentionality, and represent attempts to inscribe meaning in the environment in which men live. Any individual is confronted most fundamentally with the task of making sense of the world; this cannot be done by pure interpretation. Inasmuch as men are beings in the world, the attempt to make sense of the world is an attempt to *be* in the world in a particular manner. Such attempts constitute the projects which the individual adopts. Because they are intimately connected with the search for meaning, such projects

are greater than the simple acts themselves, they are attempted totalizations. Each and every project, being an attempt to make sense of the
world, derives from the individual's larger project of living in the world
at a certain time and place.

A project thus totalizes the world for the human subject, giving it a
coherence and order. But as attempts to be in the world, totalizations
must run the risk of failure. To examine social institutions is to attempt
to map the achievements and failings of human intentionality. Most
totalizations are failures, and history is the account of such failed
attempts at totalizations. The litter of failed or past totalizations is what
constitutes the world of dull and resistant positivity that appears to confront each individual. When individuals all pursue their own projects,
each representing differing totalizations, the search for totalization
appears fruitless. The conflict of human intentions produces results
which appear to match nobody's original project – the situation described in Engels' famed 'parallelogram of forces'.

In *Being and Nothingness* Sartre found that the ultimate value of the
human project was questionable: 'Men . . . are condemned to despair;
for they discover . . . that all human activities are equivalent and that
all are on principle doomed to failure.'[5] Since all life is ultimately a
failure to be, a profound ontological lack against which all efforts must
ultimately founder, history could contain little hope of progress. But
the *Critique* does admit of such a concept of progress. If projects can
escape from being irredeemably the intentions of isolated individuals,
and become the common property of larger groups, there may be a way
to escape the ultimate failure. If a single 'meaning', or totalization
might come to characterize the whole of society, then a totalization
might be achieved that would remove the fractious conflict that exists
between a myriad of individual projects. History may be reinterpreted
in this light. The rise of a world system and world economy dissolves the
differences of meaning that separates societies and cultures and
suggests their absorption into a single totalization.

But history is most definitely not imbued with an automatic and
irresistible logic. Along with the barriers to totalization that are erected
by distance and simple cultural difference, there are conflicts within
any given society, between classes and, indeed, within classes. The path
towards totalization is thus not evolutionary, but revolutionary. Classes
are represented by conflicting partial totalizations, expressing their
different intentions, or perhaps interests. Revolution is the unique
path to successful totalization.

Thus Sartre gives an account of history as the terrain of conflicting projects and failed totalizations. Human life has been lived in a condition of 'scarcity'. History is a history of shortage, and of a bitter struggle against this shortage, which has determined the relationships between men. Scarcity necessitates collective arrangements and efforts to extract the means of survival from an 'inert' nature. Yet the advantages of such co-operation are not unalloyed; it is, after all, only the existence of the others in the group that produces scarcity in the first place. Such a contradiction produces a specific type of group: the series. Each is bound to the other by mutual need *and* mutual hostility. Each lives in a state of hostility to nature – the inert – and further in hostility to his fellows. He is subjected to the practical arrangements sedimented by history and its institutions, and the competing needs of other people. The possibility of freedom, therefore, is negated by the domination of the 'practico-inert'.

In contrast, the paradigm of freedom is the fused group at the moment of 'apocalypse', typified for Sartre by the crowd that stormed the Bastille. It exists only on the basis of a common purpose, and that common purpose is identical to the personal project of every individual involved. No one's project is subordinated to it, because each has realized a new project, the success of which depends upon the participation of all the others. Such a group has no structure and no leaders. Sartre is under no illusions that such supremely free groups can be created at will and maintained in permanence. In *Being and Nothingness* he explained the willingness of people to accept oppression and misery in terms of a lack of imagination: 'It is on the day that we can conceive of a different state of affairs that a new light falls on our troubles and our suffering and we *decide* that these are unbearable.'[6] Thus a worker in 1830 will be impelled to revolt against his brutal conditions only if those conditions are worsened, if his meagre wages are reduced, because he can then conceive of a situation where his suffering is less than it has become. The analysis in the *Critique* reinforces this suggestion. A revolt is not produced by the simple existence of hunger, oppression and injustice. These are common and permanent features of many societies. The group that is resigned to such an objectionable practico-inert can only be transformed into a fused group by the arrival of a *threat* and a *promise*. The crowd that stormed the Bastille was produced by such a combination.

The St-Antoine district of Paris was threatened because it lay in the path of the obvious route for the rumoured advance of the king's troops.

'This possibility actualized the threat of the Bastille: it was possible that the district's inhabitants would be *caught in the crossfire*.'[7] But the Bastille also contained a promise that would negate the threat: in fact it contained cannons and rifles with which the people might defend themselves. It would appear that it is only when the practico-inert presents not simply the promise of the continued 'hell of daily life', but the threat of personal extinction, that the fused group is born to resist it.

By placing the individual at the centre of his philosophical project, Sartre has captured the depth of meaning that the revolutionary act produces for and in its participants. Anyone who has ever been involved in a meaningful collective project can testify to the transformation in human relationships and in daily experience that such a project achieves. The apocalyptic group, devoid of all complications and hesitations derived from the myriad complexities of daily life, can transact its business and pursue its goal with a speed, efficiency, willingness, and comradeship that makes formal structures and procedures practically redundant. Such a collective draws on an almost electric field of common assumptions and shared norms that allows the participants near superhuman insight into what other members of the collective wish to communicate and achieve.

Sartre's description of such a group is not dissimilar to what Durkheim described as moments of 'collective effervescence', rare moments when 'men are brought into more intimate relations with one another, when meetings and assemblies are more frequent, relationships more solid, and the exchange of ideas more active'.[8] The nature of such groups has been often discussed in the sociology of religions and crowd psychology. But Sartre's analysis offers an important insight into the process of revolution. The fact that such a profoundly joyous moment can be experienced, and the further fact that a large number of people, particularly those involved in politics, have intimations of such moments at least once in their lives, are important. Political theories can be constructed to suggest that lives, not moments, may be lived this way. In particular, in the aftermath and complications of every revolution there exists the yearning to return to the moment of primitive and uncomplicated solidarity. Not a little of this enters into all post-revolutionary oppositional movements, when the return to the routine tasks of daily life must occasion some feeling of 'betrayal', a deep sense of loss. The romantics, from the Levellers to the Trotskyists, are shot through with this nostalgia, whatever the practical merits of their oppositional programmes.

But the apocalypse *cannot* be maintained. After the immediate object of the fused group has been achieved, threats emerge which are capable of undermining the solidarity of the group. The apocalyptic group depends upon the existence of an enemy – not a theoretical or ideological one, above all not a distant one, but one that is real in the sense that it is present and immediate as a threat to the physical existence of each individual. The removal of this threat, or even its distancing, is likely to produce some kind of diversification in the projects of the group members. The assault on the enemy is after all a strictly limited task, and one likely to occasion few disagreements. Such disagreements will be tactical at most, and swept away in the rushing tide of events. But what guarantee is there that the group will be recreated in the morning, to continue the struggle against the enemy? The enemy is both more distant and more abstract. It is a ruling class and a social system, not a company of troops in the next street.

Thus the fused group of the apocalypse is a moment, not a condition. It creates no guarantees of its own permanence. It is guaranteed by no ontological status. Man has not entered the realm of freedom because no such objective kingdom of the free exists. Nor has any human essence been uncovered or liberated; there is no such essence. Freedom exists only to the extent that it is constantly recreated by the commitment of each to the common project. The return to seriality remains a possibility because only the relationship that humans adopt to their world can banish the practico-inert and seriality.

The moment of apocalypse is thus followed by the pledge, as a means of preserving the 'surviving' group. Each member must make a commitment to maintain the common project in the changed conditions. This is a defence against the internal danger brought about precisely by the fact that the individuals are now free. They are free to leave the group and change their project. The pledge is given in a moment before such defections become real, but when their possibility can be envisaged. The possibility is made obvious to all by the fact that the enemy is still unvanquished. Defection, if it be not treason, is tantamount to treason because the logic of the fused group works in reverse: if all are necessary to prevent the extermination of any, then the defection of any one threatens the ability of all others to survive.

A choice to defect cannot be construed as a real choice: it is a choice to return to the practico-inert, and is therefore an abandonment of freedom. Such individuals must be forced to be free by the common group. The pledge, therefore, is freely taken, and is a demand for violence to be used against oneself if one breaks one's word. The possibility of one's defection cannot be countered by a moral commitment. Tomorrow one's commitment may have changed and one's past be rejected. The pledge is a recognition of this possibility, and an agreement by all that such a change would be evidence of the reconquest of the practico-inert. All give the group the right to use terror against those who threaten its integrity, and by direct implication, the right to use terror against themselves. The terror may not save the individual – although it will certainly save many who might otherwise defect – but it will save the group and therefore safeguard the conditions of freedom.

The apocalyptic group does not only fade due to the passage of time; it must in fact be consciously displaced by something else. The practico-inert is not a place or a time but a relationship between man and the world. It remains, and remains until a future which can be no more than speculative. It must be combated, constantly, with will and reason; it must be worked on. The insurrectionary crowd must become an instrument for effective social change. The apocalypse is a necessary rupture with the practico-inert; it is not a considered renegotiation of the relationship between man and the world, but a practical abolition of one pole of the relationship. The rupture frees the people of all chains – both those that are part of the prior social and political arrangements, which it is the task of the revolution to destroy; and those that are part of insuperable historical conditions, or even the biological limits of the human organism itself. This group, then, is by definition utopian and *impractical*. The revolutionary crowd is saturated by a spirit far removed from any 'materialism'. The cry *Tout est possible* echoes from 1917 to 1968.

But the enemy must still be destroyed, priorities established, resources allocated, fields ploughed. Sartre underlines the transience of the apocalypse by insisting on the necessity for such considerations, and by refusing to ignore the dangers of seriality produced by the performance of such tasks. The group that successfully confronts such tasks cannot be the same group that stormed the Bastille or toppled the Tsar. The group must change, and to this extent it matters not how this change is brought about. Sartre argues against a common error that contrasts a centralizing and authoritarian tendency from above with a tendency to democracy and spontaneity that arises from below, as an explanation of the changes that occur in the aftermath of the revolution. He stresses that there is no fundamental difference in the *fact* of organization and regroupment according to whether it proceeds dictatorially from above or spontaneously from below. There can of course be crucially different effects, subtle and obvious, as a result of who originates and supervises the process. But the process itself is irresistible and indispensable. 'In short, this is not, and cannot be, an issue about Blanqui, Jaurès, Lenin, Rosa Luxemburg, Stalin or Trotsky . . . the type of formal intelligibility and rationality can be the same with organisation from above as with organisation from below.'[9] It is, therefore, crucial to understand that however democratic or spontaneous is the process of the formalization of the new organization, such a formalization is inescapable, and such a formalization is not without costs.

In this way Sartre distinguishes his analysis of the revolutionary process from the assumptions of the tradition of *The State and Revolution*. The apocalyptic group – expressed in the commune-state – cannot but disappear. This is due not to the treachery of leaders, the strategy of a bureaucracy, or the straitjacket of adverse conditions. It is inherent in the nature of the revolutionary process, because that process is itself simply a collective project pursued by human beings. Sartre, therefore, has ruptured the discourse which has previously prevented revolutionaries from grasping the consequences of acting in the world. As we have previously suggested, a utopianism that does not accept the existence of humans living and acting in a world of time, place and change does not have to be betrayed to usher in authoritarianism. Itself it betrays the reality of the human actors; it is a violation of the most fundamental fact of being human, the fact of being in the world. Being in the world compels the following changes.

An internal differentiation takes place, to allow for the performance of different tasks. A division of labour then emerges, and the group becomes an organization. But the organization does not destroy freedom; rather it creates a new freedom whereby individuals pursue the common end indirectly through their particular functions. Sartre uses the metaphor of a football team to illustrate the diverse functions moving towards a common goal, individual talents expressed in a common struggle. Thus even groups with a complex division of labour are compatible with freedom. While, compared with the apocalyptic group, there is clearly a loss in this case, this does not signify a return to seriality. But what happens in the case of a disagreement within the group? One point of view will be implemented, the other defeated. Those who lose will find themselves in a position where the project of the group has to some degree become outside and against their own project. The common project is no longer their own. Seriality has been reintroduced. The dissidents' position in the group is now one of passivity. Inertia has become part of the collectivity. The condition of the group is 'degraded' in comparison to the situation where everyone's praxis was freely expressed.

Even so, all is not lost. If the group has decided one way, it can, in its own sovereignty, decide another. So long as the processes involved are reversible, the situation is not one of seriality. If the number of those lost to inertia becomes threatening, a change can be agreed on. This remains possible so long as members of the group value their freedom above all else. But another solution is possible. Out of the organization may emerge the *institution*. As conflicts and disagreements multiply, as they inevitably will, they may be resolved by the transference of the right to decide between them to a body – or leader – standing outside and above the group. Great temptations exist to opt for this solution, especially in a situation where the group is still threatened by an enemy. Excessive discussion, and repeated tactical and strategic twists and turns in response to that discussion, threatens the efficacy of the struggle against the mortal enemy. Individuals are already partially serialized, and engrossed in their particular and vital functions. A transference of the common praxis to a leader is a slight step, legitimized by urgency. The leader does not seize power, he is the recipient of a willing abandonment of freedom by the members of the group. The return to seriality is complete as the institution establishes itself as a frozen and irreversible source of authority.

Sartre's analysis presents an incisive account of the process of revolutionary transformation, and then revolutionary degeneration. Each step can be illustrated by events and processes from the Russian experience. But the real virtue of Sartre's account lies in the fact that it does not pretend to be a history of a particular revolution, and the Russian Revolution, while present in every line of the argument, is practically absent from the text. The significance of this is simple. Sartre calls on historical example only as illustrative aids. The analysis is not an account of a revolution, of a particular problem in historiography, but of the process of revolution itself, as created by human beings. All such revolutions are made by human beings faced with the challenge of creating their own freedom. All such human beings determine the outcome of their acts. Revolutions will always take place in conditions constrained by historical limits, by unforeseen contingencies, by material and cultural shortages, by particular personalities, by specific inheritances, by problems that demand urgent solution. Without such, history would contain no revolutions, for what would there be to revolt against? Revolution does not solve these problems, rather it puts individuals in a position where they can choose how they are to be solved. And the most fundamental choice involved is simply this: will we solve them by means which reaffirm and recreate our freedom, and make it possible for us to unmake the choices we have made if we subsequently decide that they were wrong? Or do we solve them by means which recreate their dominion over us, which readmit the practico-inert as the determining element of our lives? Do we replace one set of frozen relations with another? Do we use our freedom to remain free, or do we use that freedom to decide to become, once again, unfree? Revolution is no more and no less than simply the first real choice that people have made in their lives. The unfree have been shown that they can be free. And if one free decision may be made, it follows that this freedom can structure every other decision that subsequently confronts the individual. And so the gamble is not a once-for-all attempt at liberty, but the constant nature of man's negotiation of his relationship to the world and his fellows.

## THE IMPLICATIONS OF SARTRE

Sartre's discussion is ontological, not empirical. That is, it is not a model of stages derived from an examination of concrete history like Comte's three stages or Marx's succession of modes of production. It is an attempt, by starting from the individual conceived with a minimum of assumptions – assumptions that would have to be derived *from* history – to understand the field of human actions in history, and the limits of that field. While this account has inevitably ignored, and perhaps inexcusably simplified, the complex regiment of concepts and purposes underlying Sartre's argument, we can nevertheless make some comments about its implications for revolution and freedom in the contemporary world.

It may well be that circumstances conspire against freedom in contemporary revolutions. Rather than revolution providing the ground for freedom, a divergence emerges between freedom and the security of the revolution. If that is the case, it is not yet necessarily an argument for rejecting revolution. We may, instead, consider the concept of the 'transitional period'. That is, the revolution may provoke inevitable costs in freedom, i.e. the inevitable emergence of the institution, along the road to the abolition of scarcity. If such abolition is possible, we may be prepared to bear the costs of the absence of freedom for a period. It may well be, however, that this abundance which will bring the end of scarcity, and therefore the end of the practico-inert, and therefore the disappearance of seriality, is a chimera.

Let us consider the relationship, or the tension, between revolution and freedom. The postulates of contemporary revolutions seem to emphasize the possibility of the degradation of the free group. In other words, there is clearly a conflict between apocalypse and security. Sartre has already indicated how, after the apocalyptic moment, the enemy does not disappear, but certainly recedes. The enemy is no longer the troops that threaten immediate massacre, but the troops outside the city that threaten massacre some time in the future; or the continued existence of the power complex that can raise such threatening bodies in the future; or the social system that provides the basis for such a power complex to contemplate such an act in the future. This distance loosens the bonds that held the group in such uncomplicated solidarity, but it does not lessen the need for such a solidarity, because the threat of annihilation remains: thus the need for the pledge and the terror. Their importance is greatly increased in revolutions of a more modern nature and purpose than the French Revolution. There the defeat of the enemy could be regarded in terms that were military and the establishment of the new regime of freedom in terms that were constitutional. The modern revolution, however, must refuse such a simple definition of its tasks: it proposes nothing less than the restructuring of an entire society and all its institutions. Far more than in the past, the revolutionary act itself is only the beginning, not the end: because its only success will be when it completes a global conquest. The revolution will be complete when it has transported society beyond the borders of scarcity and beyond all possible external threat. Only then is the enemy finally defeated.

The pledge, then, is the contract that will last for decades, and the terror its permanent instrument. The threat of the external world conferred legitimacy on the Stalinist institution through not only the wars of intervention, but also through the period of the rise of fascism, through the cold war and 'peaceful coexistence' to détente, and again today, to cold war. Against this threat all claims of freedom are negated. The history of the Soviet Union shows the incompatibility between the surviving group, given coherence by the pledge, and the organization which possesses democratic qualities. This does not simply refer to the rise of Stalin; for the majority of the population, even for the majority of the party, the 'institution' was established within, at most, three years of the October insurrection. In fact the period of the Russian Revolution that most clearly shows the development and free interplay of fused groups and organizations came *before* the October insurrection, not after it. This was the time when Lenin, rightly, called Russia the 'freest country in the world', and the period is saturated with demonstrations, political parties, voluntary associations and, above all, soviets, pursuing their independent projects in a common field of totalizations. This could not last, and October is the moment where the institution begins its creep to power, not the moment of apocalypse, however much it may have been reinterpreted as such in the subsequent state ideology.

The move to the pledge after the revolutionary act is necessary; in fact, the apocalyptic group is an embarrassment; it cannot in its simplicity and impracticality cope with the practical tasks of mobilization and reconstruction. The division of labour is urgently needed. This involves a cost to the group, a cost to freedom, if the apocalyptic group is the paradigm of freedom. But it is not a cost to the revolution. Those features characterized by the term 'organization', however, are problematic from both standpoints: that of freedom and that of the security of the revolution. The football team is free and efficient so long as every member agrees upon the tactics to be pursued; once there is disagreement, however, the efficacy of the group effort obviously suffers. Discussion, disagreement, opposition, mean diversion of effort by every member of the group and withdrawal of effort by those in a defeated minority. Un-freedom is ominously close; for when does a minority that has by such means distanced itself from the common project become a group which has broken the pledge, and thus, by its own prior agreement, a subject of terror? Herein may be discerned at least some of the fateful history of the Soviet Union in the 1920s and 1930s. For what is it we read in the rejection of the various oppositions by party and populace but an accusation of sabotage in the form of dissent? And what is it that makes those oppositions so impotent, so reluctant to pursue an *open* political argument, but the guilty conscience of those who are breaking a promise?

Clearly, the more radical the tasks of the revolution, the more close to being one and the same thing are the pledge and the institution. The rise of the institution is further aided by the fact that people – even, or especially, those who have made a revolution – are more often than not ready to resign the freedom so recently won. At least part of the 'institutionalization' of the Soviet Union derived from the fact that the population was exhausted by the battle for freedom and survival through almost ten years of war and revolution. Trotsky's advocacy of 'permanent revolution' may have been a fatal misnomer for that which he actually intended; but in public discourse it summed up for the population all that they had been through and from which they now wanted a respite. Berger has deftly summed up the consequences of the ideal of 'full participation' in every decision affecting one's life as 'a nightmare comparable to unending sleeplessness'.[10] At some point after the revolutionary festival the average individual retreats from constant participation to a necessary quietude. And the institution awaits.

If the rule of the institution for a period of history is the price of the abolition of the roots of alienation – scarcity – it may be a price which societies are prepared to pay. But the problem here is that for Sartre to assume that it is possible to abolish scarcity, and for him to assume further that this will entail the final resolution of the problems of being, makes little sense in terms of the rest of his system. In fact, such assumptions lead to a complete subversion of his revolutionary pheno- menology and a return to an orthodox Marxism. This is what Aronson, for example, has attempted.

If scarcity is an exhaustive definition of the source of human suffer- ing, it is possible to define the conditions for the end of such suffering. The scarcity that has conditioned life under all social formations so far will be negated by the achievement of material abundance that a social- ist revolution will bring. If scarcity is taken as the *a priori* that gives rise to the existence of multiple, diverse and conflicting individual projects, abundance will remove the root of divisions between human individ- uals. This interpretation sees the diffusion of projects as merely the consequences of the 'war of all against all' that arises due to the threat of the other to consume that which the individual needs in order to survive. The abolition of material scarcity may allow the emergence of some common human essence that will signify a permanent common- ality of projects. To establish this possibility beyond doubt, however, Aronson insists on a reinterpretation of Sartre's scarcity. He construes scarcity as a result of a historical human choice, and criticizes Sartre for his failure 'to explore the historical choice which *makes there be* scarcity in the first place'.[11] He cites the work of Sahlins on hunter–gatherer societies to suggest that the original human state was that of collec- tivities of humans who lived 'amid peace and leisure, amid a plenty based upon a systematic minimization of their needs'.[12] At some point in the life of societies, what amounts to a decision, a 'historical act', is taken to create new needs, which results in the need to labour to overcome what is now experienced as scarcity. This, of course, also coincides with the creation of classes, inequality and the struggle over the surplus – in other words the beginning of the violence of history. The practico-inert immediately becomes a less ominous concept, easily subsumed under the traditional Marxian strategies:

> if workers controlled the labour process itself, if they worked fewer hours and freely exchanged functions, if they were assured of a secure level of subsistence and co-operated in socially meaningful work – then at some point the grim rule of necessity might be brought to an end, and the practico-inert subject decisively to human control.[13]

This is a familiar road, and it can lead to only one destination. Poster has expressed his disappointment at the way in which Sartre's radical reconstruction of social theory seems to collapse into such a return to classical Marxism:

> Labour and the workplace are reaffirmed as the vortex of historical time and the only form of domination that is included in the final totalisation is that of exploited wage labour. . . . By reaffirming the primacy of labour and the mode of production, Sartre has missed the chance to transcend the limits of traditional Marxism so as to account for forms of domination that play a significant role in contemporary radical thought.[14]

If Sartre himself does not even need the corrections of an Aronson to return to the traditional Marxian political strategies, something appears to have slipped in the theory. It may be that this is due to the incompatibility of Sartre's original project with the discoveries he has presented in the course of attempting it. But perhaps it would be possible to describe Sartre's conclusions about political strategies as descriptive rather than normative. As Poster himself elsewhere points out,[15] the claims made for the power of Marxism to achieve the end of history, the final totalization, are conditional. They are conditional upon concrete history and upon existential choice.

The title *Critique of Dialectical Reason* defines the book as an attempt to establish the possibilities and limits of this form of thought. It is an attempt to define what sort of theoretical system is necessary if the assumption that history is ultimately intelligible is to be verified.

For this purpose the prospect of a single totalization is necessary, to achieve a resolution and congruence of previously conflicting or over-lapping partial totalizations. It is thus necessary to conceive of a 'total-izer', an agency which through its praxis is capable of encompassing the abolition of the practico-inert and the final defeat of seriality. It is not possible to argue with the conclusion that Sartre reaches: *if* history is to be intelligible, then it will be *only* through the agency of the single possible candidate for the role of totalizer, the working class. There is no escape from this conclusion, and Poster's regret that the *Critique* does not allow alternative paths to emancipation – of women or national minorities – is simply not relevant to Sartre's project. The totalizer must be the working class, because it is impossible to replace the 'subject–object identical', as described by Lukacs, with any other candidate for the role of 'universal class'. Thus the project of intelligi-bility is placed in doubt: first, because the working class has not played the role of totalizer, and gives less and less evidence – as history pro-ceeds, in its increasing fragmentation and incoherence – of possessing such a capability. Second, the nomination of the working class to the role of totalizer carries with it all the philosophically unacceptable and sociologically inadequate implications that permeated Lukacs' original unwieldy conception.

But the return of Sartre's project to this too familiar terminus does not render the whole enterprise futile. What Sartre has done at every point in the theory is to distinguish the assumptions that must be made if the project of dialectical reason is to be consummated. His procedure has still left open the possibility of choosing to follow the logic of the system, or to dissent from it where its consequences become unaccept-able. It may be possible to prevent Sartre's theory from leading to its own dissolution. For this, it is necessary to resist the temptation to embrace an assumption of the availability of a totalized history. Thus it is entirely possible to approach Sartre's theory by assessing his cate-gories, the coherence of his system, its legitimacy within the Marxian or radical tradition. All this can be done with the objective of establish-ing more securely the prospect of a successful outcome to the enter-prise: the end of history in the final totalization. Such approaches would, however, empty Sartre's efforts of any value and significance. The importance of his system lies in its ability to grasp the real world, not in the extent to which it satisfies demands for a perfectly coherent theoretical and strategic system. It is valuable to the extent that it manages to say something about our present condition that is signally different and more appealing than any other representation of the world that might be offered for our consideration. In other words a more valid criterion of assessment would be: as a commentary on the history of the twentieth century, does it offer an account which, by its relevance, demands our attention? It is my contention that the sociology of groups, the dialectic of revolution and freedom that it presents, does precisely this.

If we work back from this achievement we can distinguish the dichotomies and antinomies of Sartre's system, which themselves express the agonizing relationship between revolution and freedom. Sartre does not map an unambiguous path to the final totalization; he demonstrates the conflicts, contradictions and assumptions that constitute such a path. If he himself then chooses that path, that is his existential choice. But what he refuses is a theoretical 'soft option' that neatly erases the anguish of such a choice. This is expressed in his much criticized acceptance of violence as inherent in revolution. What he refuses is the attempt of those like Aronson who would dissolve the antinomies and return us to a simple and comforting world of certainties, of limited problems and neat answers. Aronson, who wishes to enforce the reconciliation of Sartre with classical Marxism, engages in no significant discussion of the theory of groups and the evolution from fused group to institution. Of this he offers merely a descriptive account.[16] The problems raised by this discussion do not appear to him as real problems at all. This is the consequence of his redefinition of scarcity. That reinterpretation was clearly intended to defend the possibility of socialism and the transcendence of alienation, and he appears to refuse any suggestion that the concept of socialism itself might have been problematized by the history of the twentieth century.

Sartre's project in fact resists Aronson's optimistic interpretation. By considering their origin and their inherent uncertainties, we can detect some incompatibility between the assumptions embodied in the original concepts (of scarcity, the practico-inert, the project and the totality) and the legitimation of the traditional Marxian centrality of the economic, and the process of economic development as the road to freedom. Even on the level of the economist interpretation of scarcity, Sartre lacked such optimism, and affirmed that 'this scarcity is a fundamental determination of man: as is well known, the socialisation of production does not put an end to it, except possibly through a long dialectical process of which we cannot yet know the outcome'.[17]

Thus it may only be possible to enter a domain of *relatively less* scarcity, and such domains may already exist. Poster points out that after 1968 Sartre himself 'accepted that elementary, material needs were by and large satisfied' in advanced capitalism, effectively dissociating his philosophy of revolution from reductionist versions of 'scarcity'.[18] Thus a distinction must be made between what could be said one hundred years ago and what may be said today: empirical history has deprived socialism of the certainty of its claim to solve the problem of scarcity, and has provided capitalism with some mitigation of the accusation that it provides for the majority of its populations a situation of permanent scarcity.

For Sartre, the unambiguous virtue of socialist revolution lies in its possibility of reconciling scarcity and needs in terms of the basic facts of hunger and survival. It is no accident that his latter-day political concerns were predominantly connected with the colonial revolution. He reminds us that 'The fact is that after thousands of years of history three-quarters of the world's population are undernourished.'[19]

The establishment of a socialist regime may lead to the elimination of this form of scarcity (or at least this is assumed to be the case, although even yet it must remain as an assumption and an assertion, not a proven fact of experience). Yet this is a very primitive formulation of the concept of *need*. Standing beyond this domain of biological need, there is a whole domain of needs that historically have developed once the biological is satisfied. The Soviet Union is impelled to consider the development of consumer goods industries in order to meet some of these 'needs' that appear to arise inexorably once 'biological' needs are satisfied. These may indeed be attributed to the delayed emergence of the 'new man' under socialism, to remnants of unreconstructed culture, even to the penetration of western ideology. However, one may believe that it is absurd and brutalizing to suggest that every need beyond the biological is unnecessary and degenerate: such a view would dismiss Beethoven's symphonies along with motor cars, books along with central heating. To select one and reject the other implies the 'dictatorship over needs' that some theorists have suggested[20] in a move that implies a return to the centralized and authoritarian plan so familiar from contemporary history. For those societies, then, that have passed beyond Aronson's very basic situation of scarcity, the problem of continuing and developing needs remains: and this very problem will confront those post-revolutionary societies that have fulfilled this basic task.

Thus, in the absence of the establishment of a 'dictatorship over needs', the problem of a disparity between needs and resources remains even on the economic level, however far we may envisage the process of economic development and technological control proceeding. Further, the modern awareness of the finitude of planetary resources may restore an appreciation of the natural components of scarcity, above and beyond those social and historical components which may be deemed to be subject to human intervention. What this dictates, therefore, is not the necessity to achieve or enter some domain wherein the problem of scarcity will be gradually eliminated; rather it is the necessity to construct processes of discussion and determination that can provide a democratic means to effect the allocation of finite resources between conflicting needs.

But a concept of 'need' that is reduced to the biological is absurd; one that is only reduced to the 'material' is exceptionally dubious. It is probably just as dubious to attempt to define human need in any positive and technical sense at all. While it is possible to view the development of civilization as the unnecessary invention of ever more infinite and redundant needs, it is also possible to reject such an attitude for its presumption. Given the existence of those human faculties about which we know, and the possible existence of some such about which we have as yet no knowledge, it is exceedingly dangerous to predict in advance – or even at some past point in history, as Aronson does – a break point where humanity moves from a situation of 'genuine' needs to ones that may be condemned as 'artificial'. Artificiality is the nature of human existence, and concepts of a golden age prior to such a situation cannot be seriously entertained. The definition of scarcity given in the glossary of the *Critique* seems to provide the necessary open-endedness to take account of this: 'the contingent impossibility of satisfying all the needs of an ensemble'.[21]

Thus, to bring Sartre's insights back to life again it is necessary to reject the Marxian concept of need that Aronson attempts to reintroduce. Sartre's concept does not derive from Marxism; rather it is a reinterpretation of the concept of *lack* developed in his pre-Marxist works. There, *lack* is an 'ontological privation',[22] the very structure of the human being. It expresses the ultimate disparity between the human subject and the world of facticity, and the ultimate domination of the former by the latter. In the Marxian version, lack is replaced by *need* and 'the resistance of the world to man is now defined in terms of scarcity'.[23]

Sartre's discussion of groups, and his tragic awareness of the transience of situations of perfection as summed up in the apocalyptic group, are hardly compatible with a scarcity defined in terms of economics, of the material needs for biological survival. It makes more sense to regard the situation of scarcity as a sub-set of a more profound human condition, his already given ontological lack. The problem of scarcity may well be the terrain for much of what has been brutal and regrettable in human history, and consequently may define the site wherein human action may minimize these consequences once and for all. This is the site of political action, where human actions combined with developing technology may reduce the problem of material scarcity to nothing more than the inevitable contingency that follows from living in a world that is ultimately natural. But this is not to enter the kingdom of the blessed. Jameson insists on the crucial element of continuity between *Being and Nothingness* and the *Critique*, an element that most commentators obscure. Just as the individual suffers from 'a lack of being, an inability to . . . reach some ultimate ontological plenitude', so the group is never a finally satisfied and stable entity, but a set of *individuals* straining towards a final consummation they can *never* achieve.[24]

Thus we may interpret Sartre in a less categoric manner than might appear necessary on first acquaintance with the theory. A more considered picture can emerge. It would seem that the condition of scarcity is just one expression of man's condition: it is the expression that is, by and large, *in* history and available to historical change. Such historical change will doubtless remove sources of alienation, as it will remove sources of hunger. This is the argument, under some circumstances, for revolution. But revolution does not bring absolute abundance and material security, and it further does not bring the end of alienation, as it cannot resolve those aspects of alienation that are locked into the condition of being humans in time. And so post-revolutionary life does not consist of a permanent end to alienation through a permanent common project: 'there is no synthetic unity of the multiplicity of totalisations, in the sense of a hypersynthesis which would become, in transcendence, a synthesis of syntheses.'[25] Similarly, pre-revolutionary life may not be the permanent hell of serial confrontation with every Other.

The extreme pessimism surrounding the consequences of scarcity is subject to modification in the discussion on groups. Sartre in fact avoids an extreme and simplistic dichotomy which would place humans under pre-revolutionary conditions in a situation of total mutual hostility, held together only by the brute demands of survival, yet permeated with a cultural loathing and fear of Others – with the post-revolutionary situation signifying a total reversal of such a state of affairs. It is much more a matter of degree. A group at any one time is of a distinct type: a fused group, an organization, a series, etc. But such groups are both inserted in temporality and located within an assembly of many groups. Each group may shift between seriality and other forms over time; each group is involved with other groups which will be of a different form at the time. Thus it is difficult to conceive of an entity as large as a nation as a group in Sartre's terms; it consists of a large number of groups, and inasmuch as it is itself a group is characterized by a permanent and shifting reconstitution of its constituent parts. 'The important thing, therefore, is to find out how far the multiplicity of individual syntheses can, as such, be the basis for a community of objectives and actions.'[26]

Individual totalizations, therefore, contain the possibility, if not of being identical to, at least of overlapping the totalizations of others, just as much as they contain the possibility of conflicting. Otherwise, surely it would not be possible to speak of people as being part of a common culture, and this concept of culture is necessary if we are not to be forced to reject Sartre's approach out of hand: a society based *only* upon the dictates of survival would be chaotic indeed, and life would be 'nasty, brutish and short'.

There is consequently a danger in Sartre's theory of groups: the danger is that the apocalyptic group may be read as the state most earnestly to be desired, and therefore to be preserved at all costs. There is a danger, in Jameson's words,[27] of a 'mystique of apocalypse'. But, to this, Sartre might reply: 'There always was.' If Sartre has spelled out to us the seductive qualities of the apocalyptic state, he cannot automatically be condemned as its high priest. For he has also told us of its transience, its impossibility as an objective, rather than as a moment. Sartre is in fact identifying and forcing the reader to recognize the danger that *already exists* in reality, and has already been witnessed in history itself. The danger is that people will be impelled to preserve what can only be a transient condition, and this is what gives the pledge and the terror their significance: as attempts to preserve the ephemeral. Thus Merleau-Ponty was wrong to accuse Sartre of 'ultra-bolshevism'[28] for his account of the terror in the revolutionary process. Sartre has done no more than analyse history and state facts: he has justified nothing.

Thus we have a disquietingly honest account of the real limits of politics. Political action cannot satisfy the ultimate ontological lack of

the individual, and the experience of the apocalyptic group is dangerous inasmuch as it suggests that politics can do precisely that. Those
who object to Sartre's honest statement of this fact are, in Jameson's
words, objecting

> in reality, to time itself. For to say that consciousness of human life is
> a lack of being, an emptiness striving towards stasis and plenitude,
> toward being itself, is only in effect to give a definition of time.

To love is an ontological failure, not because it does not exist or cannot
last, but because even love does not possess the power to 'achieve the
very end of time itself'. Politics is an ontological failure because it cannot halt the passage of time, the inevitability of change and the passage
of generations. The import of Sartre's sociology is therefore fundamentally *ethical*: 'it aims at dispelling the illusions of an ethic of being, and
at reconciling us to our life in time.'[29] And it is from this remarkable
achievement that we may, after a long detour down frightful roads,
begin the search for a politics that is, once again, ethical.

The 'myth of the apocalypse' may be the greatest specifically political threat of our age. In the light of Sartre's elucidation of the difficulty
of maintaining hold of freedom, of the dangers of placing one's freedom irrevocably in the hands of others, we may wish to avoid the
pursuit of such absolute freedom. Sartre has shown that the connection
between revolution and freedom is tenuous, and possibly negative. He
has shown that the fundamental ontological privation of being is not
accessible to solution by the act of political revolution. He has shown
the terror as the fury that is visited upon a society that is forced to
confront this, a terror that is invited by the very act of the 'pledge'
necessary to maintain the original purity of the revolutionary freedom.
Thus, at last, we are perhaps able to consider the question of revolution
as a *choice*, fully informed of its nature and consequences, of its
benefits and losses.

*The State and Revolution* is the constitutional theory of the attempt
to ontologize the apocalypse. In other words, it describes the appropriate institutional arrangements for a group which has achieved totalization: a single common project in the world, where the possibility of
differences within the group does not arise. Lenin's measures for the
control of bureaucracy, and for the extension of democracy, as argued
in chapter 2, are strikingly inappropriate for the revolutionary group at
the moment of apocalypse. Such a group has no need for bureaucracy;
indeed the concept of bureaucracy is an absurd irrelevancy. This is

because such a group is at the hour of its existence fulfilling tasks and solving problems in such a way that the grounds for a bureaucratic structure are not invoked: in other words, there is a minimal division of labour, and that which *is* necessary is highly *flexible* – no one is irreplaceable. Similarly, such a group has no need to confront and consider the question of democratic forms, because the simplicity and urgency of the tasks confronting the collective establish a necessarily narrow area of discussion and disagreement. This will be an area of *technical* issues, about how best to achieve a commonly agreed short-term objective, the defence of the people and the securing of power. Those who disagree with that aim, i.e. who adhere to a difference in *values*, rather than techniques, are by definition not part of the group. They constitute a different, and probably mortally hostile, ensemble of individuals and the differences between two such groups, obviously, are hardly the grounds for discussion and debate. Here, rather, we are in the domain of force and violence.

But Sartre's sociology has demonstrated that bureaucracy and democracy *do* become matters of substance within a relatively brief period of time, wherein the group must reconstitute itself to deal with new tasks. These tasks, it will be remembered, are the need to tackle diverse questions of economic and social reconstruction and transformation; and the need to accommodate the development of differences between members of the group over substantive issues that embrace more than technical problems. The first task produces the institutions of a bureaucracy, the second the institutions of a democracy.

Lenin's whole thesis, therefore, is startlingly *irrelevant* to the question of the state and revolution. His measures for the abolition of bureaucracy and the extension of democracy are irrelevant to the revolutionary moment because these are the natural, inevitable, components of such a moment. And his measures are similarly irrelevant to the period that succeeds the revolutionary moment in that they are simply non-functional, they cannot be applied successfully to a situation whose sociological constitution is fundamentally different from that of the revolutionary moment. Regret at the inevitability of such a 'degrading' of the initial freedom is pointless; regret is only appropriate to the extent that attempts were made to institutionalize the assumptions of the apocalyptic group. For such attempts, as I have tried to show, themselves negate the possibility of establishing securely the freedom and human dignity that *is* possible. That which is possible may indeed be a pale shadow of the moment of the apocalypse, but it is a possibility of something *real*.

We can, therefore, perhaps begin to understand the extent of the
seductiveness of *The State and Revolution*: it speaks to the consciousness of lack, and translates it into a consciousness of *loss*: that is, it
promises an end to the fundamental anguish of being, that of being in
time. It achieves this by promising an end to time itself. And so we can
see what must follow. The termination of time is only possible if it coincides with the end of human beings, with the end of the time-laden
universe of change. I have said that Lenin's problematic ensured that
politics is an ontological impossibility. Yet politics is a product of living
in time: of changing circumstances and changing interpretations of
what it is to live. In those states that have been, and may yet be, built
on Lenin's model it is assumed that politics is abolished as a result of
the abolition of time. In fact, the abolition of time is briefly, and ludi-
crously, and tragically, secured by the abolition of politics.

## NOTES

1 M. Foucault, *Power/Knowledge*,
  New York, 1980, 134.
2 ibid., 136.
3 ibid., 135.
4 M. Merleau-Ponty, *Humanism
  and Terror*, Boston, 1969, xxi.
5 J. P. Sartre, *Being and Nothingness*, New York, 1966, 561.
6 ibid.
7 J. P. Sartre, *The Critique of
  Dialectical Reason*, London,
  1976, 319. Despite the criticisms
  I make later of their arguments, I
  have to acknowledge my debts to
  the accounts of the *Critique*
  offered by Poster and Aronson,
  as well as by Jameson (see
  below), whose conclusions I find
  more persuasive. Also useful
  were R. Aron, *History and the
  Dialectic of Violence*, Oxford,
  1975; M. Cranston, 'Sartre:
  solitary man in a hostile
  universe', in A. de Crespigny
  and K. Minogue, *Contemporary
  Political Philosophers*, London,

1976; P. Chiodi, *Sartre and
  Marxism*, Brighton, 1976;
  D. LaCapra, *A Preface to Sartre*,
  New York, 1978. These secondary texts allowed entry to an
  otherwise dense and
  impenetrable work. Elements of
  the uncompleted vol. 2 of the
  *Critique* were published as
  'Socialism in one country', *New
  Left Review*, 100 (1977),
  143–63.
8 Cited in S. Lukes, *Emile Durkheim*, London, 1973, 422.
9 Sartre, *Critique*, 519, 520.
10 P. Berger, *Facing up to Modernity*, London, 1979, 19.
11 R. Aronson, *J. P. Sartre – Philosophy in the World*, London,
  1980, 255.
12 ibid.
13 ibid., 261.
14 M. Poster, *Sartre's Marxism*,
  London, 1979, 105, 106.
15 ibid., 110, 111.
16 Aronson, op. cit., 251–2.

17 Sartre, *Critique*, 138, 139.
18 M. Poster, *Existentialist Marxism in Post-War France*, Princeton, 1975, 29.
19 Sartre, *Critique*, 123.
20 Such theories are discussed by A. Arato, 'Review of Bahro: critical responses', *Telos*, 48 (Summer 1981), especially 163, 164.
21 Sartre, *Critique*, 829.
22 F. Jameson, *Marxism and Form*, Princeton, 1974, 232.
23 ibid., 233.
24 ibid., 268.
25 Sartre, *Critique*, 391.
26 ibid., 400.
27 Jameson, op. cit., 268.
28 ibid., 254.
29 ibid., 274.

# SIX CONCLUSION

Husak, the seventh President of my country, is known as the *president of forgetting*. . . . Husak dismissed some hundred and forty-five historians from universities and research institutes. (Rumour has it that for each of them – secretly, as in a fairy tale – a new monument to Lenin sprang up.) One of these historians, my all but blind friend Milan Hubl, came to visit me one day in 1971 in my tiny apartment on Bartolmejska Street. We looked out of the window at the spires of the Castle and were sad.

'The first step in liquidating a people,' said Hubl, 'is to erase its memory. Destroy its books, its culture, its history. Then have somebody write new books, manufacture a new culture, invent a new

history. Before long the nation will begin to forget what it is and
what it was. The world around it will forget even faster.'
Milan Kundera, *The Book of Laughter and Forgetting*, London,
1982, 158–9

Politics is a matter of time. Life is lived in time, and for modern man
life is lived in an awareness of time, as the source of our discontents,
ultimately our mortality, and of our delights. Political efforts to
extinguish the source of our discontents, even and perhaps especially
when they are successful, must also rob us of the essential delight of
being human: the promise of always new and different sensations,
emotions, understandings, relations and meanings. Politics, as the
European tradition has successively refined and redefined it, is the field
for the exploration of this ambiguity of a life in time, and also the only
civilized mode for expressing and confronting and controlling those
problems to which civilization gives rise.

But politics not only allows us to explore the possibilities of freedom
within a world of time; it must also be remembered that politics itself is
a product of time, in the sense of being a result of history. Politics is
certainly not compatible with all and any sets of social arrangements: it
remains, as yet, a minority experience. It seems to follow, then, that
history can rob us of politics, perhaps with greater ease than that with
which it emerged in the first place. At this point in history we could do
worse than to spend some time considering how easily, and with what
apparently convincing and virtuous motives, we may be robbed of politics. This I have in the preceding pages attempted to do. But a theoretical argument may have little effect upon the course of events. The
threats from those forces that reject politics, because they refuse to face
the complexities and responsibilities of a life in time, may yet prove
strong enough to turn any literary defence of politics into a mere
epitaph. When all is said and done, history, to paraphrase Galileo,
does move, despite any efforts of those who wish to see and construct
the end of history. Within the turmoil that is history, there can be no
assumption that politics will be a survivor. If it is true, as Max Weber
passionately argued, that 'it is a gross self-deception to believe that
without the achievements of the age of the Rights of Man any one of us,
including the most conservative, can go on living his life',[1] where can
we find any reassurance that life will go on?

In my argument against Lenin, I have insisted that the monolithic
utopia will always founder on the rock of divergent human values.

Such an argument, of course, is only sustainable on an assumption that the human passion for values will transcend and survive any set of social and administrative arrangements, however efficient and all-pervasive these may be. This does, however, bring the argument dangerously close to demanding a metaphysics, dependent upon a supra-historical human nature, an ever present commitment to freedom and individuality.[2] To subscribe to such a view would return us to the embrace of those secular teleologies that contemporary thinking finds so unconvincing, and recent history has proven so dangerous. But to accept the opposite, a view of freedom and individuality as no more than an ephemeral historical construct whose vitality will not outlive the social arrangements that gave it birth, is not only to vitiate my entire argument against Lenin's commune-state. It is also to plunge us into the sea of absolute moral relativity, and further concede that 'old European dignity' is not only an accident in historical terms – a perfectly acceptable analysis – but also an accident in ethical terms. My argument has been directed to a defence of the institutions of liberty, a defence of politics. But if my argument cannot raise that concept of liberty to something more than the effect of a structure, it is as contingent as the rest of morality is proclaimed to be in Marxist ideology, and one may with equanimity view its disappearance from the world.

There is no terrain to be easily found between metaphysics and Marxism. If the intellectual 'French revolution' of the past twenty years has done anything, it has at least profoundly undermined the concept of the metaphysical, essentialist, transhistorical, humanist subject.[3] But ethical humanism is not reduced to a vacuity as an automatic result of the revealed vacuity of philosophical humanism. In other words, just because we cannot ground the free and responsible human individual in indisputable theoretical or historical argument, it in no way follows that we should not continue to believe that human beings should be free and responsible, should be treated as end and not means. Indeed, the shock of the philosophical collapse may bring us to appreciate more keenly the value of the freedom we inhabit in its very uniqueness, delicacy and unlikeliness.[4] The reconstructions of ethical theory that must be undertaken in the light of philosophical anti-humanism I must leave to others. But my argument has now to seek a reconstruction of a political theory in order to deny the Leninist assault on politics. This may yet be possible through pursuing a sociological argument, which will suggest that while the human subject at the heart of western concepts of politics may have been precariously born of a specific time, place and conjuncture, it is a historical innovation of such uniqueness that it may, at least to some degree, escape its dependence on history and social structure, and from being an effect become a cause.

For this, we must once again return to the unsurpassed insights of Max Weber, who at one point reflected on the possibility of the 'end of politics' and the advent of the 'totally administered society' as follows:

> A progressive elimination of private capitalism is theoretically conceivable, although it is surely not so easy as imagined in the dreams of some literati who do not know what it is all about. . . . Together with the inanimate machine [the bureaucratic organisation] is busy fabricating the shell of bondage which men will perhaps be forced to inhabit some day, as powerless as the fellahs of ancient Egypt. This might happen *if* a technically superior administration *were to be the ultimate and sole value* in the ordering of their affairs.[5]

Clearly, the threat that Weber is addressing is not that of the totalitarian police state whose power may only be established by revolutionary violence and guaranteed by permanent repression. Those, ultimately, are simple and primitive organisms of limited novelty, and their lack of effectiveness and permanence has been amply suggested in contemporary history. Weber is rather considering that frightening situation wherein domination is, in Marcuse's words, 'non-terroristic, democratic, spontaneous-automatic', that is, a society that is the outcome of the psychology and technology of the dialectic of Enlightenment – mass gratification, market research, and so forth. This was the spectre that for Marcuse was haunting America. In Weber's words, it was something as apparently anodyne as 'a rational bureaucratic administration with corresponding welfare benefits', but in human terms an unbreakable 'shell of bondage' that will be 'as austerely rational as a machine'.[6]

Giner has indicated Weber's confidence in countervailing institutions; Habermas has suggested that the worst of fears have not come to pass, and perhaps need not; Piccone validly points out the acute problems that must befall a bureaucracy that absorbs all sources of negativity. Perhaps it will be possible to recast these arguments in a stronger and more fundamental form, if we direct our attention to the problem of values once more. Weber's stress on the conditions necessary to produce the totally administered society is a stress on values. He is not a technological – or organizational – determinist. He allows that bureaucratic domination may come to pass – but only '*if* a technically superior administration *were to be the ultimate and sole value*'. The question is, could such a condition come to pass? Or can we offer convincing evidence against such a possibility?

Weber offers the historical analogy of the Egyptian *fellah* who inhabited those ancient bureaucratic empires. Egypt and China worked, and worked for some thousands of years, because the human subject at the heart of those institutional arrangements was profoundly different from and alien to the inhabitant of modernity. The forms of domination that prove effective depend fundamentally upon the human subjects that suffer and sustain them. The pluralist politics that I have sought to defend depend fundamentally upon a unique historical product: to revert to conceptual and historical shorthand, the West European post-Enlightenment Helleno-Judaeo-Christian human subject. Our necessary rejection of teleology indicates that there was no immanent logic in the world-historical process which conspired to produce this subject as the ultimate (or, for some, penultimate) consummation of the evolution of the species. Weber's work rather suggests that we are likely to be no more than the outcome of a series of rather bizarre and unpredictable historical accidents. Certainly, the way in which recent non-European experience has obstinately refused to bear out Engels' dictum about the west showing the rest of the world the image of their own future might offer some negative confirmation of this suggestion. (But neither, of course, is the reverse obstinately true. There is no inherent reason why the products of Europe may not become the property of other societies and cultures.)

We find an evocative expression of the nature of the West European subject in Martin Luther's paradigmatic declaration: 'Here I stand; I can do no other.' Of course, Luther was not the first to take such a stance as a mode of being in the world, and perhaps not even the most important. And it should be realized that the significance of the statement has little to do with the particular issue upon which Luther chose to stand. After all, Sir Thomas More took an identical stance in defence of a diametrically opposed belief. What matters is not *where* anyone chooses to stand; what matters is the belief in the irrevocable *right to stand itself*. Thus, when I argue that bureaucratic domination will founder on the complications introduced by the continued existence of political wills, in other words on people's beliefs, I am not nominating as *the* contradictory element one particular belief or set of values. I mean essentially that the western subject is constructed around a belief in the *value of values*.

The Lutheran moment is a critical historical turning-point because, in the words of Hirst and Woolley, of 'the socially explosive nature of this concept of the person as the steward of his own soul'.[7] The rise of modernity, with all its ominous consequences in terms of the rationalizing process, also produced this concept of the individual conscience as the supreme court of judgement, and transformed it from the possession of a few 'saintly' and charismatic characters into the bedrock of modern culture. Here is the basis of modern politics and political institutions. The historical consequences of this moment are well known. The 'conscientious' individual possessed a shattering dynamism, and it is precisely those countries overwhelmed by this concept that generated the distinctive history of classical capitalism: a history wherein individuals, groups and institutions – disparate, autonomous, localized, spontaneous – produce in economy, polity, culture, technology and civil society that which elsewhere must *ab initio* be sponsored and directed by the state. At the root of this dynamism is a simple possibility, the possibility produced by 'conscience', the possibility of choice. This is the ambiguous burden which the world of modernity inscribes in the heart of the human subject.

Clearly, there will be no dispute over how obviously this fact of choice produces the domain of political will-formation and the continuous debate over values which gives the political sphere its unique character. What is perhaps less obvious is how this concept of choice is also central and indispensable to the apparently counterposed process of rationalization and bureaucratization. Rational bureaucracy, as Weber understood it and as I have expounded it, exists only to the extent that it is *also* organized around the concept of choice. Rational bureaucratic procedures are those that proceed, and justify themselves, by norms of technical efficiency. In other words, the bureaucracy does not consist of mere clerical executors of orders – were that so the whole fear of bureaucracy would itself be redundant. Bureaucracy does not legitimately choose ends; but it must certainly make choices between means towards prescribed ends. It must therefore implicitly claim the right of appeal to the court of *judgement*, it must itself make choices. This leads to a simple question: what kind of people are these who can make choices on the basis of scientific rationality and technical efficiency? What kind of people must inhabit and staff the bureaucratic machine if that machine is to produce acceptable results? What kind of personnel are required to ensure that the bureaucratic apparatus is one that does not repetitively, in the end fatally, produce inefficiency, incompetence, inadequate results, confusions and acute economic problems, with their consequent crises of legitimation? Perhaps the appropriate kind of people are precisely, and only, those in the mould of the West European individual.

We are back, of course, with Gouldner's perceptive redefinition of those who must staff the administrative machine in a contemporary late- or post-capitalist economy. These, we may recall, are not 'ritualists'; they regard nothing as acceptable purely because 'things have always been done that way', they refer to *reason*, not to authority. This is because their tasks are not only more complex but qualitatively different, inasmuch as they hold responsibility for processes and outcomes that cannot be successfully achieved through mere repetition and precedence. But this must have *cultural* implications. Can we conceive of an individual who proceeds by a *genuine* scientific method – in other words by the weighing of evidence, the testing of hypotheses, the comparison of competing explanations, the defence and explication of procedures and conclusions to peers and colleagues – and who is not the product of, who is not embedded in, the western culture of critical discourse? In other words, must not such people be precisely those West European subjects whom we claim to be already, today? And, if they must be such people, and if no other character-type can successfully comprise a modern bureaucracy, does this not suggest that those who would allegedly rule us as a new breed of scientific monsters must in fact remain integrally and inextricably inhabitants of the culture of liberty and conscience that we today envisage them threatening and subverting?

These optimistic suggestions may be buttressed by a consideration of a theme which has been undeservedly neglected. When Luther made his grandiloquent gesture at the birth of conscience, history coincidentally provided the technology whereby the conscience might prove victorious over the tomb of forgetting. The printing press initiated the typographic culture, against which all savage dictators and all perfect utopias may ultimately labour in vain. The connection between the printing press and liberty is not a new discovery. But the connection goes deeper than the necessity of a technology for the dissemination of critical and dissenting views. What is involved is the nature of the human subject created and secured by a typographic culture. In fact, the crucial change occurs much earlier in history, at that moment when the written word itself established its primacy over a previously oral culture. The printing press is simply the technology which turns the privilege of a few into the possession of the many, and thus implants literate culture as the dominant mode of thought for entire societies.

Oral thought has the character of being 'emphatic and participatory rather than objectively distanced'.[8] It denies the possibility of the separation of the knower from the known; or it prevents the emergence of that crucial foundation upon which the entirety of western knowledge, scientific and moral, is based – the distinction between subject and object, the awareness that the world is distinct and radically separate from the self and therefore an appropriate and irresistible object of study, investigation, manipulation and control. In other words, oral thought prevents history. Havelock[9] offers a fascinating account of Plato's assault on the poetic mode of pre-literate Hellenic culture motivated precisely by his desire to *make knowledge possible*.

Oral cultures are consequently homeostatic, that is, they live in a permanent present. In the nineteenth century the British colonial service attempted to record the oral histories of the tribes of Ghana. The Gonjas gave the following account of their history: the founder of the state of Ghana had seven sons, each of whom became a ruler of one of the seven territorial divisions of the state. But when the myths of the state were again recorded some sixty years later, this history had changed. Now the founder king had only ever had five sons. During the intervening sixty years, the territorial divisions of the state had in fact altered, and boundary shifts had reduced the number of territories to five. According to the oral history, there had never been more than five sons, just as there had now never been more than five territories. Oral history is capable only of reflecting and justifying the present, and is incapable of explaining origins, changes and development.[10] Now, can we not see the Gonja syndrome as a potent explanation of why the march to the Leninist state seems so irresistible in so many parts of the world? Winston Smith spends his life destroying yesterday's books and newspapers and writing the history that will justify the alliances and enmities of today. *The Great Soviet Encyclopaedia* is recalled in 1953 and the entry on Lavrenti Beria is replaced by an extended essay on the Bering Straits. Books, libraries and archives are memory, and they offer to each citizen the possibility of choosing between varied and competing accounts of any event in the past or present.

But it is not only a question of objectified technology. Books, after all, can be burned, educational systems policed, printing presses nationalized. The typographic culture also gives birth to something that is not at all as freely reversible: it creates the mind and the psychology of the independent free-thinking moral individual. Literate thought establishes the distance between the individual and his or her world, and it is this space alone that is the country of conscience. Totalitarian domination, in other words, exists only to the extent that it can recreate the pre-typographic culture and the pre-literate individual. Indisputably, the countries where the party regimes have established the most successful dominion are those where there was a high rate of illiteracy. The essentially literate and independent subject of modernity may, therefore, possess precisely those qualities that will prove resistant to the strategies of totalitarian utopians; it certainly offers impressive obstacles to the evolution of liberal democracies into regimes of rational bureaucratic dominion.

In this admittedly speculative and tentative manner I want to ground my argument for the continued existence of humans as value-oriented and motivated in a manner that will not succumb to the society of bondage. Only a culture of individuation, of conscience, of critical judgement, can produce and sustain a rational bureaucracy that may successfully pursue its tasks; any other culture will, conversely, produce a bureaucracy that must suffer from incompetence, public cynicism and a chronic lack of legitimation. As long as the autonomous subject exists, therefore, scientific bureaucratic procedures are a possibility, but bureaucratic domination is negated. Where the autonomous subject does not exist, bureaucratic domination is – and has been – a real possibility; but not one that can anticipate a lengthy reign in the world of modernity. For this world no longer provides a home for Weber's Egyptian *fellah*. Weber pointed out that China, Egypt, latter-day Rome, Byzantium worked as totally administered societies under 'highly *irrational* forms of bureaucracy'.[11] This irrationality proved an adequate basis for up to 3000 years of stability precisely because they were formations of a profoundly static nature. This static quality was no accident and no choice. As pre-modern formations they were devoid of the contradictions that must inhabit a modern 'total administration': growth, development, science, technology, mobility, 'progress', the very concept, in fact, of 'the future'. The members of such societies, then, defined themselves by a set of meanings that were appropriate to such frozen social stasis. They were not 'individuals' and they knew nothing of 'choice'.

What we see in the contemporary party regimes is the pale and crippled ghosts of these ancient empires. They indeed are ruled by 'highly irrational forms of bureaucracy', proceeding according to precedent, routine, instinct and unquestioned authority. The error committed by the contemporary prophets of absolute bureaucracy was to read in the Soviet development the logic of western history and the dialectic of Enlightenment. They fell victim to a debilitating Marxian fallacy: believing in history as a process of logical and immanent progression, they assumed that what comes later must also stand higher. Such an error at various times lay behind widely held Marxist characterizations of imperialism and fascism.[12] In the case of the Soviet Union, because it emerged after industrial capitalism in the west, it had to represent a development out of, beyond and transcending that prior social formation (despite the fact that in all aspects – economy, culture, technology, individuation, polity, etc. – the Soviet Union and its imitations possessed and continue to possess a level of development far lower than their putative evolutionary predecessors). Only an oppressive and facile historical schematism can make such an assertion seem necessary – or intelligent.

More precisely, total administration – the current reality of the Soviet Union and the inevitable future reality of the west – was alleged to grow out of the dialectic of Enlightenment, the Protestant ethic, the capitalist mode of production, the rule of rationality, the scientific culture and the modern state. On the contrary, on the evidence offered, these allegedly guilty parties must be declared innocent of the conspiracy Horkheimer and Marcuse claim to have detected. The party regimes must ultimately fail because of their profound discrepancy with each and every one of these elements of modernity. The Soviet Union, despite replicating the institutional arrangements of the ancient empires, experiences steering – and legitimacy – problems of a magnitude unprecedented, and the likelihood of any of them lasting 3000 years is obviously comically absurd.[13] The reason for this is simply that the ramshackle Russian variant of oriental despotism is polluted by elements of occidental modernity, elements which work against, and not for, bureaucratic domination. It is shot through, at subterranean and undetectable levels, with the bacillus of the human subject born of modern western culture.

This refers not simply to those dissidents who may conveniently be confined in psychiatric hospitals or marched on to airliners to Paris.[14] It is a disease to which every organ and component part of the society is to some extent victim. Pre-Soviet Russia was for some time at least marginally inserted in the orbit of Western Europe, and the consequent pollutions are still present, however desperately the borders may be policed and however many returning prisoners-of-war Stalin may have had executed. But the pollutions are not merely the remnants of pre-Soviet history, remnants which the passage of time might, after all, eliminate. The western discourse is also lodged fatally at the heart of the Soviet regime. Precisely because it is a Marxist, and therefore legitimately European, experiment, it is grounded upon concepts, justifications and meanings that are essentially *dynamic* and *rational*: history, progress, growth, development, science, technology, the belief in *a future that will be different from the present*. If it therefore assumes the possibility of different futures, the discourse at the same time must admit the possibility of different presents. In other words, within even the hermetic discourse of the Soviet Union, the revolutionary concept of choice must be present. However fast it runs, the bureaucracy cannot escape its own shadow: that concept of choice that gave it birth in the first place and which continues to be the only legitimate grounding of its existence. This not only points to a contradiction in economic terms, in terms of promise and performance, although it certainly is important that the bureaucracy is unable to make the right choices, to fulfil its plans and promises due to the absence of formal rationality, the deadweight of bureaucratic and structural ineptitude. The rickety and crisis-prone Russian version of the frozen empires also testifies to the ability of the western subject to resist dissolution at the hands of those institutions that conspire towards entropy. And, by extension, it might again confirm the unlikeliness of the emergence of societies of perfect bondage out of those social formations that have achieved a genuine level of modernity. Such societies, which have constructed, and been constructed by, the western subject in full flower and maturity, offer the very opposite of the *tabula rasa* of mind, memory, morality and culture that would allow a transition to 'irrational bureaucratic domination'.

These concluding theses are, of course, speculative, as any discussion of the future must be. It is not my intention to suggest that no threats exist or can be created that are capable of subverting the structures of civilization that I have identified. Do we genuinely live in a *mass* literate culture? Is the literate culture threatened by the displacement of the book by the data bank, or more pointedly, of the word by the audio-visual image? If genuine literate culture is still the property of an élite, how resistant will those outside it remain to the seductive appeals of those who would abolish time as an alleged solution to economic and social crisis, or simply as escape from an escalating crisis of meaning? If humanism is exposed epistemologically as a myth, with the decline in religions, both spiritual and secular, will it be possible to persuade people that, nevertheless, the myth is worth living? Can we avoid a creeping and subterranean *trahison de clercs*? That is, are our administrators sufficiently aware of the weight and the limitations of their responsibilities, or do they conspire, from inadequate training and culture, obtrusive and illegitimate political predilections, or myopic personal and career considerations, to change their own nature to something similar to the Russian version? Can those of us, ultimately, who are in a position to recognize the threats that do exist fulfil our responsibilities for the necessary undogmatic, open and political defence of politics? For in a society where literate culture is still as yet the property of an élite, the surest way to effect the dissolution of that culture is for the élite to actively participate in its dismantling. Few phenomena are as bizarre and paradoxical as those of us who devote a fair part of our lives and a fair portion of our energies to the project of creating a society in which we, of all people, would find it intolerable to live.

Few people will read this book because, apart from whatever inherent defects it may possess, few people in the world we live in are yet much interested in such matters. Those who actually derive some satisfaction and fulfilment from the dialectic of argument and the confrontation of ideas remain a small minority. Yet too often have we been ready to succumb to the fatal temptation to turn all these energies to one appalling end. It is possible that many people would not find Lenin's – or even Andropov's – utopia too difficult to live in. Most men live lives of quiet consummation. For the rest of us, however, efforts on behalf of the birth of utopia amount to the most peculiar form of suicide. In simple terms, utopian society would be the most fundamentally and stupendously *boring* place in which to live: no problems, no arguments, no sufferings, no joys, no defeats and no victories. We would have to survive without a large part of that which today gives us life, and makes a life worth living. It is difficult, therefore, to decide whether the activities of the intelligentsia towards the end of politics belong more appropriately in the theatre of cruelty or the theatre of the absurd.

It would be an insensitive reader who reached this part of my argument with the impression that, because certain current and traditional assumptions, institutions and practices have been defended, it follows that the entirety of existing social arrangements should be left undisturbed, for fear of something worse. We do not, any longer, need to inhabit such a universe of exclusive alternatives. The argument I have developed had among its purposes the desire to show how the character of political change is perhaps safest and most effective when it addresses the fundamentals of political process delicately and thought-fully. Within an understanding of the virtues of European institutions and liberties, the opportunities for genuine radical change are not at all diminished; quite the opposite. For I believe it has been, and continues to be, the failure of many to appreciate the nature of a truly political system, their unknowing insistence upon an attenuated and inade-quate understanding of the European political and intellectual tra-dition, that has condemned so much that is valid and necessary in the way of political change to a barren, dogmatic and fruitless repetition of failure. Within, and only within, a genuinely political approach, and a genuine political arena, may politics be audacious, and may it be creative, and may it be successful.

The validity, and the necessity, of politics was what, obliquely but undeniably, was demonstrated so recently in Poland: not the mythical revolutionary qualities of some classical proletariat, but the resilience of the political mind. After forty years of enthusiastic reconstruction in the Leninist-Pharaonic school, 'old European dignity' emerged un-scathed and, I believe, ultimately irrepressible. The struggle of man against power, says Kundera, is the struggle of memory against forget-ting. Against all the odds, there is evidence enough that memory will overcome forgetting.

### NOTES

1 Max Weber, *Economy and Society*, 2 vols, Berkeley, 1978, 1403.

2 Religion, or more convincingly, Christianity, does provide the metaphysical basis for such an assumption. It may yet prove to be the only basis. But what counts here is not the logical validity of Christianity as such a grounding for freedom, but the sociological likelihood of it so being. In an age characterized by secularization and disenchant-ment, Christianity as a basis for democracy does not offer an opti-mistic picture of democracy's future.

3 Paul Hirst and Penny Woolley, *Social Relations and Human Attributes*, London 1982, chapter 7, 'Theories of the personality', is a superb and dignified account of the conse-quences of this 'revolution' which confronts the ethical ques-tions involved. Alex Callinicos, *Is There a Future for Marxism?*, London, 1982, offers in the first four chapters a very clear and competent introduction to these philosophical developments, although the second half of the book is a profound disappoint-ment as it resolutely marches us all back into the embrace of

Lenin, Trotsky and the revolutionary party. This shows a strange combination of intelligence and naivety. Alternatively, it may be possible that he has done no more than speak the truth, in demonstrating that even the most sophisticated of marxisms will lead to the politics of manipulation and mysticism.

4 Hirst and Woolley, op. cit., 137, 138.

5 Weber, *Economy and Society*, 1402 (Weber's emphasis).

6 ibid.

7 Hirst and Woolley, op. cit., 137.

8 W. J. Ong, *Orality and Literacy*, London, 1982, 45, 46. Chapter 3, 'Some psychodynamics of orality', establishes in some greater detail the different ways in which pre-literate and literate cultures must think about themselves, the world, the past, present and future. Apart from the factors mentioned in the chapter, oral thought is distinctively (a) additive rather than subordinative, i.e. it is purely narrative, and cannot cope with elaborate subordinate expressions which might render the narrative less monological; and (b) aggregative rather than analytic – the culture may only be maintained by casting it in the form of rote traditional phrases and formulae. Analysis – breaking up established concepts and thoughts – threatens to dissolve the whole cultural inheritance. (c) It is redundant or 'copious': written discourse allows referral back and forth to different parts of the text for confirmation or interrogation. The oral statement must simply and repetitively reinforce the line of argument that is its historic responsibility: it allows no *distance* from the statement itself with its consequent analytic and critical potential. (d) It is conservative or traditionalist: because there is no recording process other than memory and repetition, energies must be devoted to saying over and again that which has been arduously learned over the generations. There is little opportunity or energy left for creativity. (e) It is close to the human life-world: the absence of analytic and abstractive possibilities renders knowledge and thought little more than a reflection of the familiar world; the distant and unfamiliar are reduced to versions of homely reality. The sum consequences of these features for knowledge and politics will be obvious to the reader.

9 E. A. Havelock, *Preface to Plato*, Cambridge, Mass., 1962.

10 Ong, op. cit., 48.

11 Weber, *Economy and Society*, 1401.

12 The Marxist movement was certainly – and probably in large part still is – susceptible to such a naive error regarding the other version of the society of total domination, fascism. Mihaly Vajda, nevertheless, offers a convincing and sensitive Marxist account of Italian and German fascism as products of *backwardness*, in contrast to those theories that would label it as the final, *highest*, stage of capitalism. See M. Vajda,

*Fascism as a Mass Movement*,
London, 1976.

13  The reasons are summed up by
Castoriadis in acid fashion:

> Russia, the grain basket of
> Europe even before Herod-
> otus' time can hardly feed its
> population, while Western
> countries subsidize the agricul-
> tural sector not to pro-
> duce. . . . the system does not
> always meet the population's
> solvent demand for consumer
> goods; the manufacture of
> products of a constant satisfac-
> tory quality remains an un-
> solved problem. . . . After
> sixty years of 'socialism' and of
> over-exploitation of the popu-
> lation, the per capita national
> product is the same as in
> Spain, if not in Greece. This
> 'socialist' regime has not yet
> been able to solve the prob-
> lems already solved in Neo-
> lithic times: how to assure
> continuity between one crop
> and the next; nor others,
> solved as far back as the
> Phoenecians: how to provide
> commodities to those who are
> willing to pay the price. . . .
> Apart from repression, the
> only cement of bureaucratic
> society is cynicism. Russian
> society is the first cynical
> society in history. (C. Castori-
> adis, 'The social regime in
> Russia', *Telos*, 38 (1978–9),
> 37–8)

14  One of the most interesting of
dissident accounts is V. Bukovsky's *To Build a Castle*, London,
1977. First, Bukovsky was not an
intellectual or a disenchanted
member of the Soviet élite, but
instead that remarkable animal,
a 'born' dissident. Second, most
striking is his claim, simple and
unshakable, throughout his
trials, to be treated as a *citizen*
enjoying the benefits and protection of an alleged rule of law.

# INDEX